WITHDRAWN

OUR LADIES
OF DARKNESS

Joseph Andriano

OUR LADIES
OF DARKNESS

Feminine Daemonology
in Male Gothic Fiction

The Pennsylvania State University Press
University Park, Pennsylvania

Library of Congress Cataloging-in-Publication Data

Andriano, Joseph, 1948–
    Our ladies of darkness : feminine daemonology in
male Gothic fiction / Joseph Andriano.

        p.   cm.
    Includes bibliographical references and index.
    ISBN 0-271-00870-9
    1. Horror tales—History and criticism.   2. Gothic revival
(Literature).   3. Archetype (Psychology) in literature.
4. Demonology in literature.   5. Femininity (Psychology) in
literature.   6. Anima (Psychoanalysis) in literature.   I. Title.
PN3435.A54   1992 3
    809.3'8738—dc20   92-5019
                                                                   CIP

Printed in the United States of America

Published by The Pennsylvania State University Press,
Suite C., Barbara Building, University Park, PA 16802-1003

It is the policy of The Pennsylvania State University Press to use acid-free paper for
the first printing of all clothbound books. Publications on uncoated stock satisfy the
minimum requirements of American National Standard for Information Sciences—
Permanence of Paper for Printed Library Materials, ANSI Z39.48–1984.

What is this being?
Beautiful shall I call her,
or inexpressibly terrible?

—Giovanni Guasconti,
in Nathaniel Hawthorne's "Rappaccini's Daughter"

CONTENTS

ACKNOWLEDGMENTS

Conceived in 1985, this project has undergone many alterations, expansions, contractions, and renovations. At the beginning, Professor Ralph Flores helped me narrow the focus from an initial "plethora of texts." John Ehrstine, Al von Frank, and especially Alexander Hammond guided me through the manuscript in its first phase. In its second, I am deeply indebted to Professor Burton Raffel, not merely for his stylistic suggestions that helped me refine the work, but especially for his constant encouragement— for continuing to "believe in it" when I had my doubts. In its final phase, I am grateful to Bettina Knapp and Cecile Nebel for their valuable suggestions and support.

The section of Chapter 4 on "Ligeia" appeared in slightly different form in *Poe Studies* 19, no. 2 (December 1986), and parts of Chapter 5 have been published, also somewhat modified, in two Greenwood Press volumes: *Contours of the Fantastic* (1990; ed. Michele Langford) and *Selected Essays from the Ninth International Conference on the Fantastic in the Arts* (1992; ed. Lloyd Worley). I am grateful to the editors of the journal and to Greenwood Press for permission to republish.

The book would never have been completed without the financial and moral support of Catherine A. Duffy, the technical support of Becky Patterson, and especially the emotional support, love, and patience of Gail Lloyd Andriano.

INTRODUCTION

What if the fiend should come in women's
garments, with a pale beauty amid sin and
desolation, and lie down by your side?
                    —Nathaniel Hawthorne,
                        "The Haunted Mind" (1835)

Demoness, succubus, female vampire—this "fiend" has been haunting men
at least since Lilith and Adam. When Hawthorne raised this rather hysterical
question in his odd little sketch, he conjured the familiar figure in order to
give readers a clearer sense of the hypnagogic state to which his title refers.
He left the question unanswered. But even if it was merely rhetorical, many
male artists in the nineteenth century agonized over the compelling image
of the demonic feminine—as Mario Praz, Nina Auerbach, and Camille Paglia
have most vividly shown.[1]

The scenario of a demoness haunting a sensitive young man, at first
animating but then enervating him, became a pervasive motif in Gothic
fiction in about 1820, when the genre was being transformed from the
hackneyed formulas of the 1790s to the more sophisticated "Ambiguous
Gothic." This simultaneity is no coincidence. As G. R. Thompson has
demonstrated, Ambiguous Gothic texts were created partly out of the

---

1. Praz devotes a chapter of *The Romantic Agony* to "La Belle Dame sans Merci," whom he
sees as a stereotype that embodies a "chronic ailment," male masochism (191). According to
Praz (189), her frequent recurrence in literature can be explained in terms of real-women
prototypes; one need not evoke archetypes. On the other end of the spectrum from this
misogyny, feminist Nina Auerbach, in *Woman and the Demon*, sees the haunting female
apparition in Victorian literature as the heroine of a myth that reasserted the power of woman
in a male-dominated society. Barbara Fass sees the haunting feminine daemon as a muse figure,
and Virginia Allen reads her as an "erotic icon." Most recently, Camille Paglia, in her book
Sexual Personae, views the daemonic feminine as an assertion of Dionysian, chthonian, and
pagan natural forces ("earth-cult") in eternal opposition to masculine, Apollonian, Christian,
civilizing forces ("sky-cult").

consciousness of boundaries breaking down—including the boundary between Self and other.[2] In the early 1860s, Emily Dickinson was acutely
aware of this trend in the Gothic imagination: "One need not be a Chamber,"
she reminds us, "to be haunted—"

> Far safer, through an Abbey gallop
> The stones achase—
> Than Unarmed, one's a'self encounter
> In lonesome place—
>
> (Dickinson, 169)

A great discovery of Romantic Gothicism was the realization that even
when a man is haunted by a feminine demon or ghost, he could still be
encountering himself—or part of himself.[3] The haunting Other may be a
projection of the haunted Self: outer demon is inner daemon, a psychic
entity unrecognized as such by the male ego. The Romantics were in fact the
first to name the disorder experienced by such a hapless male: they called it
nympholepsy.[4] And though nympholeptic male artists seemed to proliferate
at the *fin de siècle* (Praz, 206), the "fiend in women's garments" haunts us
still. Something about her transcends time and place. Something about her,
as the Romantics first fully realized, is archetypal.[5] They were anticipating
the psychology of Carl Jung, who started using the word *anima* to signify a

2. See G. R. Thompson, *Romantic Gothic Tales*, 26–28. Thompson's "Ambiguous Gothic" is
similar to Tzvetan Todorov's definition of the Fantastic: the text seems suspended between
supernatural and psychological explanations. "Supernatural malevolence" is not explained away
in terms of Enlightenment psychology as in Anne Radcliffe and Charles Brockden Brown; rather
it remains a threat, though its nature is ambiguous: "is it in the nature of the universe or of the
human mind or both?" (Thompson 26). If the latter, then boundaries begin to dissolve: Self
merges uncannily with Other (28).

3. Cf. Rosemary Jackson, *Fantasy: The Literature of Subversion*, 24: "the history of the
survival of Gothic horror is one of progressive internalization and recognition of fears generated
by the self." And, more relevant to the motif here, Barbara Warren, in her feminist textbook
The Feminine Image in Literature, states that "the phantom lady is essentially the man's most
vital spirit, his soul, without which he is inwardly dead, merely existing, wandering lost in a
gray world" (8); the phantom "reflects more about what [the male] neglected, denied, or
repressed in his own nature than about the true nature of woman" (10).

4. See the *OED* (1933 ed.), vol. 7; see also herein pages 97–98.

5. Blake's Vala, Coleridge's Geraldine, and Keats's "Belle Dame sans merci" come most
readily to mind as archetypal figures consciously created by Romantics. Charles Lamb's famous
comment in "Witches and Other Night Fears" that "the archetypes are in us, and are eternal"
(114), and Thomas De Quincey's "Levana and Our Ladies of Sorrow" may also be cited (see
Chapter 5 on De Quincey).

female image perceived by a man as *numinous*—in Rudolph Otto's sense of evoking a "*mysterium tremendum et fascinans*, a frightening yet fascinating mystery" (Varnado, 10). Nympholepsy became *anima* possession. (Jung, *CW* 9.1: 39; Neumann, 5).

Using a post-Jungian approach, this book provides a possible answer to Hawthorne's question: what if the haunting demon manifests feminine signs, appearing also to be both beautiful and deadly? And why does this scenario recur so frequently in Gothic fictions? It appears to meet a psychological need, shared by many male human beings. The phenomenology of the female demon reveals that she is a persistent symbol of our two most impelling instincts, the erotic and the thanatotic. When the demoness is a numinous image rather than a consciously manipulated stereotype or a mere reflection of male ego anxiety, she seems often to be associated with these primal instincts. The haunted man's "sacred terror"—the haunting demon ess's numinosity—is a sign of her bipolarity: she is both feared and loved. My concern, then, is not merely with supernatural *femmes fatales*, but especially with *belles dames sans merci*: feminine daemons that both animate and enervate, inspire as muse yet threaten to destroy (cf. Fass, 17–18).

A "post-Jungian" approach avoids the most problematic Jungian assumptions. I do not assume that the collective unconscious is a noumenal center or psychic ocean from which phenomena or archetypes leap out like breaching whales, nor do I take a Platonist or essentialist view of the archetype as a transcendent Idea. The readings in this book are based on the premise that the anima and the related mother archetype are not signified Givens but rather signifiers (i.e., utterances, words or images) whose meaning derives first from interaction with (and difference from) other signifiers in the text, and second from connotations and associations (from other texts) the reader brings to bear on the text at hand. Rather than work deductively from Jungian premises, then, I have sought out *signs* of the archetype. When enough of them appear, making an archetypal interpretation plausible, I create a secondary text using those signs to illuminate the primary text.[6]

6. Cf. Martin Bickman, *The Unsounded Centre*, 149. Bickman's "mythodology" is also pragmatic rather than dogmatic: Jung's symbology equips the reader with "analogies" that may "illuminate" the text. Similarly, Van Meurs (246) distinguishes between "the critic who uses psychological notions to bring out . . . the concrete complexity of human experience" and the critic who "imposes a psychological scheme on the literary text," which destroys that complexity. For a guide to variations on orthodox Jungian theory, see Andrew Samuels, *Jung and the Post-Jungians*, and Karin Barnaby and Pelegrino D'Acierno, eds., *C. G. Jung and the Humanities*.

One cannot simply assume that every time the demoness appears she is an archetype. One must instead endeavor to disentangle merely conventional or diachronic elements from the truly primordial or synchronic, for only the latter are archetypal, at least in Jung's sense of the term. Northrop Frye's definition of an archetype (*Anatomy*, 365) is more broad—a symbol or image "recurring often enough in literature to be recognizable as an element of one's literary experience as a whole." This definition includes literary conventions, stereotypes, and stock characters such as the Braggart Soldier (see *Harper Handbook*, 48). Here, on the other hand, I restrict the term to recurring figures that (1) show signs of primordial—or at least extremely archaic—origin, and (2) seem to be associated with human instinctual drives.

Frye also makes a distinction "between psychological and literary treatments of archetypes": "In psychology their central context is a private dream. . . . The dream is not primarily a structure of communication: its meaning is normally unknown to the dreamer. The literary archetype, on the other hand, is first of all a unit of communication" (*Handbook*, 48). But what about dreams as they appear in literature? They are in effect the same as a person's discourse about a dream. They are therefore units of communication between text and reader. A dream may or may not communicate something to a dreamer; but a dreamer, in his or her retelling, always communicates something to a listener or a reader. Moreover, some of the archetypes that appear in myths may have originated in dreams. As Frye himself explains, a myth is a narrative that tells a society what it most needs to know about itself. We cannot simply distinguish literary from psychological archetypes: the latter must appear in literature and in myth.

In the 1960s, Jungian criticism acquired a poor reputation because it was either too reductive or too "mystical" and nonscientific. Neo-Freudians and ego psychologists attacked it (see Appendix B), and structuralists made sure to distance Lévi-Strauss from Jung.[7] More recently, some poststructuralists have dismissed archetypal psychology on the grounds that it posits a "center," the collective unconscious, in which may be found the "archetype

7. See, for example, Jeffrey Mehlman's article, "The Floating Signifier." Mehlman views Lévi-Strauss's idea of the unconscious as collective yet "resolutely un-Jungian" (16), but he offers no convincing argument that Jung and Lévi-Strauss are incompatible. Both, it seems to me, reveal "the condition of mental life for all men in all ages" (16). For a fairer assessment of the compatibility of post-Jungian archetypalism with Lévi Strauss's structuralism, see Annis Pratt, "Spinning among Fields." See also Kugler, 310: Lévi-Strauss's distinction between the "subconscious" and the "unconscious" is "almost identical to Jung's earlier subdivision of the unconscious into a personal aspect composed of imagos and a collective aspect consisting of archetypal structures."

an sich" (Jung's term: *CW* 8: 213), which is a signified concept underlying the archetypal figure, or signifier. But the patterns of what *appear* to be archetypal phenomena may be traced without disturbing the noumenon, which need not be summoned from the abyss.[8] Archetypal figures appear like tracks in a bubble chamber. And like elementary particles, archetypes "as such" are known only by their traces and effects. The interaction of signifiers (self, ego, id, anima, animus, shadow) may create a synchronic image, a momentary mental picture (not a solid icon) that somehow manages to transcend time and place. It may well be an illusion, but as Derrida says of meaning in general, it is an illusion "absolutely necessary to us" (Brooke-Rose, 46).

Men often need to conjure certain numinous images of women, which usually have little or nothing to do with real women.[9] These illusions, whether Madonna or succubus, become delusions only when men forget that they are signs men themselves create to guide their way through life, love, and death. Only when men mistake them for real "demons" on the one hand, or real women on the other—or when men expect women to conform to archetypal patterns (expecting them always to fall toward that center)—do they run the risk of "nympholepsy." The Gothic texts explored in this book all share this motif: men mistaking their own daemon for a fiend, or casting the women in their lives into archetypal molds, forgetting where the molds were formed. What these men fear most is the crossing of gender boundaries. The haunting is an incursion into the male ego's dominion: the female demon is seen as a usurper; she inhabits and insidiously attempts to exert her influence, to feminize the male.

Since most men view femininity and masculinity hierarchically, they feel that the feminization of the ego is an insult to its integrity. This feeling is derived mainly from the view, unfortunately widely shared by cultures in the East as well as the West, that it is better to be male than female; it is therefore better to be a "manly" man than a "womanly" man (cf. Paglia, 125: "Effeminate men have suffered a bad press the world over"). To be manly has

8. Lauter and Rupprecht (13) also reject the "essentialist (Platonic)" idea of the archetype (Jung's *archetype an sich*). Archetypes are not "absolute or transcendent or unchanging. . . . if we regard the archetype not as an image whose content is frozen but . . . as a tendency to form and re-form images in relation to certain kinds of repeated experience, then the concept" remains a useful one for poststructuralists. See also Eric Gould, *Mythical Intentions in Literature*, 20 and 32; and my Appendix B.

9. Cf. Pratt, 98: When a man "experiences his anima" it is not at all "equivalent to understanding the experience of a real woman in the real world." Agreed, but isn't it better than his denying inner femininity completely? Doesn't it at least help him begin to empathize?

always meant to be important, to be on top of things and of women, to show "manly courage," to be in charge when the going gets tough. But now we know there is such a thing as manly nurturing, manly sensitivity, manly yielding, and manly love.

These Gothic protagonists do not know this, however. As alter egos of the male authors who take these personae, they fear the feminine in themselves because they do not want to be changed, having been conditioned by culture that gender boundaries must be maintained, that only women should be feminine (which can only mean soft, smooth, unassertive to the point of submissiveness, receptive, open, deferential to men, nurturing, sensitive, motherly, daughterly), and that only men should be masculine (which can only mean hard, rough, firm, courageous, penetrating, fatherly, protective, assertive, aggressive or, better yet, dominating yet gentlemanly and deferential to ladies). Then this Lady of Darkness arrives. Her very being defies gender boundaries, for she is aggressive both sexually and intellectually. She invades, inhabits, attempts to effect change, which often occurs in spite of the man's conscious will.

Why does she do this? She is the return of the repressed, the exiled goddess coming back to demand her due. Or she is the cast-out prematurely buried twin sister, Madeline Usher, who comes back to destroy the hysterical Roderick. Like most nineteenth-century men, he failed to come to terms with the feminine within him, causing an uncontrollable eruption of femininity that overwhelmed him. In Poe's day, the term *hysteria* was, as its etymology in the womb attests, largely confined to women. Poe knew that this restriction was based on untenable presumptions: that women are less able to control their emotions than men; that women, by nature more submissive, more readily succumb to the symptoms of hysteria. But Roderick is the passive one. Madeline is the embodiment of energy out of control, superhuman enough to break open her own tomb, aggressive enough to kill. Poe undercuts the idea that only women are "feminine" and only men are "masculine."

The psyche appears to have been primordially androgynous, as thinkers from Plato to Freud have suspected. The psychic norm may well be androgynous, but the social norm in most cultures is hierarchically dualized. For a man to fit in as a man in society, he must deny certain feelings and modes of behavior that society has labeled "feminine"—meaning qualities the society has decided are more fitting a woman than a man. But these feelings, whatever they be—anything from the need to nurture to the desire occasionally to be dominated—are feelings we have because we are human, not because we are a particular gender.[10]

To consider the psyche archetypally androgynous is not to suggest that androgyny is a social panacea (cf. Paglia, 489), but rather to realize that inside of every man and woman are drives that seek that primal unity. This book focuses on men for the simple reason that it is not merely a scholarly but also a personal book, and its author is a man. Some men are more able than others to harness and focus those drives toward androgyny, to integrate the "feminine" into their psyches. Perhaps they are genetically predisposed. In any event, they manifest this androgyny in any number of ways, from more moderate behavior modification (like becoming more nurturing, receptive, sensitive, less macho, etc.) to the extremes of cross-dressing (dresses and lingerie being metonymic signs of femininity) and even transsexualism. Some men simply are more "feminine"; the most obvious ones are labeled "effeminate" by those who consider "womanliness" in a man a sign of inferiority. Other androgynous men do not evince obvious mannerisms that social custom has signified as "womanly" but manage to express their "feminine side" in other ways, like actually discussing their feelings openly, giving in to emotion rather than holding it in, even crying unabashedly when they must, without worrying what people will think. Contemporary popular culture seems for the most part to encourage androgyny, as in the film *Tootsie* (1982), which expressed the need for a man to become more sensitive, but to do it "without the dress"; or Sam in *Quantum Leap* (NBC, 1990–91), who occasionally "leaps" into a woman's body, always learning empathy for that gender men once thought unknowable, wholly other. He even learns what it is like to be a victim of rape (30 October 1991).

To become more androgynous is not necessarily to become a transvestite priest of the Great Goddess; androgyny need not be the abject submission to the chthonian so brilliantly described by Camille Paglia in her recent book. It is rather a matter of precarious balance, a surfacing of what was once submerged, a conscious attempt to place masculinity and femininity into a dialectic rather than a hierarchic dualism.[11]

---

10. Cf. Edward Whitmont, "Reassessing Femininity and Masculinity," 121: "Either sex may partake in any of the masculine or feminine determinants in various constellations or degrees, comparable to a zodiac wheel in which any of its sections can be accentuated to different degrees in different people."

11. For Paglia, androgyny as evinced in Romanticism—especially the "male heroines" of Coleridge as Christabel and Poe as narrator of "Ligeia"—is decadent, solipsistic, and "self-

Every man who is able will find his own way to integrate the feminine; others will remain polarized. One hopes that as society becomes more androgynous (giving up the whole idea that there are *proper spheres* for each sex), these "manly" men will have less political power. But to the man who *fears* that he will be "feminized," the drive toward androgyny appears as a terrifying embodiment of a female Other because he cannot accept her for what she is—the deepest part of his own soul, or *anima*.

Of the many texts I found exhibiting strong signs of the anima, I have selected those which I think best answer Hawthorne's question, and which most vividly illustrate Dickinson's haunting verse. For when the female demon appears as a man's alter ego ("one's a'self")—when the "female garments" are worn, as it were, by a male consciousness (the succubus actually an incubus in drag)—then we may best perceive the "critical difference" in Barbara Johnson's sense: femininity *within the male* is indeed "a rhythm of multiplications, divisions, and fusions . . . an appearance and disappearance of partition" (18).[12] Discerning signs of the anima in this breakdown of boundaries between masculine self and feminine "other," perhaps we may better comprehend the psychodynamics of the male ego in action. These succubi and lamiae may help us understand men's attitudes not only to their art (as Barbara Fass has shown) and to the women in their lives (Nina Auerbach) but also toward their own femininity, which so many men spend so many conscious hours denying even exists at all.

---

emasculating" (323). For me, it is the *fear* of archetypal androgyny that these writers express through their "sexual personae." Ironically, this enervating fear makes them more passive, creating the very "feminization" they fear. It is a vicious circle or vortex (an image common in the Gothic). Paglia then goes on to "the modern androgyne [who] seeking only self-realization, forfeits the Spenserian energy of opposition and conflict" (489). My point is that androgyny need not be solipsistic and narcissistic: men can relate better to other men and women if they effect a synthesis of inner genders, rather than the usual polar dualism.

12. Cf. Samuels, *Jung and the Post-Jungians*, 223: one's "manifest gender" is determined by one's perception of difference with what he or she senses as Other. Masculine and feminine are relative, co-defining signifiers (cf. Ulanov, 156), "shifting elements" (Barthes, 17) that create a "mirage of structures" (20) rather than a fixed concept. Femininity may variously signify grace, softness and smoothness, tender deference, self-effacement, weakness, passivity, submissiveness, cavernous (chthonian) earthiness, darkness, unconsciousness, enclosure, intuitiveness, sensitivity, and affiliative behavior—all depending on the perceiving consciousness (See *OED* [1933 ed.] 4:152; Appignanesi, 1–19; Bradway, 276; Stevens, 180–92; Zabriskie, 267). When any of these "feminine" elements within a man are perceived by him as "Other," they become uncanny, demonic. But the otherness is illusory: as Shoshona Felman puts it, femininity is uncanny when it "subverts the very opposition between masculine and feminine" (42); i.e., it asserts the existence of a man's own androgyny, which most men do not want to admit.

1

BIONDETTA/BIONDETTO
Le Diable amoureux as Archetype

She look'd at me as she did love
And made sweet moan—
—Keats, "La Belle Dame sans merci"

The prototype of "the fantastic," according to Tzvetan Todorov, was *Le Diable amoureux* (1772) by Jacques Cazotte.[1] A close analysis of this Gothic text's ambiguities, especially those concerning androgyny, will reveal that Cazotte's is a seminal work in this genre, undeserving of its obscurity, containing important prototypes for Romanticism. One of these, the female demon, is a Judeo-Christian icon of feminine evil. But might she actually be prehistoric, primordial, predating the religious system that defines her as a devil? May the prototype actually be an archetype? And if so, so what? Does it really matter to us, here and now?

Camille Paglia has recently asserted that "the femme fatale began in

---

1. Cazotte (1719–92) was a French civil servant who wrote popular tales, fables, parodies, and satires. He became a mystic and, during the Revolution, a royalist who supposedly predicted his own execution during the Reign of Terror. See Shaw, chapter 18.

prehistory and will live forever" (339); the demonic feminine, in *all* its manifestations, evokes "the daemonic spirit of archaic night" (346). I do not think that every female demon in literature is this powerful or evocative. Some are mere bugaboos, embodiments of various personal fears and anxieties, not necessarily of transpersonal terrors shared by many men in many cultures. Cazotte's demoness Biondetta is a perfect "test case" because she is obviously an embodiment of the male protagonist's personal fear of female sexuality, yet when she first appears, she seems frighteningly primeval.

Le Diable amoureux was widely read, especially influencing later Gothic and Romantic writers—M. G. Lewis, Gérard de Nerval, Charles Nodier, E.T.A. Hoffmann, and Charles Baudelaire.[2] Nothing quite like Cazotte's work had appeared before, even though its temptation plot, with its prototype in the life of St. Anthony, was familiar to all Catholics. The text seems a curious hybrid of several popular genres of the time—*contes licencieux, contes morales, contes de fées*—but it has long had the reputation of being the first of a new genre—*le conte fantastique*, not only in Todorov's narrow sense of reader hesitation but in a broader one: Cazotte simply added the mimetic techniques of realism, already apparent in some *fabliaux* and *contes*, to the marvelous.[3] The result was an exquisitely ambiguous work in which a fairly ordinary young man is confronted with both the supernatural and the perfectly natural "realistic" problem of choosing a mate. *Le Diable amoureux* may also be considered Gothic in that term's broadest sense. It has the trappings—ruins, diabolism, sexual pursuit—and it gives a little *frisson*.

With elements of all these genres, *Le Diable amoureux* had something to please almost everyone: humor, light titillation, periodic chills, and moral messages. Only a thoroughly ambiguous work could provide such conflicting needs. Todorov has already shown the structural ambiguity of the text in terms of the protagonist's (and the reader's) hesitations between dream and reality; the reader is never sure, even at the end, how much of his adventure was dreamt and how much was "real" (Todorov, 45, 52). My concern is with

2. See Shaw, 66–68; Castex, 39–41; and Winkler's article. For the irony of Cazotte's becoming the hero of the early Romantics, see Fleurant's article "Mysticism in the Age of Reason." He sees Cazotte as a staunch conservative whose antirevolutionary views made him an unlikely pre-Romantic.

3. Shaw, chapters 7 and 11. Breuillac, as early as 1906, defined the *conte fantastique* as "*un genre intermédiaire entre le merveilleux proprement dit et le réel*" (quoted by Shaw, 57). Cf. Castex, 34–35.

ambiguities that give rise to ambivalence over sexuality and gender. In order to consider the female characters as possible images of archetypal femininity, the conventions Cazotte was consciously manipulating must first be considered. Ambiguities that cannot be explained in terms of Cazotte's controlling consciousness may have archetypal significance.

A largely unknown work in this country, *Le Diable amoureux* is not readily available in translation.[4] I have therefore included a paraphrase based on the definitive French text.[5] Aspects of the work not directly related to my theme will be merely summarized, while scenes revealing the complex relationships between masculine and feminine will be described in some detail.

The Devil in Love

The narrator-hero of *Le Diable amoureux* is Don Alvare, a twenty-five-year-old Spanish naval officer employed as a royal guard in Naples, where he and his comrades lead as dissipated a life as their purses will allow, gambling and living it up with "femmes du jeu" (315). Alvare gets into a conversation with a pipe-smoking older officer, Soberano, who turns out to be a Flemish cabalist and necromancer. At Alvare's eager insistence, he proves his conjuring ability by evoking a fire demon to light his pipe, impressing Alvare so much that he wants to learn the tricks of Soberano's trade.

Bored with mundane reality, Alvare is anxious to communicate, even to "bind himself" (*se lier*) to a spirit. "Je le veux, Je le veux!"—such is his rash enthusiasm that Soberano has to warn him that although humans have the power to command spirits, sometimes our weakness of will, "notre pusillanimité" (317) allows them to possess and control us. Conjuring can be dangerous, especially if the conjurer is not prudently and gradually initiated. With cavalier braggadocio, Alvare assures Soberano that he could handle any demon, including the devil himself, whose ears he would even offer to pull to show his courage. Apparently to teach the presumptuous young man a

---

4. It was first anonymously translated into English in 1793, then in 1810 as *Biondetta; or the Enamored Spirit* (a title that is already an interpretation, since it leaves out the word "devil"). The only other translation I know of is *The Devil in Love* (Boston: Houghton Mifflin, 1925), of which only one thousand copies were printed.

5. The most reliable text is in Marguerite de Cheyron, ed., *Romanciers de XVIIIe siècle* (Paris: Gallimard, 1965), vol. 2: 311–78. All parenthetical references to *Le Diable amoureux* are to this edition

lesson, Soberano agrees to show him how to conjure. With some friends of his, he takes Alvare to the recently excavated ruins of Herculaneum in Portici. There, under a well-preserved vault made up of twenty-five stones, Soberano draws a pentacle, bids Alvare enter, tells him to recite "Béelze-buth" three times, and withdraws with his friends (318). Alone, Alvare experiences a moment's apprehension, but realizing that he must now prove himself in front of Soberano and his friends, who are waiting to gloat over his fear and trembling—his "pusillanimité"—he resolves to go through with the conjuring (319).

Reciting the formula, he immediately feels a chill in his veins, his hair rising. There is a flash of light, and through the window of a ruined wall comes a horrifying apparition: a huge camel's head, "horrible, autant par sa grosseur que par sa forme," equipped with disproportionately large ears. It opens its ugly mouth to speak: "Chè vuoi?" (Italian for "What do you want?"). Although Alvare is frightened, he manages to show courage; but more significantly, he also feels mentally and emotionally stimulated, suddenly aware that the soul of man is vast, filled with a multitude of conflicting emotions, ideas, reflections, all making their impression simultaneously (319).

Alvare, mindful of Soberano's assurance that the spirit must obey him, chides the demon for taking such a hideous form, and calling it a slave he orders it to assume a more agreeable persona. He thinks of a dog, and tells the apparition to take the form of a spaniel, whereupon it vomits one forth. The dog's ears, also too large, are dragging on the ground.

The frightening apparition gone, Alvare has no trouble offering to pull the dog's ears. As it cowers, lying on its back as though to beg for mercy, he notices that it is "une petite fémelle" (320). Again calling it slave, he orders it to create a suitable environment for him and his friends to have a snack. He calls the dog Biondetta (Italian for "little blond one"), and orders it to take the form of a servant and to fetch Soberano and his friends. The vault has become a room where Alvare, outwardly confident but inwardly worried, now offers his astonished companions wine and fruit. The dog has become a page boy, referred to now as "il" rather than "elle"—a beautiful youth who pours their wine. Alvare rakishly toasts the most beautiful courtesan in Naples, and after he drinks he gives the page a stealthy look. "Figurez-vous," he tells the reader, "l'amour en trousse de page" (322). Since Alvare perceives the page as male, he calls him Biondetto. After the snack, he tells him that a certain Signora Fiorentina, the famous singer and harpist, is waiting outside. Biondetto leaves and a veiled woman comes in carrying a

harp. She plays and sings for them. Thus, through a series of transformations, the demonic camel's head has become an angelic harpist. Her
performance is so moving that Alvare almost forgets that he himself is "the
creator of the charm that ravishes" him (323).

While his creation sings, she looks at him over her veil with a penetrating
stare yet with "une douceur inconceivable." He recognizes Biondetto's eyes,
thinking it is a page boy disguised as a woman; then he wonders whether it
is actually a woman pretending to be a page boy disguised as a woman. Such
confusions concerning the sex of the apparition continue through the first
half of the narrative.

The harpist leaves, and Biondetto returns. Alvare has him escort them
home in pomp. On the way, Bernadillo, one of Soberano's friends, admonishes Alvare, warning him that he must be moderate, rather than indulge in
immediate gratification ("on précipite ses jouissances"—325), for which
Soberano warns him also that he will have to pay dearly. So when Biondetto,
"flambeau à la main," escorts Alvare to his apartment, he is ready to end the
adventure. He feels guilty, thinking of his parents, especially his mother, "la
femme la plus réligieuse, la plus respectable" (325) in all Estramadura—what
would she think of her son if she saw him dabbling in sorcery? He inwardly
gives her his word that it will not continue. But he finds it is not so easy to
get rid of the page. Trying to dismiss Biondetto, he is astonished to hear the
page respond as a woman. She is insulted, remarking that even if she were
one of his courtesans, Alvare would show more respect. Reminding him
several times of her true sex, she feels humiliated that he would send a
decent girl out on the streets so late at night. She wants to remain in his
bedchamber. Giving him the sweetest, most innocent looks, she seems
vulnerable, helpless without his protection in an alien world (326). On her
knees, she embraces his.

The chivalrous cavalier is no match for such entreaties. Alvare agrees to let
her stay in the farthest corner of his room, where she is to be neither seen
nor heard, or else he may say in his turn, "Chè vuoi?" (327). He goes to bed,
and through a translucent curtain he sees "le prétendu page" undress. There
is for the moment no longer any question of her sex. She extinguishes the
lamp. He finds he cannot sleep, for he keeps seeing above him the alluring
figure of the page; but he suddenly recalls the terrifying image of the camel's
head, from which he cannot completely dissociate "cet objet ravissant,"
Biondetta. Remembering her moving song, her "voix ravissant," which
seemed to come from her heart and resound in his, he cannot believe a devil
could be so convincing. Can a devil have a heart and "une âme sensible"

(327)—such an impressionable and sensitive soul? "Ah! Biondetta!" he cries, "si vous n'étiez pas un être fantastique" (328). He tries to remind himself that if she does indeed have a heart, it must be filled with "cruel poison." So agitated is Alvare that he tosses and turns until his bed collapses. Biondetta gets out of bed and comes to him, afraid he has hurt himself. The moonlight shining into the room and through her chemise enables him to see her beautiful body, her thighs—the moonlight aids and abets Biondetta, and once again Alvare begins to forget her bestial origin. She hugs him, but he orders her back to bed, to her corner, where she goes, crying softly.

Next morning, Biondetta is Biondetto again, up and dressed as a page boy, and referred to as "il." But that long blond hair reminds Alvare of her femininity. Addressing the reader a second time, he invites us to imagine the dawn in springtime, issuing from "les vapeurs du matin avec sa rosée, ses fraicheurs et tous ses parfums" (329). The dawn image transforms Biondetto into Biondetta again. Alvare gives her a comb for her hair, which she fixes to look like a boy's. Now he tries to dismiss "Biondetto" again, but Biondetta reminds him that she is helpless without him, for she is a spirit who has taken a vulnerable body, become mortal for love of him (329–30). She explains that when she saw his heroic countenance confronting that horrid apparition the camel's head, she fell in love with him.

Her ruse in dissociating herself from the camel's head alerts Alvare: "Vous parlez d'amour, vous en présentez l'image, vous en empoisonnez l'idée" (330). He thinks her a devil once again, but instead of declaring, "Get thee behind me," he decides to continue the adventure, asking only how he will be able to separate himself from her when he wants to. She replies, "Il suffira d'un acte de votre volonté" (330). Beset by ambivalence, our hero is in no position to make an assertion of willpower. One moment he sees the horrid Beelzebub; one moment he sees Biondetta, naive, *sympathique, timide, embarassée*, and so obviously in love with him that, now "outside of himself" (331), he runs away with her to Venice. He has to leave Naples because he may be arrested any moment for practicing necromancy. Biondetta lends him money, and they travel in separate carriages.

When he arrives at the inn, she does not come right away. For a moment he is relieved; perhaps she is gone, and after his imprudence, he would feel fortunate to lose only his job and nothing more (332). He wonders what this imp (*lutin*), which has taken such a seductive figure and given him money, could possibly have wanted? Then he thinks he would like to return the money—only then does she reappear, for inwardly he wants her back; he is merely rationalizing about repaying the loan. She arrives at the inn dressed as a page boy again, and they share a suite. Letters from his mother arrive, making him feel guilty again, but all he is able to do is ignore Biondetta; he cannot get rid of her. She amuses herself by putting a harpsichord together in her room. Submissive, docile, she serves him his dinners and publicly pretends to be his page boy; so convincing is she in this role that the innkeeper considers her the prettiest and most affectionate young man he has ever seen (334).

It is carnival season in Venice, and Alvare, avoiding "l'être dangereux," loses himself in revelry. When he returns dissipated from his gambling, Biondetta greets him at the door, "flambeau à la main" (34). Ten days pass, until he finally loses all his money. Biondetta then teaches him how to win by understanding the laws of chance. So he wins again and pays his debts, but he is more worried than ever about the designs of "this dangerous being," as she is so often called. He does not have the will to be rid of her, however, so he continues to avoid her, now seeking the companionship of courtesans. One of them, Olympia, takes a fancy to Alvare. She is about his age, very beautiful and spirited. They form a liaison, but she can tell he is preoccupied with something. She gets jealous of the pretty page boy with whom Alvare seems so infatuated, but whom he never takes to town. Using spies who see Biondetta naked through a keyhole, Olympia discovers that the boy is really a woman. Alvare denies it, but Biondetta has been seen crying all alone, neglected. "Tu l'as abusée," cries Olympia, "comme tu m'abuses, et tu l'abandonnes" (338–39). She angrily orders him to send the miserable young girl back to her parents, but he continues to deny that his page is a woman.

Learning of her rival, Biondetta simply feels more sorry for herself. Alvare, spying on her through a keyhole, listens to her sing at the harpsichord a lament in which she bemoans her fate: a daughter of heaven who has abandoned her airy element, lowered herself, put herself into corporeal chains for the love of a man who scorns her (341–42). The song throws Alvare into extreme confusion. Is this a fantastic creature, a dangerous imposter who knows he is listening? Realizing he must leave before her sirenlike song lures him—not to death but to sexual initiation—he flees to Brenta. Biondetta follows him, but she is attacked by a masked Olympia and stabbed.

Wounded and apparently dying, Biondetta now completely enchants Alvare; all misgivings concerning her true nature vanish. Alvare sees only an adorable woman, victim of ridiculous prejudice, sacrificed by his and others' cruelty (343). When a doctor undresses her and Alvare sees her lovely body afflicted with two wounds, he is overcome with love and pity. But that night he has a dream in which he tells his mother his whole adventure, and when he tries to take her to the ruins at Portici she says, "N'allons pas là, mon fils . . . vous être dans . . . danger" (344). Then he feels a hand trying to push him over a precipice; it is Biondetta's. He falls but his mother catches him, and he finds himself in her arms. Despite the dream, he continues to pity the wounded *lutin*.

After weeks of convalescence, during which Biondetta delightedly learns that Alvare is now in love with her, Alvare becomes convinced she is not a fantastic creature. When she is strong enough to speak, he eagerly asks her for the truth—who or what is she? She finally tells him, "Je suis Sylphide d'origine" (346). She claims that Soberano tricked him into conjuring the most frightful of all fiends, but his courage in the face of the apparition drew the admiration of all the elemental spirits—the gnomes of the earth, the undines of the water, the salamanders of fire, and the sylphs of the air. She was especially taken with him, so she abandoned the air and her vague existence there without sensations or pleasures. When she took a body, she found she had a heart.

To Alvare, it all seems like a dream, and he muses, "mais la vie humaine est-elle autre chose?" (347). Why shouldn't women be made of dew, of mists and rays of light, of the debris of a condensed rainbow? "Où est le possible? Où est l'impossible?" (348). Alvare is now completely enchanted, but instead of having sex with her, which is what she wants, he proposes. "Ma mère veut absolument que je me marie" (349). But Biondetta is afraid that marriage will poison their love (350). She sees dona Mencia as a rival who will never approve of her. It is necessary, she adds, for Alvare to grow up, to triumph over his mother's possessiveness, to make his own decision based on his heart's passion, not his mother's will. She is not persuasive enough, however, and Alvare attempts to fulfill his filial obligation, to get his mother's approval of his marriage. After doing this duty, he swears he will sacrifice the rest of his life for Biondetta, becoming her slave (353).

On their way to Spain, however, Biondetta arranges a storm and various illusions to prevent their arrival in Estramadura. Their carriage overturns with a broken axle, and the house they come upon for help is in the midst of a wedding reception. At first it seems curious that Biondetta would create this particular illusion, since she wants Alvare without the bothersome duty of matrimony. But then there are gypsies at this party, which slowly becomes a bacchanal. Biondetta dances the fandango as passionately as they, but

Alvare finds it vain, and leaves her for the company of two gypsy crones who tell him his fortune—that he is soon to unite with a fair young lady (364).

After the reception, Alvare and Biondetta are given a room by the lady of the house, who thinks they are married. Biondetta is angry and jealous that Alvare seems to prefer the company of the gypsy hags to her. But he tells her that their fortune confirms his love, and that he is convinced there is no need to go to Estramadura—they will go to Rome, Paris, anywhere she wants. But she will not be consoled; she is worried that her enemies Bernadillo and Olympia will destroy her if Alvare is so ready to abandon her. Her tears are what finally win him: "O pouvoir des larmes! . . . mes défiances, mes résolutions, mes serments, tout est oublié" (369). Kissing her tears, engulfed in her sweet breath, he cannot resist. They finally make love, an act indicated in the text by two lines of ellipses (369).

Afterward, Biondetta feels like the happiest of all creatures, but Alvare is confused, ashamed, immobile. Biondetta dashes to the foot of the bed; she is once again at his knees. Then, in bed in the dark, in a tone of enchanting sweetness, she tells Alvare the truth: "Je suis le Diable, mon cher Alvare, je suis le Diable" (370). Alvare is still petrified. She wants him to place his hand on her heart, which is animated by his, to let that "flâmme délicieuse" run in his veins as it does in hers, and to recite tenderly (as Charles Baudelaire later would), "Mon cher Béelzebuth, je t'adore."

At this fatal name, albeit so tenderly uttered, a mortal fright seizes Alvare; astonishment, stupor, overwhelms his soul. Only "la voix sourd du remords" saves him from annihilation. The devil then shows Alvare its true form again. The whole room is suddenly lit by giant, wriggling, luminescent snails, by the light of which he sees beside him in bed the frightful camel's head. Alvare falls, hides under the bed. He feels now that he is suffocating, totally unable to breathe (371).

The next morning she is gone, and Alvare wonders if it was just a bad dream. He goes home finally to his mother, an "ange tutelaire" who will protect him from monsters and phantoms. He resolves to cloister himself in a monastery, where he thinks he will be sheltered from these "chimères engendrées dans [son] cerveau" (373). He renounces "le sexe charmant," which he now sees as an "infernal larva" disguised by all the graces he had idolized. Though moving as an "automate," Alvare makes it home, where he falls into his mother's arms and embraces her knees (373).

After he tells her his dream, she sends for a wise old doctor of Salamanque, Don Quebracuernos, who, on hearing Alvare's adventure, assures him it was no dream. The devil did indeed tempt Alvare in the flesh, but he is uncorrupted; his remorse has saved him. Finally, the doctor informs him that to ensure no further temptations he should not become celibate but should marry, letting his respectable mother preside over his choice. Her graces and "talents célestes" will help him choose a girl he will never mistake for the Devil. Here the novella ends.[6]

The Female Demon as Feminine Daemon

Le Diable amoureux was long considered a *conte moral*, a didactic fable of temptation with no moral ambiguity at all. Even readers aware of its psychological sophistication (relative to other *contes* of the time) saw no ambivalence either in the narrator or in the authorial voice behind him (Shaw, 60). Todorov paved the way for more sophisticated analyses, as he showed that "the devil is woman as the object of desire" (27), and the flight to the mother in the work is regressive rather than progressive (130). The ending may therefore be read as an unhappy one, for Alvare remains adolescent in his flight from Woman (Porter, 8; Knapp, 117–18). Critics then began to realize that this was not simply a *conte moral*, for it seems continually to undercut the didactic intention by providing voyeuristic titillation and vicarious participation for less pious readers. Laurence Porter even goes so far as to assert that Cazotte was writing soft-core pornography (5).

How can the same story be variously considered pornographic and didactic? Cazotte himself made his intentions deliberately unclear in his preface, where he writes of the work that it was dreamed in a night and written in a day, and that it was written mainly for his own "plaisir" and only "un peu pour l'édification de ses concitoyens" (312). He goes on however to emphasize his didactic purpose in warning young men against ardently amorous women, whom indeed he misogynistically equates with "le diable" (312). But if one accepts his claims about both the oneiric origin of *Le Diable amoureux* and the speed with which it was dashed off, and if one considers

6. Cazotte actually tried three different endings. The original one had a corrupted Alvare become the tool of the devil, helping him spread disorder. Cazotte did not, however, publish this. In his second attempt at an ending, he omitted the scene in which Alvare has sex, and ended the tale much too abruptly for his readers' tastes, with the retreat to mother but without the Wise Old Man. The present ending first appeared in the second edition. See Cheyron, 1941–44, and Shaw, 64–65.

his insistence on pleasure and that phrase "un peu" qualifying his didactic intent, one must conclude that Cazotte could not have written anything but an ambiguous work. Here is a work intended to give pleasure to both writer and reader, and much of that pleasure is in the imagining of the irresistible Biondetta; and yet here too is a work about the dangers of sexual temptation, personified by the fiend in women's (and sometimes men's) garments, Biondetta. One reader may be edified by the moral, but another may read the work as a *conte licencieux*. The writer's pleasure in creating Biondetta becomes the reader's. Some will see her as lovely sylph, others as repulsive and deceitful demon; which side wins—the erotic/licentious or the Christian/didactic—cannot be determined by the text even though the latter has the last word. As O'Reilly puts it: "The hero's libidinal urges are admitted and satisfied, as are his responsibilities to family and church. Neither the devil nor the church . . . nullifies the other" (241).

Cazotte's novella is ambiguous in another way that has not been emphasized. Boundaries between subject and object, between masculine and feminine are constantly being strained throughout the text, both in the French grammar and in the imagery. When Biondetta is disguised as a page boy, Alvare always refers to her as "il," as though he mistakes the garment for the person. But "Biondetto" is really an image of Alvare himself—as servant of the demon he has conjured. Or, if one reads erotically, Biondetta/Biondetto provides a fantasy for both hetero- and homosexual male readers.

Alvare seems at first quite confused over whether this creature is male or female. Not until she is stabbed does he relate to her totally as female, for it is at that point that he is convinced she is a real woman and not "un" (masculine) être fantastique." *Le Diable amoureux* makes vividly concrete Barbara Johnson's and Shoshona Felman's ideas about sexuality:[7] here is a perfect example of gender boundaries uncannily breaking down, for Alvare, in his confusion, does not know whether to relate in a masculine or a feminine manner with Biondetta. If she is a woman, then he must act as a man, but if she is a "chimère" engendered in his brain, he has no idea how to act, and his very inaction feminizes him, makes him submissive to the demon. The genders are signified in the text through gestural language—the relationship between Alvare and Biondetta is always one of "feminine" submission and "masculine" dominance.

7. See Barbara Johnson, *The Critical Difference*, part 1; and Shoshona Felman, "Re-reading Femininity." Femininity, Felman writes, "inhabits masculinity as otherness, as its own disruption" (42).

Each of the characters alternates these roles. At first, Biondetta is feminine slave and he is masculine master; she embraces his knees and devotes herself, almost dying for him. Then he offers himself as her slave (in his letter, 353), and indeed through enchantment becomes so. She pursues and seduces him, in a reversal of Gothic roles, but she does so by crying and acting helpless without him. After sex, she "abases herself" once more, at his feet. He is master again, but then she reveals that she is not a woman but the ultimate male demon, and he is reduced to utter helplessness, hiding under the bed.

Androgyny, then, is structurally apparent in the grammar and in the gestural language of the text. But what is the significance of these masculine/feminine oscillations both within the apparition itself (Biondetta/Biondetto) and in Alvare (as master/slave)? Carl Jung considered androgyny an archetype.[8] A dreamlike narrative like Le Diable amoureux seems a good place to "test" whether an androgynous figure is archetypal. Is there anything about Biondetta that evokes the pre-Christian, the archaic? And if there is evidence for a primordial archetype, does it help explain the themes of sexuality in the text?

Consider first the historical aspect of the demon. Cazotte had read Jean Bodin's De la Démonomanie des sorciers (1580), Balthasar Bekker's Monde enchanté (1691)—both mentioned in the text (375)—and, most important, the Abbé de Villars's Le Comte de Gabalis (1670).[9] From these and other works on demonology, Cazotte learned that a controversy over the nature of demons, especially incubi, had been raging since the time of Paracelsus. The latter, as well as the Neoplatonists, did not consider incubi evil; men could benefit themselves by uniting with succubi, which were daemons rather than demons (Kiessling, 57, 75–77). The patristic tradition, however, saw them as evil spirits, tempting men to sinful pleasures of the flesh but not necessarily to damnation (Kiessling, 63).

Villars's Rosicrucian count in Le Comte de Gabalis claimed that the Church Fathers mistook the elemental spirits identified by Paracelsus—earthy gnomes, fiery salamanders, watery undines, airy sylphs—for devils. According to the count, a man should consider himself fortunate to form a sexual union with such creatures, who surpass real women (Kiessling, 59).

---

8. See especially Aion (CW 9.2) and Psychology and Alchemy (CW 12). Cf. Busst, 6.

9. For Cazotte's reliance on de Villars, see Milner 88–90. Although there is no explicit evidence that Cazotte read Le Comte de Gabalis, the book was so popular in the mid-eighteenth century that it is highly unlikely that anyone interested in demonology would not have read it.

Bodin's book held the contrary opinion; written as an aid to judges trying witches, it reinforced orthodox ideas on the evil intentions of incubi and succubi (Robbins, 54). Bekker's work, on the other hand, was an Enlightenment document—spirits, whether good or evil, if indeed they did exist, could "exercise no influence over human affairs" (Robbins, 45). All three views may be supported by Cazotte's text. The pious reader preferring the didactic interpretation would take Biondetta as evil, the erotically oriented reader would see her as Sylph, and the "enlightened" reader would take her as the ultimately harmless product of Alvare's overheated brain.

Cazotte drew on two prototypes for Biondetta, then. The first is the evil succubus, a devil who takes a woman's form for the purposes of sexual seduction, like the ones that supposedly tempted St. Anthony and the monk Richard Rolle (Kiessling, 29–33). The second is the essentially good Paracelsan elemental spirit (here a sylph), which takes the form of a woman so that, by uniting with a man, it can acquire a soul or immortality (Hartmann, 156). (As will be seen, Biondetta significantly varies the motivation.) Before testing these two historical prototypes as possible archetypes, one must discern to what extent Cazotte consciously manipulates them. Once that is determined, the more intriguing archetypal possibilities may be considered.

Take first the evil prototype. Alvare conjures up the devil itself, which appears as a camel's head. This unusual choice for a diabolic beast enabled Cazotte to avoid clichés like goats and serpents. But why specifically a camel? The symbol of sexual appetite must of course first appear as some sort of animal (that is indeed part of the devil prototype—see Rudwin, 38–45), so the moral will be clear; but a camel seems an odd choice. The only associations of the demonic with camels were in the Jewish midrashim and the cabalist Zohar (Langton, 12), which Cazotte could have known secondhand through cabalistic writings (Milner, 79). Both sources interpret the serpent of Eden as a winged camel. In his desire to avoid clichés, however, Cazotte created only more ambiguity: conventionally the camel was not an evil symbol; it was often a symbol for submission, obedience, temperance, fortitude, endurance (De Vries, 78)—all positive qualities.

When the beast becomes a dog, the reader is on more familiar ground. Dogs have long been associated with the satanic (Rudwin, 39). But one expects a black menacing mastiff, not a cowering spaniel. Again the prototype itself aids Cazotte's didactic purpose, while his variation of the type seems to undercut that purpose. On her back, the dog reveals that the demon has taken female form. The actions of the dog prefigure Biondetta's later strategy of submissiveness. When the female dog becomes a woman dressed as a page boy, Cazotte is again following conventional ideas about the devil. It is not only bestial but androgynous. A common belief since the Middle Ages held that the devil could take either sex (Kiessling, 26; Rudwin, 52). Icons of devils were often grotesquely androgynous (e.g., the picture of Aziel in Rudwin, 47), as those of Christ were beautifully so. Again Cazotte varies the prototype, for Biondetta's androgyny is not grotesque. Her hermaphroditic beauty (as Biondetto) perhaps reflects the historical conflict between the Platonic/alchemical notion of the androgyne as symbol of prelapsarian unity, and the common fear of bisexuality.[10] The latter is given a demonic mythos, as in stories of demons who could change sex, appearing first as a succubus to receive human seed, then as an incubus to transmit that seed (Kiessling, 26). Biondetta does not go that far, of course, but her androgyny can certainly be explained in historical terms of which Cazotte was fully aware.

Cazotte was familiar with these aspects of the devil from Bodin and Bekker, from whom he could also have gotten the idea that the devil can perfectly imitate virtue. Biondetta acts like the kind of girl any gentleman would want to marry. Don Q., the doctor of divinity who appears at the end, thinks that this is a new quality of the devil, but it was commonly believed that the devil could convincingly imitate goodness—even Christ himself (Rudwin, 121). Thus, for his didactic purpose, Cazotte simply relied on the conventions of demon lore.

He manipulated the positive prototype, the sylph, more liberally. Sylphs desired to unite with men so they could obtain a soul or immortality. Paracelsus wrote that they and the other elemental spirits were below humans in the cosmic hierarchy because they did not have souls (Hartmann, 151). Biondetta, on the other hand, already has "une âme sensible"; moreover, she explains to Alvare that she has sacrificed immortality— lowered herself on the Great Chain of Being to love him. She gains a heart, not a soul (346). The pious reader would interpret this passage as a clue that if Alvare knew anything about occult writings, he would see that Biondetta doesn't really know anything about sylphs. He would then know she is lying about being one. It is just the devil again imitating goodness, the goodness of ultimate self-sacrifice.

Less pious readers, however, may see this "kenosis" as more than mere

10. See Busst and especially Schwartz, who shows how the positive image of the androgyne in the early Renaissance gave way to the image of the hermaphrodite, "the figure not of inner harmony but of grotesque, unnatural sexuality" (127).

pretense. This sylph is even more enchanting than the traditional one because of her self-sacrifice. Her story is true—she is not the camel's head. The proof? Every time she is seen alone, through a keyhole, she is acting like a sylph, not a devil, and when delirious with fever she speaks only Alvare's name. Again, the pious reader would retort: the demon knows it is being watched; it is still pretending. But the text can support either interpretation.

Cazotte, then, using these prototypes, may have been consciously warning men of the dangers of lawless passion, but he was not "in complete control of his material" (Porter, 10). It gets out of his control in the same way (though on a much smaller scale) Blake said of Milton that he wrote in fetters about angels but in freedom about devils—the most stirring passage in the novella is when Biondetta eloquently celebrates passion as "une flâmme celeste," which is threatened by repression of natural impulses ("élans naturels"). The orthodox want to snuff the flame (355). Only through passion, she says, may humans achieve a union of body and soul. This passage leads to what may be called the Romantic reading of the work. Biondetta is the dawning ("l'aurore") of Eros ("l'amour") within a man. She symbolizes a dangerous feminine force, demonic in its insistence, potentially but not necessarily destructive. Sylph can become demon in the Romantic synthesis, and both are symbols of inner forces (Kiessling, 75–77).[11] The text is didactic, then, but not in the manner consciously intended. The point is not that lust is bestial and premarital sex—indeed woman herself as a sexual being—is to be shunned, but that the supression of "élans naturels" transforms the sylph into a demon. Eros becomes poison (327, 330, 350). When Alvare succumbs and has sex with Biondetta, he presumably enjoys it, but is immediately ashamed. His guilt and remorse turn the beautiful girl into a monster.

This sense of guilt, of course, comes from his mother, who appears, as Todorov observes (130), at every decisive moment in the plot. The major conflict is not, however, between Biondetta and Alvare's actual mother (as Shaw thought, 63–64), for they never meet; it is rather between Biondetta and Alvare's imagined, dreamed, fantasized, introjected mother—what Freud and Jung called the mother imago.[12] She is more than a personal mother; she is Mother Church itself, she is the Virgin Mother. The conflict

11. Nodier and Baudelaire both were haunted by this synthesis. See Milner's second volume for an exhaustive treatment.

12. The idea of the mother imago goes back at least as far as Nietzsche (Ellenberger, 708).

is between fleshy Venus and Blessed Virgin. This inference is easily drawn from the text, especially in the scene in which Alvare sees a statue in a church "become" his mother (352).

The transformation of sylph into demon through the catalyst of guilt occurs in the text in spite of Cazotte's conscious intent. But is Biondetta the *anima* and dona Mencia the *mother archetype*?[13] Can such signifiers, if applicable, help in understanding the conflict between these two characters any better? Biondetta's androgyny is easily explained in terms of historical prototypes— the anima hypothesis is not necessary to understand her form. But what about her function as antagonist of the mother image?

In order for Biondetta to be a possible anima figure, she must exhibit certain definite characteristics. First, she should at least appear to originate in the mind of the haunted man. Second, she must either be a part of him (his "feminine side"), a fantasy-girl, or an unconscious projection onto a real woman. Third, she must be a soul figure and an animating force controlling Alvare's impulses and moods, energizing his actions, instigating change. Fourth, she must be bipolar, like a magnet, having one pole that attracts and another that repels; that is, she must be numinous both in the sense of the *numen*—a guardian or guiding soul (psychopompos)—and in Rudolph Otto's sense of being "over-powering, fascinating, terrible" (Neumann, 5). Finally, she must evoke a "genuine primordial experience."[14]

I think one can safely say that Biondetta herself was not used by Jung, Neumann, Hillman, and Jacobi, from whom I have gleaned these characteristics, in their formulations of the anima archetype. She does seem to meet all the criteria. Her bipolar and numinous natures have already been sketched; she is both daemon and demon, sylph and succubus. To these, one may add the archaic prototype of the siren (Biondetta sings twice for Alvare,

13. Bettina Knapp and Laurence Porter have already labeled Biondetta an anima figure. In her chapter on Cazotte, Knapp practices the kind of Jungian mysticism Kaplan and Kloss complain about (see Appendix B). Although she comes to some conclusions similar to mine, she *starts* from the assumption that Biondetta is the negative anima, without attempting to demonstrate this role. Porter, on the other hand, uses Jung when it suits him (like Leslie Fiedler); halfway through his article, he decides that the best way to explain Cazotte's indecisiveness concerning the ending is through Jungian archetypes, which Porter uses primarily as mere labels. He also confuses the issue when he sees the devil as a combination of anima and shadow (10), which in my opinion ignores the bipolarity of the anima.

14. This phrase is from Jung, "Psychology and Literature," 162. The four criteria have been gleaned from the following sources: Jung, CW 9.1, 26–39; Neumann, 3–38; Hillman, "Anima I," 97–106; Jacobi, 42–47. Cf. Hillman, "Anima II," 134: "We may call 'anima' only that particular gestalt which . . . signifies the core quality of my soul . . . she must stir my loving, and link backwards through tradition to prehistory, trailing the archaic, the phylogenetic."

and both times she enchants him), which is at least as old as Homer, and was originally a "positive" wind spirit or soul-bird as well as a "negative" harpy (Rose, 28, 245). Furthermore, Biondetta seems clearly to emerge from Alvare's mind, not only in such references to her as a chimera of the brain (373) and a fantastic being (*passim*), but also in the curious scene in which Alvare first names her (320)—he doesn't formally name her; he seems already to know her name, though she has not mentioned it. And the volcanic ruins are directly linked to Alvare: the twenty-five stones of the vault under which he conjures could represent the twenty-five years of his age. Béelzebuth/Biondetta erupts out of the ruins of Alvare's unconscious. Notice also that in one of his dreams, Alvare tries to take his mother to the ruins, but she sees them as dangerous and begs him to stay away from them.

Biondetta also seems to be Alvare's feminine side in her role as Biondetto, whose submissiveness gives the pattern for Alvare's later role as slave. But more important is Biondetta's obvious role as Ideal Beloved, ultimate fantasy-girl. She is not only an object of desire as Todorov saw her; boundaries between subject and object break down in this tale. She is Alvare's own desire. She is clearly not projected onto a real woman, but to be the anima she need not be projected if she is an autonomous fantasy. She must be a soul figure, however, which I think is seen most clearly in her role as sylph, creature of the air, the soul's element (Hillman, "Anima I," 106; cf. Onians, 168). She is, like Psyche, imagined with "flambeau à la main"; she is a guide to the dark regions. Cazotte's variation of the Sylph legend—she is not a soulless Undine or Melusine seeking a soul—seems a tribute to his intuition that the legend had it somehow wrong; it was the men who acquired souls by marrying these beings. Much fiery and volcanic imagery is associated with Biondetta, but she is not the flame of Eros itself; she is the air that allows it to burn, the fuel that feeds it (cf. Hillman, "Anima I," 106). She is therefore an animating force, even when she first appears in horrid aspect (319). Through her, Alvare is stimulated—he feels more alive (until they have sex). She also causes him to act spontaneously, impulsively, to "précipite ses jouissances," seeking immediate gratification. Finally, the words "âme" and "animée" are most frequently linked with Biondetta (e.g., 323, 360), and Alvare feels "animé" by her (e.g., 353).

There is enough textual evidence, then, to consider Biondetta an anima figure. The next question concerns dona Mencia. Is she an image of the Great Mother? She must show similar signs: the image of the mother must be in the mind of her son, but there must be something about her that is transpersonal—as here the definite link between personal mother and Holy

Mother Church. The mother archetype also has two poles, but instead of being a dynamic transformative force, she is a static, elementary entity. At her positive pole is the nurturing Good Mother who protects but at the proper time lets go; at the negative pole is the Terrible Mother or antimother, who sucks in and devours (Jung, *CW* 9.1: 82–83; Neumann, 24–27; Ulanov, 192–211).

The archetypal feminine (at least as conceived within the male) comprises both the mother archetype and the anima; the dynamics between the two are crucial in the development of a boy into a man. The boy must liberate most of his psychic energy (including libido) from his mother, who is also the first woman onto whom he has projected anima, and invest that energy in relationships with girls. If the detachment of anima from mother is incomplete—that is, if the boy either identifies with his mother or continues to relate to her in a feminine/submissive way—the mother will remain dominant (Jung, *CW*, 9.1: 83). When a young man is able to overcome the tendency to see real girls as goddesses, which is a vestige of infantile dependency on the mother, he is then able to relate well to girls. He may still project anima onto them—romanticize them—but now he is more conscious of the process, which he can therefore control.

Again, the possibilities of this model applying to *Le Diable amoureux* are strong. Dona Mencia is clearly a goddess figure for Alvare; she is always described in superlatives—"la plus religieuse," "la plus respectueuse," "la plus digne"—and in vision she attains the stature of a saint (32). Most revealingly, she is seen as a "tutelary angel" who will protect her son from monsters and phantoms (372). He remains, however, unconscious of her "negative" aspect; it is only perceived by those readers who do not see the ending of the story as happy; only to them do the mother's arms (into which the twenty-five-year-old man falls) become the devouring womb of the Terrible Mother.

Cazotte's text reveals two more compelling transpersonal symbols: the volcanic ruins of Portici and the incubus. The former gives a pre-Christian, primitive aspect to the story (as does the camel's head), and the latter is almost certainly primordial. That is, the incubus myth seems to result directly from the experience of primeval man, whether it was the fear of predators leaping on one's sleeping body and crushing it or the shared human experience of sleepers gripped by night terrors, feeling paralyzed, unable to breathe (Kiessling, introduction and 86)—as Alvare feels after sex with Biondetta. That Cazotte consciously uses the succubus for moral purposes does not necessarily preclude its possible archetypal significance, especially if he did indeed, as he claimed, dream the work before he wrote it.

Jungian terms may lend support, then, for the interpretation of Biondetta not as "object" but as "subject." The melodramatic plot involving diabolic temptation, illuminated with a Jungian perspective, becomes a mental mythos involving daemonic forces vying for dominance in the male psyche. The unfamiliar, uncanny (*unheimlich*) *conte fantastique* is transformed into a familiar *heimlich* (homely) family drama, played out as follows: Alvare at twenty-five is at an age when he should be concerned about marriage. His mother has been reminding him of this duty (349). He has been avoiding the issue, however, by leading a dissipated life with "femmes du jeu." (315). Beelzebub's frightening bestial appearance—the instinctive eruption of unconscious contents to the surface—indicates psychic upheaval over anticipation of a change in his life, an entrance into a new phase of development. The revelation of the apparition as feminine identifies her as the anima, which is necessary to guide the man in his selection of a mate. She appears as his Ideal, showing utter devotion and desire only for him. But she also appears as his dread, because the Ideal is so desirable, and he has been taught by his mother and church that desire is lust. Guilt therefore torments him. Because he still childishly mythologizes woman (she is perceived as a deity of Love and the Dawn), he is unable to relate to real women. They must be either Madonnas or courtesans: white or red goddesses. He wants to worship woman, to be her slave; he wants to relate to her pusillanimously, as infantile son to Great Mother. But she cannot be his mother; she is a transformative figure—she fuels his desire. Since he is still dominated by the Virgin goddess he has made of his mother, however, he tries ridiculously to reconcile the positive anima (sylphan Venus) with the positive mother archetype (nurturing protectress). The two poles repel each other—anima stirs man to give up maternal security.

Alvare is in what Ulanov calls the first stage of anima development. He need not be aware yet of his feminine side—he needs now to be a man (Ulanov, 228; cf. Jung, *CW* 9.1: 71–76). But he should be able to distinguish real girls from his idealizing fantasies. He cannot even do this. As my paraphrase reveals, the rising action of the story—up to the climax in sexual experience and revelation—is punctuated by a series of forgettings that Biondetta is an "être fantastique." He keeps seeing her as a real person, then reminding himself that she is not. She flickers back and forth between reality and fantasy. Her actions, seeming so real, are simply reflections of his own ideals of what he wants from a mate. But these ideals clash with those that have been inculcated upon him. He tries to repress his desire, but she then uncannily takes on an autonomy, and he mistakes her for a real woman.

One may interpret the sex act with Biondetta, then, as an act of onanistic narcissism. Instead of going out and relating with real women (other than his courtesans), Alvare would rather masturbate, dreaming of the ultimate fantasy-girl, a picture in his mind created out of the archetype of desire, the sylphan Venus. But a strongly ingrained sense of guilt, a superego forged out of the most powerful archetype in the child's mind, the mother imago, flips the fantasy-girl over, as it were, revealing her negative pole: daemon becomes demon.

These inner conflicts are vividly reduced to sexual terms as the climax occurs. Whether over sex with a woman (Todorov's interpretation of Biondetta as object), or over masturbation (my interpretation of Biondetto as subject), shame and guilt win out; Alvare is repulsed by the idea of the vagina, which he imagines as an infernal worm (373). And so he retreats into the womb of his mother's arms, a cozy, heavenly place. It keeps him safe from the terrifying vagina, the *janua diaboli*.[15]

Alvare knows he cannot have his fantasy-girl, but instead of decisively affirming her positive aspects as a guide for selecting a mate, he refuses to admit her to consciousness: anima retreats to unconsciousness. When she does so, Alvare is completely drained of will—he becomes an automaton (373), until his soul feels reborn, regenerated by his mother ("mon âme semble renaître"—373), his child's anima. Biondetta said it would take an act of his will to be rid of her, but it is not his own will that keeps Alvare from an affirmation of sexuality; it is his mother's, whose knees he has embraced (as he had embraced Biondetta's). Mother will select a proper wife in her image. Alvare has no will; he is pusillanimous.

Alvare's adventure, then, may be read as a mythos following an archetypal pattern. Cazotte was the kind of intuitive, visionary author Jung discussed in "Psychology and Literature" (155). And even if one does not accept the archetypal hypothesis, one may see the Jungian reading as a psychological development of the Romantic one. Regardless of how it is interpreted, *Le Diable amoureux*, while no masterpiece, is a remarkable text. Its ambiguities regarding dream and reality created a new genre, and its ambivalence over sexuality gave it conflicting messages—equal homage to the Virgin and

15. For the idea of the vagina as the gate to hell, see Kiessling, 38. Cazotte's work reveals the same misogyny promulgated by the Church Fathers (cf. Rudwin, 267), but as I hope I have shown, Cazotte's unconscious was working against him.

to Venus. Its light style conceals the guilt theme (so much so that Porter [5–6] thought it was about pleasure without guilt), which is nonetheless present to remind the reader that Venus and the Virgin are irreconcilable. Most importantly, *Le Diable amoureux* gives a fresh, vivid representation of the inner world of a man's psyche. Cazotte paved the way for the Romantics, who would come to create greater works than he by following his suggestion that a man's own sexuality—his soul's succubus—can be far more dangerous than any demon summoned from some outer hell.[16]

16. In this first chapter, I have attempted to illustrate the process by which I skeptically inquire whether a particular demonic image is indeed archetypal—archaic and daemonic. For further "testing" of the Jungian hypothesis on a text, see Appendix A, "Recognizing Anima." In the remaining chapters, to avoid becoming tedious, I will no longer present exhaustive delineations of the inductive process. My conclusions, however, are nonetheless derived from it; I never assume ahead of time, deductively, that the female demon is the dark side of the haunted man's soul. I look instead for her signs.

2

THE FEMININE IN *THE MONK*
From Sublime Madonna to Bleeding Nun

Matthew Gregory Lewis's *The Monk* (1796) is one of the most notorious minor novels in English literature: notorious for its lurid scenes of rape, necrophilia, and torture; minor for its melodramatics, histrionics, bombastics, its inconsistencies in character and its awkward double plot. The novel is more important historically than artistically—more an extravagant curiosity than a literary masterpiece.[1] It does not work as a whole, but it works very well in parts: some of the poems scattered throughout the text are fine contributions to the genres they imitate,[2] and its occasional psychological

---

1. The historical significance and artistic worth of *The Monk* have been explored by Praz (191–95), Birkhead (66–68), Summers (210–23), Railo (88–92), Varma (147–54), Fiedler (129–35), Brooks, Kiely (98–117), and Punter (90–97).
   2. John Berryman, in his introduction to the Grove Press edition of *The Monk*, refers to the

sophistication, relative to other Gothics of the time, paved the way for the "mature Gothic" of Maturin, Poe, Hoffmann, and Hawthorne (Frank, 25).[3]

As Frank explains, "Lewis advanced the psychological excitement inherent in Gothic villainy and exposed the reader to the torn mind and soul of this strange and terrible creature" (25). In fact, Lewis actually attempts to "psychoanalyze" his protagonist; he devotes many long passages to a sort of anatomy of Ambrosio's psyche (e.g., 64–66, 84–89). And he lets the reader know early that Ambrosio is unaware of his own true desires: "A thousand opposing sentiments combated in Ambrosio's bosom," many of which "did not obtain his notice" (84). Unlike Cazotte, whose unconscious was working against his conscious intent, Lewis was writing consciously about the unconscious.[4]

The Monk is not a visionary work like *Le Diable amoureux*; it is an early and crude example of the psychological novel (in Jung's sense in "Psychology and Literature," 154–55). Since it is a self-conscious and manipulative work rather than a "naive" visionary one, archetypalism is more difficult to assess in the text. Further compounding the problem are Lewis's liberal borrowings. Many of his contemporaries flatly denounced him as a plagiarist.[5] The character of the female demon Matilda, for example, was thought for a long time to have been a simple development of Cazotte's Biondetta (Railo, 260–61). Louis Peck, however, in an admirable piece of detective work, showed that this particular charge of plagiarism was based on the poor 1810 translation of Cazotte, which was dedicated sarcastically to Lewis by the translator. This anonymous person, eager to reveal that Lewis had plagiarized from Cazotte, actually inserted into *Le Diable amoureux* a passage from *The Monk* in which Ambrosio sees Matilda's bosom in the moonlight, instead of the woman's thighs as in the original French (Peck, "*The Monk* and *Le Diable amoureux*," 408). Railo read the 1810 translation (called *Biondetta,*

---

poems as "far from contemptible" (17). All citations to *The Monk* will be to this edition (New York: Grove Press, 1952), which was edited, with variant readings, by Lewis Peck.

3. Cf. Robert Hume, "Gothic vs. Romantic," 285: the shift from Radcliffean terror-Gothic to horror-Gothic enabled "the suspense of external circumstance [to be] de-emphasized in favor of *increasing psychological concern* with moral ambiguity" (emphasis mine).

4. Here I am in disagreement with Robert Kiely, who sees the work more in terms of surface rather than depth psychology (107). According to Kiely, "*The Monk* is not an early account of identity crisis, but an exploration of imposture" (108), which in Jungian terms would make it more concerned with the persona than the anima.

5. For detailed accounts of Lewis's alleged plagiarism, see especially Peck's articles and Railo (90–95, 260–61).

or the Enamored Spirit), thought he had found a passage lifted from Cazotte by Lewis, but was actually reading the translator's devious insertion of Lewis. Thus, Peck concludes, Lewis probably did not lie when he claimed he had not read Cazotte.

I cannot agree with Peck, however, when he claims that the similarities between Matilda and Biondetta are "negligible" and "incidental" (406). Enough of them exist to suggest that Matilda may also be an anima figure. Both women start as men subservient to a male master: one a page boy, the other a novice protégé. Both are loved as men, perhaps because each is an image of the male protagonist's self—the homoerotic love is really a form of narcissism. Like Biondetta, Matilda "flickers" between sexes, suggesting not a "transvestite game," as Kiely puts it (116), but a serious theme of the collapse of boundaries between subject and object, self and other—making *The Monk*, if only in part, an early example of Ambiguous Gothic.

Further similarities are no less negligible. Matilda is,, like Biondetta, compared and contrasted to an ideal maternal figure (discussed in detail below), which appears also in the protagonist's dreams. Moreover, the haunting female claims to have sacrificed everything for the haunted male (see *The Monk*, 68, for Matilda's echo of Biondetta's self-sacrifice). That both women are sirens with harps may be incidental, since the siren was conventional, but as previously mentioned, the siren is more than a mere convention, since this prototype seems old enough (pre-Homeric) to be considered primordial.

Their demonic aspect too is similar—both Biondetta and Matilda, when revealed as female, begin as sympathetic feminine/submissive characters, but become dominant aggressive sorceresses. A major difference in their demonism, however, presents a serious problem for the archetypal inference. Matilda, unlike Biondetta/Beelzebub, is not revealed as the devil itself, which in *The Monk* is unequivocally masculine, but as "a subordinate but crafty spirit" (418). Here Lewis was closer to conventional devil lore than Cazotte; the symbol of absolute, aggressive evil was seen as male, whereas many lesser demons were androgynes (Rudwin, 164). Matilda's androgyny is probably conventional (cf. Grudin, 140).

All the similarities between Matilda and Biondetta may merely be the result of both authors' use of the same traditions and conventions. And since the similarities are not "negligible," they suggest that Lewis probably was more familiar with Cazotte's work than he let on. Moreover, *Le Diable amoureux* was still well known on the continent; if Lewis had not read it, he could have heard enough about it to give him ideas for Matilda. Influence does not however completely preclude the possibility of archetypes; it only makes the task of discerning them more difficult.[6]

The episode of the Bleeding Nun presents a similar problem with a source.[7] One needs to look within the text rather than outside it for the most convincing evidence. Again, if enough signs of the archetypal feminine appear in the text, they may help the reader comprehend the psychodynamics of male sexuality, in terms not merely of what may have been peculiar to the late eighteenth century, but especially of what may be synchronically present in the human male. This archetypal perspective will then add yet another dimension to a text abounding in psychological themes, as Kiely, Punter, and Brooks have already demonstrated.[8]

Matilda and the Madonna

The protagonist Ambrosio, abbot of the Capuchins, famous in Madrid for his eloquence in preaching, "is reported to be so strict an observer of chastity, that he knows not in what consists the difference of man and woman" (44). In the beginning of the novel, he is so proud of his celibacy that he considers himself immune to sexual temptation; he feels superior to other men, for unlike them, he has "subdued the violence of strong passions" (64). Lewis is quick to reveal, however, that Ambrosio is deceiving himself. In his cell, the monk looks upon a picture of the Virgin, which for two years has been an object of his adoration. The portrait is the first compelling evidence of a feminine archetype, for it is perceived as a divinity by Ambrosio, as an "ideal . . . superior being," in comparison to whom mortal women are

6. In fact, influence itself may involve archetypal situations, like the Oedipal situation in Harold Bloom's concept of "the Anxiety of Influence."

7. See Peck, "*The Monk* and Musaeus' 'Die Entführung,'" and Syndy Conger's dissertation (93–105). Cf. Peck's biography (22).

8. Kiely shows how Lewis is able "to fashion remarkable psychological portraits even out of the crude materials of melodrama" (105) through the interplay of public and private aspects of the self; Punter gives a Freudian/Marxist reading of the literature of terror in general, including *The Monk*, in which he analyzes "social and psychological tendencies . . . in extreme and grotesque form" (85); Brooks, in his article using Otto's ideas on the numinous, also analyzes *The Monk* in terms of Freudian repression and guilt, concluding that the reassertion of the numinous during the desacralized Enlightenment led not to a reaffirmation of the Sacred but to an exploration of the unconscious: "The epistemology of the irrational leads rather into ourselves . . . primal numinous awe puts us in touch not with Godhead but with the unconscious" (262).

"tainted" and "disgusting." No real woman could be "lovely as you—Madona!" (*sic*; 65–66). Praising her in conventional rose/lily imagery—then even longing to "press with [his] lips the treasures of that snowy bosom" (65)—Ambrosio unconsciously reveals what Brooks (258) calls the "latent erotic content" in the Madonna. She is both a maternal figure and an object of desire: the original object of desire in the man.

A further archetypal suggestion may be in the figure of Rosario, who first appears in the novel immediately after Ambrosio's Madonna "revery" (66). Rosario seems to be a young novice, beloved protégé of Ambrosio, who calls Rosario "son" and would like to mold him in his image. But Rosario, after much hinting, reveals to Ambrosio that he is really a woman, whose name is actually Matilda. As a female hidden in a male, Matilda too begins strongly as a possible archetypal figure. Rosario, so closely associated with the Madonna portrait, could be an image of the youthful Ambrosio, whose desire is first hidden under a cowl, then revealed as a feminine force. Matilda/Rosario is, in Brooks's words (258), "not a wholly other, but a complex of interdicted erotic desires within" Ambrosio. As in *Le Diable amoureux*, the personification of desire within the man is imagined to be female. Because of this blurring of subject and object, *The Monk* begins promisingly as an Ambiguous Gothic text. Matilda may be seen as either a part of Ambrosio's psyche or an other. The problem is that it is impossible to sustain such ambiguity for four hundred pages, even with the intrusive subplot. The Ambiguous Gothic genre works best in the novella (*The Turn of the Screw* being the fruition of the form). Lewis later does make Matilda "wholly other"—as she becomes clearly a demon whose supernatural existence he finally asserts not as a metaphor for unconscious eros but as a polemic against Enlightenment rationalism. Matilda at the end is revealed to be an incubus from a literal hell.

In making Matilda thus an agent of cosmic darkness, Lewis forgets or deliberately ignores several earlier passages that unequivocally evince Matilda's humanity. Beginning as "not wholly other," she quickly becomes a real woman, then a real demon. Her metamorphoses are not consistent, nor can they be explained away, as Peter Grudin attempts, with the suggestion that Matilda is only the illusion of a real woman created by a demon.[9] She

9. See Peter Grudin, "Matilda and the Rhetoric of Deceit." Only Frederick Frank agrees. Most other commentators think that Lewis simply changed his mind about the nature of Matilda as he wrote the novel. Most recently, Camille Paglia has asserted that Matilda has been male all along, and that "the meltingly delicious sex between Ambrosio and Matilda . . . has been homosexual and daemonic, not heterosexual" (266). Ambrosio prefers the "feminine pseudo-

is not, as Frank claims, "consistently presented as a demon of carnal desire" (24). In several passages, the omniscient authorial voice obviously sees her as innocent of anything except womanly desire. For example, after Ambrosio is bitten by the serpent "concealed among the roses" (92), he is convalescing and she thinks him asleep—she gives an impassioned soliloquy that is pointedly undemonic (99–100). In this and several similar scenes, Matilda is clearly a real woman, so much in love with Ambrosio that she will do anything to have him. At first, her desire is innocent, but as she becomes more frustrated (he demands that she leave the monastery after he discovers her sex), her desire becomes more carnal. Eventually, she is consumed with lust for Ambrosio's "person," and will stop at nothing to have him. She will even sell her soul to the devil to have him. Frustrated by rejection, she becomes more and more desperate, until she finally seduces Ambrosio and they become clandestine lovers in the abbey, where she remains disguised as Rosario.

Matilda's degeneration is completely human here, and indeed Ambrosio's follows the same pattern: love that is at first nonerotic (or at least so the person in love thinks) is eventually supplanted by lust. But then Matilda's degeneration goes one step further—once she has Ambrosio's body, she wants his soul. It is this desire that begins to demonize her: she is no longer a woman who has sold her soul to the devil but a fiend in women's garments who becomes more and more masculine—only male demons can win men's souls (233).

When Ambrosio meets the Clarissa-like Antonia, she inspires in him (or so he deludes himself into thinking) a higher passion, not lust. Matilda's amorousness seems disgusting in comparison, as she "apes the harlot" (243). He bluntly informs her that he no longer wants her. She soon becomes his "friend" again, changing from the desperate yet feminine woman in love to the masculine sorceress. Ambrosio, noticing her metamorphosis into a "manly" woman (267), is at first frightened but finally submits to her influence, as she tells him she will help him seduce Antonia. Of course, no real woman would help a man seduce the very woman for whom he has spurned her. Matilda's motivation is developed realistically at first, like a Pamela's or a Clarissa's, as Lewis wants to dramatize the dynamics of

---

male" Rosario over the "masculine woman" Matilda. This view fails to account for Ambrosio's fixation on the female bosom, although I fully concur with her conclusion that *The Monk* "redaemonizes sex," reflecting the return of repressed Paganism and demonstrating "the occult compulsiveness of sex" (266).

frustration in woman and repression in man. But then he abandons psychological realism for Gothic melodrama. Matilda becomes a mere device, a cog in the Gothic machinery, an agent of supernaturalism.

Since she begins as a possible projection of an ideal, then becomes a real woman, then finally and most inconsistently becomes a male demon, Matilda is ultimately problematic as a possible anima figure. One could perhaps argue that this inconsistency is a reflection of archetypal bipolarity, but Matilda's ambiguity is too obviously manipulated by Lewis to make such an inference plausible.[10] Biondetta, on the other hand, was a consistently numinous figure appearing as a reflection of a man's ideals, desires, and dreads. Cazotte seemed largely unaware of her psychological significance. Lewis, however, seems almost too aware of Matilda's, and he decides to use her for several different purposes. Although her androgyny (as Rosario) may at first appear to be an indication of anima in Ambrosio, her subsequent masculinization as an external demonic aggressive force merely reflects the history of ideas on demons as androgynes (cf. Grudin, 140). Matilda, then, is not a compelling archetypal presence in *The Monk*.

Lewis was nevertheless a precociously intuitive psychological novelist. He seems to have realized that men form their impressions of women by comparing them to internal ideals. But if he did indeed stumble upon a picture of what Jung would later call the anima, it is not the problematic Matilda (nor can it be Antonia, as Fiedler seems to think),[11] because any character presented as a mortal woman cannot be the archetype. Thus, in *The Monk*, if the anima is present, it must be in the two numinous images that appear like opposite panels of a diptych—the Madonna portrait and the Bleeding Nun.

The portrait of the Virgin, which turns out to have Matilda's face, recurs in several key passages throughout *The Monk*. The picture obviously represents an ideal: "What charms me," Ambrosio says to himself, "when ideal and considered as a superior being, would disgust me, [if it were to] become woman . . . tainted with all the failings of mortality" (65). In the

10. Cf. Robin Lydenberg's article "Ambivalence in *The Monk*." She shows that Lewis orchestrates and carefully manipulates ambivalent attitudes in *The Monk*, not only over the nature of Matilda, but also concerning superstition and rationalism. Sometimes Lewis is ridiculing Catholic superstition; other times he is undercutting Enlightenment dismissal of the supernatural. He is simply inconsistent.

11. In *Love and Death in the American Novel*, Fiedler throws around Jungian terms like *anima* and *animus* when they suit him. His claim that Ambrosio and Antonia are projections of each other's anima and animus (131) is, I think, unfounded. Antonia is not herself a projection; she is a woman upon whom Ambrosio projects.

next passage in which the portrait appears (88), Ambrosio kneels before it and asks its assistance in stifling his "culpable emotions"—the desire for Matilda, who has just told him she is a woman but whose face still remains hidden under Rosario's cowl. Then Ambrosio goes to sleep, dreaming of "none but the most voluptuous objects."

> Matilda stood before him in his dreams, and his eyes again dwelt upon her naked breast; she repeated her protestations of eternal love . . . he clasped her passionately to his bosom, and—the vision was dissolved. (89)

It is replaced by one of the Madonna:

> He fancied that he was kneeling before her: as he offered up his vows to her, the eyes of the figure seemed to beam on him with inexpressible sweetness; he pressed his lips to hers, and found them warm: the animated form started from the canvas, embraced him affectionately, and his senses were unable to support delight so exquisite . . . while sleeping, his unsatisfied desires placed before him the most lustful and provoking images. (89)

In this description, Lewis deliberately psychologizes a common Gothic motif—that of a portrait coming to life. Ambrosio's dream reveals his unconscious attempt to reconcile the sublime feminine ideal with the object of desire.

Ambrosio, however, continues to resist temptation, until Matilda (in another soliloquy that would be nonsense if Lewis had already conceived her as demonic) addresses the Madonna. Matilda is envious of "this happy image" that has received all Ambrosio's affections:

> "'Tis religion, not beauty, which attracts his attention; 'tis not to the woman, but the divinity that he kneels. Would he but address to me the least tender expression which he pours forth to the Madona! Would he but say, that were he not already affianced to the church, he would not have despised Matilda." (100)

Here is the familiar situation in which the mortal woman envies the ideal apparition (as Olympia did Biondetta). Matilda does not seem aware that Ambrosio has overheard her, and her lament is a revelation to him: he knows without doubt that she loves him. It is significantly at this point that the Madonna portrait is revealed to have Matilda's face (101). This revelation is a remarkable instance of projection; in Jungian terms, if the Madonna is the anima, Ambrosio projects it onto the real woman Matilda, who then takes the form of the ideal. When he dreams again (104), the Madonna no longer appears; now there is only Matilda.

As an inward numinous force, with both sublime and erotic elements (the latter being perceived as negative in the bipolar structure), the Madonna evinces the most compelling signs of archetypalism in *The Monk*. Matilda is "a mere mortal" (103) who is at first contrasted with the ideal. But once the celibate man realizes that the ideal is unattainable, he tries to overcome his childish notion that real woman is "tainted" and "disgusting" by projecting the Ideal onto her. Only then is he able to possess her (109), overcoming her Otherness by investing her with part of his own soul. It is only when Matilda takes on a more sublime aspect as a "preserver of his life" and "adorer of his person," who has almost sacrificed her life for him (by sucking out the serpent's poison), that he is, ironically, able to succumb to erotic temptation. Ambrosio thinks he has made love to the Madonna. The delusion cannot last, however—the two poles, Virgin and Venus, are irreconcilable—the projection dissolves and Matilda is revealed not as Madonna but as whore (243). Then, Ambrosio must reproject Madonna onto Antonia, whom he at first loves nonerotically:

> The monk returned to his cell, whither he was pursued by Antonia's image. . . . He felt not the provocation of lust; no voluptuous desires rioted in his bosom; nor did a burning imagination picture to him the charms which modesty had veiled from his eyes. (243)

By contrast, Matilda, with whose sexuality he now feels glutted, seems a disgusting prostitute (243–44). This sublimation of Antonia does not last, however, as Lewis once again insists that refusal to admit erotic desire leads to a deadlier form of that desire. In a magic mirror provided by the suddenly demonic Matilda, the monk sees the naked Antonia preparing for a bath; lust supplants affection, and he eventually rapes and murders the Madonna-like heroine. After violating her, Ambrosio "felt himself at once repulsed from and attracted toward her, yet could account for neither sentiment" (371). Lewis, however, with precocious psychological insight, accounts for both: the attraction is to the projected Madonna/anima (the mirror suggesting a self-reflection); the repulsion is once again for the whore the monk's ambivalence has made of woman. His confusion is seen as a direct product of celibacy, an "unnatural state" that attempts to sublimate Eros, but only ends up perverting it into a deadly aggressive force. As Lewis traced the degeneration of a man from a paradigm of the holy to one of the damned, he anticipated both Freudian insights into repression and sublimation, and Jungian theories of archetypal projection. The two systems are complementary, for anima theory gives concrete form to sublimation.

The Bleeding Nun

The other numinous feminine apparition in *The Monk* is that of Beatrice, the Bleeding Nun. She appears as part of the subplot involving Raymond and Agnes. In a novel filled with extremes of good and evil, this couple seems to represent the median position. Ambrosio and the prioress succumb (respectively) to the worst erotic and sadistic tendencies of which human beings are capable; the Clarissa-like Antonia is actually too perfect—too naively good for her own good. Raymond and Agnes, on the other hand, are portrayed as flawed but sympathetic human beings. If the female ghost that haunts Raymond is archetypal, then the psychodynamics associated with it should be more normative than those associated with the Madonna and Ambrosio.

Agnes's family is opposed to her engagement to Raymond; they keep her locked up in their castle. Agnes has told Raymond about the legend of the Bleeding Nun, a ghost that is yearly supposed to haunt the castle. The two lovers plan an escape by which Agnes is to disguise herself as the ghost, for whom the doors are always left open. On the appointed night, Raymond comes to fetch the disguised Agnes and escorts her to his coach. The agitated horses know what Raymond soon discovers to his horror: he is in the company of the real ghost, an "animated corse" (170).

Agnes is led to believe that Raymond never came for her; her family convinces her that he does not love her, and she becomes a nun. But Raymond eventually convinces her that he does indeed love her, and in "an unguarded moment" they make love on the convent grounds. She becomes pregnant, and is locked by the prioress in a dungeon, where she is subjected to prolonged torture, becoming a species of what she had not believed existed—a bleeding nun. She gives birth to a stillborn child, but in contrast to Antonia, who (the novel suggests) is too good for this world, Agnes is saved and marries Raymond in the end.

The above summary suggests that the Bleeding Nun's ghost is used as a mere stock device, both to advance the plot and to enhance the Gothic melodrama.[12] In spite of Robin Lydenberg's contention that the ghost is nothing more than "a composite of clichés" (72)—a stereotype rather than an archetype—the text presents some evidence that David Punter was closer to the truth when he asserted, "the Nun may be a projection" (77). In Punter's Freudian view, she is a projection of Raymond's guilt about elopement. But may she also be a projection not just of something he feels but of something he is? Could she be an archetypal figure rather than a mere composite of shudder-romance stereotypes and *Volksmärchen* prototypes?

She first "appears" in a portrait painted by Agnes (151). When Raymond first sees it, he is "unconscious of what [he is] doing" because he is upset by the jealous rage of donna Rodolpha. The ghost in the portrait is described as

> a female of more than human stature, clothed in the habit of some religious order. Her face was veiled; on her arm hung a chaplet of beads; her dress was in several places stained with the blood which trickled from a wound upon her bosom. In one hand she held a lamp, in the other a large knife. (151)

At the outset, the ghost is promising as a possible anima figure. She appears when the man is upset, preoccupied, in an emotionally extreme state.[13] She is numinous—larger than life yet terrible because part of life—and she is bipolar, carrying a lamp like a guide and a knife like a murderess. Further bipolarity is suggested when Agnes, in her scoffingly sarcastic description of the legend of the Bleeding Nun, says of her that, as she haunted the castle, she alternately recited paternosters and "the most horrible blasphemies. . . . In short, she seemed a mighty capricious being: but whether she prayed or cursed, whether she was impious or devout, she always contrived to terrify her auditors out of their senses" (153).

The spectral figure, like the Jungian anima, is in conflict with a real woman—Agnes. Because she has been unconsciously projected onto Agnes, she seems to emanate from her; Agnes paints her even though she does not believe in her and ridicules anyone who does.

---

12. A conclusion suggested implicitly by Kiely, who sees the work largely in terms of theatrics (105–7), and explicitly by Lydenberg (71): "The ghostly conjurings in *The Monk* [are] theatrical and mannered."

13. In Jungian theory, archetypes tend to surface when people are either at turning points in their lives or in states of emotional upheaval (Ellenberger, 707–13).

The ghost, then, starts out promisingly, but like Matilda she threatens to become a mere device used to undercut Agnes's smug "enlightened" scoffing at superstition.[14] The actual appearance of the ghost thwarting the planned elopement of Raymond and Agnes may only be a piece of "forensic" drama, arguing against rationalism. But Raymond, haunted by the Bleeding Nun, appears self-haunted even as the external reality of the ghost is asserted.[15] When she first appears, he tells Lorenzo, "I *fancied* I perceived a female figure with a lamp in her hand moving slowly along the apartment" (166—emphasis added). He thinks it is Agnes disguised as the ghost, but when he sees the face of the animated corpse, he reacts to it as to a Gorgon and becomes "inanimate as a statue" (170).

> Her eyes were fixed earnestly upon mine; they seemed endowed with the property of the rattlesnake's, for I strove in vain to look off her. My eyes were fascinated, and I had not the power of withdrawing them from the spectre's. (171)

At first, she is not just an outer ghost. Like a lamia, she draws energy from the person she haunts, enervating him.[16] A boundary between haunter and haunted therefore breaks down. Lewis immediately equivocates further when "the charm ceases"; the horror at the sight of the apparition returns, and Raymond passes out. He seems now to be in a fever dream. Medicines bring him around, but then he sleeps and has more "fearful dreams" in which "Agnes and the bleeding nun presented themselves by turns to my fancy, and combined to harass and torment me" (171). The ghost begins to haunt him regularly, and unlike the legendary one, "was not even visible to any eye but mine" (173).

These psychological implications fizzle out, however, as Lewis relies on a

14. It is therefore misleading to call Lewis "an Enlightenment conservative like Diderot," as Lydenberg does (73). Lewis was young (not quite twenty) when he wrote *The Monk*; his feelings concerning superstition versus rationalism, as *The Monk* reveals, were mixed—he asserts the supernatural but scoffs at any peculiarly clerical superstitions.

15. A ghost's "flickering" between psychological projection and actual external entity is of course a staple of the Ambiguous Gothic genre. But such equivocations must be sustained through the whole text. *The Monk*, as has been seen in the main plot with the female demon, ultimately becomes a work of the Marvelous, unequivocally supernatural. Even if one takes the Bleeding Nun episode as a self-contained tale (as it was indeed published), it is not Ambiguous Gothic. The ghost is not simultaneously real and projected; she is first projected, then real.

16. Thus creating a kind of psychic vampirism, as Twitchell defines it in his book *The Living Dead*.

folktale motif to finish the story of the Bleeding Nun. It turns out that she is haunting Raymond because she needs him to help her get her unburied bones properly interred.[17] Thus her existence is ultimately supernatural: she is a ghost because her body was not buried. (She had been a monstrously evil woman, an adulteress and murderess.) She degenerates into stereotype.

Lewis seems nevertheless to have been aware of the possibilities, the potential for psychological symbolism in the haunting apparition. Its clash with the real woman is suggestive of a fairly normal situation—Raymond may unconsciously not want to marry his fiancée, or at least may have mixed feelings about her. When the Bleeding Nun appears alternately ghastly and charming, she may reflect Raymond's ambivalence as he attempts to choose a mate. But Lewis never goes further than a mere suggestion. He is an intuitive psychologist only incidentally; the bulk of his book is Gothic melodrama and alternately anti-Catholic, anti-Enlightenment, polemic. Nevertheless, in select passages, the female apparitions are more than mere stereotypes of castle specters used as devices. Raymond's first-person narrative (anticipating those of Poe) especially helps give the tale a modicum of psychological sophistication lacking in the Gothic novel before Lewis.

In fact, when the tale of the Bleeding Nun is placed next to its source—a German tale by Johann Musaeus called "Die Entführung" ("The Abduction")—one can clearly see how Lewis, in spite of his desire to please the audience of shudder-romances, lends some psychological sophistication to the original. Syndy M. Conger, in a dissertation on the influence of German literature on Lewis, has already demonstrated the author's indebtedness to Musaeus.[18]

From Musaeus's piece (an essentially comic *Kunstmärchen* making fun of superstition), Lewis got the idea of a nun's ghost appearing to thwart an elopement. He has Raymond recite a verse, clearly lifted from Musaeus (Conger, 97, 151), in which he vows himself to Agnes (actually the ghost). What is more suggestive is the way Lewis alters a part of Musaeus. In "Die Entführung," Fritz says to the ghost whom he thinks is his Emilie, "Ich bin dein, du mein, ich dein, mit Leib und Seele" ("I am thine, thou mine, I thine with body and soul") (Conger, 151). Raymond almost but not quite echoes this sentiment:

17. See Stith Thompson's *Motif Index of Folk Literature* or Ernest Baughman's similar index of English and North American Folklore, which uses the same categories. Motif E334 is the closest to the Bleeding Nun.

18. Conger thus refutes Peck's contention (in "*The Monk* and Musaeus," 347) that "it is by no means certain that Lewis was dependent upon Musaeus." There are too many echoes and exact parallels to be coincidental (Conger, 93–105).

> "Agnes! Agnes! . . .
> "Thou art mine!
> "I am thine!
> "Thine my body! Thine my soul!" (*The Monk*, 166)

Lewis deliberately alters the original from loving *with* body and soul to *identification* of the man with the apparition.[19] (As Raymond later discovers, he has unwittingly made a pact through this verse not with Agnes but with the ghost.) "Thine my soul!" This is perhaps the most compelling evidence of anima signification in *The Monk*; the author in his manipulation of a source is consciously asserting that the haunting female is actually the soul of the haunted man.[20]

The haunting females in *The Monk*, when they are not mere stereotypical devices, reveal some striking archetypal aspects that cannot be dismissed as mere conventions or plagiarisms. If they are anima figures, the Madonna and the Bleeding Nun are vividly polarized: the Madonna reflecting the ultimate wish fantasy (that the beloved woman echo the inner ideal) and the Bleeding Nun reflecting the ultimate dread fantasy—that the beloved turn out to be the worst possible image of the feminine ("an animated corse"). One might think that Raymond's psyche, haunted by such dread, would be more pathological than Ambrosio's, haunted by desire. Yet Raymond (along with Lorenzo) is the hero of the piece. Lewis was, I think, giving the final blow in his bitter attack on the Catholic practice of celibacy. Raymond is able to overcome his fear of marriage and woman, which is not abnormal in a young man even with so grotesque a manifestation. But Ambrosio cannot overcome the destructiveness of his wish fantasy: the unconscious desire to make love to the Madonna. Lewis, unlike Cazotte, realized that desire can be unconscious; he understood that men have an erotic instinct that cannot be suppressed or sublimated without danger. Further, he saw that men reveal their desire through projected ideals, and since Ambrosio has been trained to make his ideal woman the Virgin, he attempts to reconcile his erotic instinct with his sublime ideal. Thus Biondetta/Venus's *thighs* become

19. Louis Peck, in his presentation of variant readings of *The Monk*, reveals that Lewis had originally written the passage as practically a word-for-word translation of Musaeus. He altered it as shown for later editions (*The Monk*, 440).

20. One may also note another change from Musaeus—actually an addition. The ghost in "Die Entführung" did not carry a dagger or a lamp. The dagger Lewis apparently borrowed from another German source (Conger, 103); the lamp he added himself, transforming her into Psyche, giving her that guiding aspect of *psychopompos* also present in Biondetta.

Matilda/Madonna's *bosom*, as sexuality is displaced from below upwards. Only the breasts contain a potential reconciliation of the maternal ideal with the erotic reality. As in *Le Diable amoureux*, the vagina remains a place of horror, tainted and disgusting. It is the reality of woman that so disgusts the celibate monk; it is this perception of woman that ultimately damns him.

3

"UNCANNY DRIVES"
The Depth Psychology of E.T.A. Hoffmann

The first glimmerings of a sophisticated "literary psychology" in the Gothic were in *The Monk*, for Lewis seemed intuitively aware of mental entities to which Freud and Jung would later give a habitation and a name. But it was, appropriately, the German Romantics who first fully realized the psychological implications of the supernatural, not only in the fairy tale, which they raised to high art (*Kunstmärchen*), but also in the lowly genre of the *Schauerroman*. The masters of psychological horror in Germany were Schiller, Tieck, and especially E.T.A. Hoffmann.[1]

Hoffmann was profoundly interested in the philosophers who were forebears of Jungian thought—Kant, Schelling, and G. H. von Schubert, to

---

1. Schiller's "Der Geisterseher" (1789) was especially influential on later, more psychological horror (Frank, 145–46). Ludwig Tieck was the more innovative, blending Gothic and märchen elements in "Der Blonde Eckbert" (1797) and "Der Runenberg" (1812).

name the most important.[2] He was, for example, intrigued by Schelling's conception of the world soul (*Weltseele*), and Schubert's idea that the Unconscious provided a bridge between the world soul and the individual (Taylor, 78; Ellenberger, 729). Like Schelling and Schubert, Hoffmann believed that the unconscious was a person's link to cosmic forces, if only he or she could understand its language.[3]

Unlike Cazotte and Lewis, who had much less control over their material, Hoffmann deliberately makes his supernatural beings into numinous symbols of the *Weltseele* or the *Geisterreich*. The green snake Serpentina in "The Golden Pot," for example, is clearly both a Nature figure and an image of feminine forces within Anselmus.[4] A Jungian reading of Hoffmann, then, should reveal how thoroughly and how profoundly this "literary psychologist" anticipated Jungian ideas about the archetypal feminine and its relation to men.[5] A post-Jungian reading should avoid the Platonism of *Geisterreich* and *Weltseele* as forerunners of the Collective Unconscious. Instead, I will examine specific texts for signs of archetypes.

Whether Hoffmann was psychoanalyzing himself in these works I will not conjecture;[6] my focus remains on the universal, on what the texts reveal—

2. Hewett-Thayer (113–21) provides a concise summary of Hoffmann's reading of these and other philosophers. See also McGlathery's exhaustive source study *Mysticism and Sexuality: E.T.A. Hoffman. Part One: Hoffmann and His Sources*, 136–50.

3. Cf. Tymms, 60: "To Hoffmann, the apparent absurdities of dreams, visions, and other figments of the irrational mind imply deep mysteries of cosmic proportions, which might be revealed to man if he were but able to . . . decipher the symbolism." Other readers draw direct links between Hoffmann and Jung. Prawer asserts: "For Hoffmann, the personal unconscious is a means of gaining contact with something larger and deeper . . . which we may equate . . . with Jung's collective unconscious" (302); Peters (62) agrees: "the Other Realm exists at a deep subconscious level . . . common to all human beings, not unlike C. G. Jung's concept of the Collective Unconscious."

4. Hoffmann's masterful "märchen for modern times" therefore inspired one of the best Jungian interpretations of literature: Aniela Jaffé's monograph. Prawer (302) and other non-Jungians have praised her study. Another Jungian interpretation more relevant to this essay is Elardo's dissertation, "The Chthonic Woman." But his study, heavily dependent on Neumann, overemphasizes the negative aspects of the feminine, forgetting the bipolarity of the archetype. She cannot be "always the vixen, never the virgin" (2704A); she is often imagined as both.

5. In a sense, Jungian analytical psychology is a "formulation . . . of the confluence of traditions that shaped . . . Romanticism" (Bickman, 5), but it must be remembered that Jung did not derive his theories from the Romantic philosophers. He made inferences, often in agreement with theirs, based on observations of dreams and fantasies of patients. Hoffmann seems to have made similar inferences based on his own observations.

6. Kiernan (310) thinks "The Sandman" is "an autobiographical sketch of Hoffmann's childhood." McGlathery (*Part One*, 35–37) sums up the psychobiographical interpretations. See

albeit parabolically—about the problems of growing up a male human being. The Ambiguous Gothic, which Hoffmann learned from Cazotte, Tieck, and Schiller,[7] is an excellent vehicle for psychological parables, especially fables of identity crisis, since (as has been seen) the genre tends to break down boundaries between self and other, male and female.[8]

Hoffmann's two stories "The Sandman" (1815) and "The Mines of Falun" (1818) are perfect examples of this Ambiguous Gothic. They mingle the moral with the macabre, the humorous with the grotesque, the horrific with the absurd. Both may be read as cautionary stories of sensitive young men who go mad. Though merely absurd and anomalous to some early critics,[9] these tales have more recently found readers and rereaders (e.g., Hertz and Fass) who have created brilliantly coherent texts out of Hoffmann's ambiguities. Below are two post-Jungian attempts to create coherence out of the seemingly anomalous numinous figures haunting Hoffmann's protagonists.

"The Sandman": The Failure of Vision

Dramatized in Offenbach's opera *Tales of Hoffmann* and analyzed by Freud in his famous essay "The Uncanny," the much anthologized "Der Sandmann" is perhaps the most familiar of Hoffmann's tales. The close reading offered below, to some extent an elaboration on Freud's, involves a study of the language of archetypes; that is, how they attempt to communicate to the protagonist, who misinterprets their message.

---

also Mahlendorf's article, which reveals "the thin line between creativity and pathology" (232) in Hoffmann. Nathanael in "The Sandman" is that part of Hoffmann he wishes to exorcize. McGlathery (*passim*) sees Hoffmann's protagonists as "self-ironic" portraits.

7. *Le Diable amoureux* was one of Hoffmann's favorite books (McGlathery, *Part One*, 122; cf. Winkler), but it was probably mostly from Tieck that Hoffmann learned the techniques of Ambiguous Gothic—e.g., of refusing to explain away the supernatural, seeing in the uncanny a psychic reality that is not mere delusion.

8. Cf. Daemmrich, 23: The unconscious alter-ego projections appearing in the Romantic fiction of the Germans are "the first indication of the modern crisis in man's identity." This identity crisis involves doppelgängers of both sexes—it is a crisis also of gender identity, as Nathanael's identity in "The Sandman" dissolves into Olimpia.

9. Sir Walter Scott (467) missed their moral significance completely, seeing Hoffmann's tales as mere raving, the "feverish dreams of a lightheaded patient . . . requiring the assistance of medicine rather than of criticism." Goethe agreed that they seemed meaningless. Their ambiguity has resulted in conflicting interpretations, from Neoplatonic Idealism (Negus) to Romantic Irony (Tatar) to the Absurd (Daemmrich, 75, and Prawer, 307).

The tale opens with a letter from the student protagonist, Nathanael, to his friend Lothar, the brother of his fiancée, Klara. Worried that his friend, fiancée, and mother are disturbed and angry with him, Nathanael is writing to convince them that he is not "a crazy visionary" ("einen aberwitzigen Geisterseher") (K, 137; W, 7).[10] As the story will ironically reveal, however, Nathanael's problem is that he is *not* a visionary and that he *is* a ghost-seer.

Archetypal implications begin with Nathanael's description of Klara, his "pretty angel-image, so deeply imprinted in heart and mind" ("holdes Engelsbild, so tief mir in Herz und Sinn eingeprägt") (K, 137; W, 7). Immediately, Hoffmann reveals that the young man perceives the beloved as a divine figure within him. She seems his guardian angel. She even accepts the role (K, 146), but for her it is only a figure of speech, while for Nathanael it is a literal reality. Unfortunately for him, however, she cannot live up to the role he has projected onto her from his own Idea of Woman. Klara is a fairly complex character in her own right, refusing to be inflated to the archetypal or reduced to the stereotypical angel.

In his letter to Lothar, Nathanael attempts to explain his apparent paranoia by going back to his early childhood, when he formed an obsession with that goblin of the nursery, the Sandman, whom he identifies with a friend of his father, Coppelius. Freud has shown that Coppelius is really the boy's image of his father (*Vater Imago*), who seems to have made a diabolic alliance with this ominous figure of horror.[11] But why does Nathanael come to view his father as the ally of the evil one? At first, before he knows about Coppelius, Nathanael describes the father in nostalgic terms. When he was little (he writes to Lothar) he enjoyed the "marvelous stories" his father told the children while he smoked his pipe, which Nathanael loved to light for him (K, 138; W, 8). But "*mother was very sad on such evenings*, and hardly had the clock struck nine when she would say: 'Now children, off to bed with you! The Sandman is coming, I can already hear him'" (K, 138; emphasis added). And Nathanael would hear someone clumping up the stairs. The child perceives a conflict here between the parents. His mother does not seem to share his enthusiasm for the father's marvelous tales. She is sad and nervous. At such a young age (he is still in the nursery), he remains very

10. All references in English to "The Sandman" and "The Mines at Falun" are to Knight and Kent's edition, *Selected Writings of E.T.A. Hoffmann, Volume One*, hereinafter abbreviated as K. References to the original German, given for key words and phrases, are to *E.T.A. Hoffmanns Werke*, vol. 2, hereinafter abbreviated W.

11. Freud, 384: "The figure of his father and Coppelius represent the two opposites into which the father-imago is split by the ambivalence of the child's feeling."

attached to his mother (K, 142), whom he perceives as angelic. Unconsciously, then, the father's smoke is seen as issuing not from a genial pipe but from hellfire.

Nathanael does not yet realize the reason for his mother's sadness: the lawyer Coppelius is coming over to continue on some mysterious alchemical work with Nathanael's father. She tells her son that in fact there is no Sandman—"it only means that you are sleepy, that your eyes feel *as though someone had sprinkled sand in them*" (K, 139; emphasis added). But he does not believe her; he is already frightened, traumatized by the first rift he has ever seen between his parents. He knows that it has something to do with the Sandman. Asking the nurse, he discovers that the Sandman is "a wicked man who comes to children when they refuse to go to bed and *throws handfuls of sand in their eyes* till they bleed and pop out of their heads." (K, 139; emphasis added).

Here the possibility arises that Nathanael is an unreliable narrator—anticipating Poe's insane narrators. There may actually be no nurse; she could be a hag projection of the mother—an image of Nathanael's *interpretation* of his mother's words, which were supposed to comfort him. A figure of speech, a simile, becomes a literal horror, magnified in the lens of the child's soul, which is troubled by a disharmony between his parents. The simile "feeling as though" sand is in the eyes transforms into literal sand thrown in the eyes by an ogre, who is really a father: "Then he throws the eyes into a sack and takes them to the half-moon as food for his children" (K, 139). The half-moon ("Halbmond"—W, 9) could also be a sign of partition, the splitting of the parental image. The boy's fantasy, in any case, attempts to assert that the father is an Other father, one who may steal his eyes. Freud considered this anxiety to be that of castration, an idea that remains controversial among critics.[12] Eyes are complex symbols; as "windows of the soul," they are more than mere sexual symbols. They are metonymies for vision. "The Sandman" is about the failure of vision, what Hoffmann calls "faulty vision" (K, 142; "Augen Blödigkeit"—W, 13). Nathanael fails to see the real Coppelius, who is indeed a wicked man, but a man only. The youth has magnified the lack of harmony between his parents into an archetypal conflict between the maternal feminine—which he knows to be angelic—

---

12. McGlathery (*Part One*, 36) considers Freud's equation of the fear of eye-loss with castration anxiety "unacceptable," since Freud was more interested here in supporting his theories than in understanding Hoffmann. Cf. Prawer, 303. For Prawer, the intrusion of the *unheimlich* into the cozy *heimlich* domestic circle is a matter of much more than sexual consequence.

and the paternal masculine, which must therefore be diabolic. When Nathanael realizes that the clumping footfalls belong to Coppelius, and that Coppelius is the source of the parental rift, he jumps to the only conclusion that makes sense—Coppelius, not father, is the diabolical sandman.

But "his intimacy with my father occupied my imagination more and more" (K, 139). Try as he might, he cannot separate the father from the Sandman. The boy consciously likes his father, however. The tales he tells stimulate Nathanael's imagination and probably help develop his later aspiration to be a writer. But the conflicts struggling just below consciousness create ambivalence; "I liked nothing better than to hear or read horrible tales about goblins, witches, dwarfs [*Kobolten, Hexen, Daumlingen*] and such; but at the head of them all was the Sandman, of whom I was always drawing hideous pictures" (K, 141–42; W, 9). He likes what he fears; he is compelled to draw pictures of his nightmare, and the pictures give him pleasure. When he concludes, however, that the Sandman is not just a "hobgoblin of the nurse's tale," but is actually a creature of flesh and blood named Coppelius, fear dominates, and all of the lawyer's grotesque features are magnified (K, 140–41). In his presence, the father magically changes—all of his good qualities vanish: "As my old father now bent over the fire, he looked completely different. His mild and honest features seemed to have been distorted into a repulsive and diabolical mask. . . . He looked like Coppelius" (K, 141–42).

As the boy observes the diabolic alliance between his father and Coppelius, he begins hallucinating. His father is some sort of demon now, servant to the satanic Sandman. This delusion precipitates a nightmare in which Coppelius treats Nathanael like a doll, twisting his hands and feet, saying, "There's something wrong here! It's better the way they were. The Old Man knew his business" (K, 142). The Old Man, the reader does not realize until later, is the scientist Spalanzani. The nightmare has revealed, before Nathanael has even met the scientist, that he too is a father image; but why Nathanael sees himself in the dream as the mechanical creation of the old man is not yet clear. The nightmare ends when "a gentle warm breath passed across my face" (K, 142) and his nurturing mother revivifies him, kisses and cuddles her reclaimed darling. In a revealing synecdoche, the mother is represented by her breath—as the child's inspiring soul image, she is his first incarnation of anima.

So far the tale has been narrated by Nathanael, and there is no way of telling which events are objectively true and which are psychic realities. The conflict between the parents has something to do with the mysterious experiments Coppelius and the father are conducting. When they result in an explosion that kills the father, Nathanael blames Coppelius, the "vile Satan" (K, 143). But if this is a tale told by a madman, the father may not literally be dead. In a story in which figures of speech become uncannily literal, it is also possible that apparently literal events are really figurative. The father does not die; only the good in him does. He leaves, and in so doing undergoes another transformation—into Spalanzani. When Nathanael swears to avenge his father's death, he may really be saying that he will get revenge on his father's real or imagined desertion of his mother. The original father/mother unity is completely severed now.

The second part of the story is a letter from Klara·to Nathanael, who in his distraction has accidentally addressed the letter meant for Lothar to Klara. This young woman, somewhat reminiscent of Lewis's Agnes, is a bright levelheaded girl whom Hoffmann presents as a kind of Enlightenment heroine, toward whom he is therefore somewhat ambivalent.[13] She is perceptive enough to realize that "all the fears and terrors of which you speak took place only in your mind," and that "dark powers within" Nathanael seem "bent upon his destruction" (K, 145–46). She goes on to give a psychological analysis of doppelgängers:

> If there is a dark power . . . it must form inside us, from part of us, must be identical with ourselves; only in this way can we believe in it and give it the opportunity it needs if it is to accomplish its secret work. If our mind is firm enough and adequately fortified by the joys of life to be able to recognize alien and hostile influences as such . . . then this mysterious power will perish in its futile attempt to assume a shape that is supposed to be a reflection of ourselves. (K, 146)

She goes on to reveal that she and Lothar have come to grasp the mechanism of what psychoanalysts would later call projection; the "dark power" within frequently introduces in us "the strange shapes the external world throws in our way, so that we ourselves engender the spirit which in our strange

13. That Klara may be an Enlightenment figure is further supported by the German word for Enlightenment: *Aufklärung*. Hoffmann's distrust of Enlightenment science is apparent in his sinister portrayal of Spalanzani, a prototype for Frankenstein and Rappaccini (see Cohen's article).

delusion we believe speaks to us from that shape" (K, 146). But Klara's sanity goes too far in the other direction; this Enlightenment heroine dismisses Nathanael's Sandman as a "phantom of the ego"—mere figment of an imagination overpowered by uncanny drives ("unheimliche Treiben"—W, 16). Hoffmann's tale reveals, on the contrary, that the phantoms have their own psychic reality, even if it is not an external reality.

Nathanael, however, sees them as literal monsters. He has been unable to outgrow his childish fears because he still takes them literally, in a failure of vision that originates in a misconstruction of his parents as diametrically opposed entities (mother/angel/moonlight; father/devil/hellfire). Another important—and related—split in the story is the dissociation of sensibility that also originates in Nathanael's bifurcation of the parental image: feminine/heart versus masculine/head. He is therefore, in his next letter to Lothar, outraged by Klara's letter, which he finds too "logical" and "analytical" for a girl. He can only believe that Lothar has poisoned her feminine sensibility with lessons in masculine *Logos* (K, 147). And no sooner is his disenchantment with Klara spoken than he sees (through peeking, as usual) the "divinely beautiful face" of Olimpia, Spalanzani's supposed daughter (actually a mechanical doll). He does not realize that what he sees in her is a reflection of himself: "Her eyes seemed fixed, I might almost say *without vision*. It seemed as if she were sleeping with her eyes open" (K, 148—emphasis added; cf. Freud, 385 n. 1). But it is Nathanael (whose eyes have been "stolen" by the Sandman) who has no vision, who is the automaton. He has automatically withdrawn anima (*Engelsbild*) from Klara, no longer worthy of it, and projected it into Olimpia, his feminine ideal.

Hoffmann then switches to an omniscient narrative (K, 148),[14] prefacing it with a reminder that Nathanael's case is not an anomaly: he should be recognizable to the reader, "and you may feel as if you had seen him with your own eyes on very many occasions. Possibly also, you will come to believe that real life is more singular and more fantastic than anything else and that all a writer can do is present it as 'in a glass darkly' " (K, 149). Nor is Nathanael's anima projection of Klara unusual (though his withdrawal of it certainly is). The authorial narrator himself has a tendency, he admits, to apotheosize Klara, likening himself to poets and musicians who cannot "look

14. Thus complicating his tale even further. As several readers have noticed, the narrator who comes in after the epistolary first half seems yet another reflection—another "alter-ego projection" either of Nathanael (his sane self perhaps) or of Hoffmann himself. See Tatar's article for an explanation of these multiple reflections in terms of Romantic Irony. I see this narrator as an authorial voice of sanity.

at the girl without sensing heavenly music which flows into us from her glance and penetrates to the very soul until everything within us stirs awake and pulsates with emotion" (K, 150). But in reality, Klara is not a muse. "Dreamers and visionaries" have bad luck with her because she is practical; her "clear glance and rare ironical smile" seem to dissipate their "shadowy images." Yet she is tenderhearted and intelligent (K, 151); in short, she is not a mere reflection (" 'That is nonsense about a lake and a mirror!' "), magnified in the convex lens of the dreamer. She has her own substance. But Nathanael can only see the reflection of his own projected image—the guardian angel inherited from his sense of the Feminine, formed from his perception of his mother. Unable to "dissolve the projection" (Jung, CW 9.1: 84) and recognize Klara as a woman rather than an *Englesbild*, he simply withdraws it and reprojects it onto Olimpia, who fits the mold.

Much has been made by critics of Nathanael's aspirations as a poet.[15] A common misreading of the tale, in my opinion, is to see Klara as a domestic philistine and Olimpia as the Romantic artist's true muse (cf. Veronika vs. Serpentina in "The Golden Pot"). But Nathanael is not a poet; he is at best a poetaster. Rather than a visionary, he is a literalist. Believing in the objective, external reality of those "dark powers" Klara wrote to him about (K, 151), he imagines himself their "plaything." He also believes that poetic inspiration comes from external powers, rather than from an inner light. Consequently, his tales and poems are "really very boring" (K, 152), for he has reified the archetypes, mistaken them for external beings, for Others.

He writes a poem about his presentiment that Coppelius will destroy him:

> He portrayed himself and Klara as united in true love but plagued by some dark hand which occasionally intruded into their lives. . . . Finally, as they stood at the altar, the sinister Coppelius appeared and touched Klara's lovely eyes, which sprang onto Nathanael's breast, burning and scorching like bleeding sparks. Then Coppelius grabbed him and flung him into a blazing circle of fire. (K, 152)

The poem turns out to be prophetic, but not in a visionary sense; it is a self-fulfilling prophecy. Nathanael refuses to see that he himself is the

---

15. Mahlendorf, for example, sees Nathanael as a Romantic poet. Although she recognizes in the tale "the thin line between genius and madness," she does not see that Nathanael, as a reifying literalist, is no poet. Nor does Kamla, for whom Olimpia is "the mirror image of the [Romantic] solipsistic poet" (95).

impediment to their marriage, not only because of sexual cowardice, as McGlathery points out, but because of a fragmentation of his personality.[16] Klara implores him to realize that what burned into his breast were not her eyes but the drops of his own heart's blood—a heart torn apart by the hands of his own inner daemon, an animus run amok, dissociated from anima.[17] The two must be in harmony for a man truly to love a woman. But all Nathanael can see in Klara's eyes now is death, which "looked upon him kindly" (K, 153). And as he gets more enrapt in his poem, more self-possessed, she cries out for him to throw the "mad, stupid tale into the fire." This is not philistinism; she knows rather that his poem is mentally dangerous, a blind rehearsing of his inner turmoil in occultist terms. But Nathanael is indignant: He "thrust Klara away, and cried, 'You damned lifeless automaton!'" (K, 154).

He is the automaton, of course, and though there are a few remissions from his mental disease when he manages momentarily to restore "Klara in his heart" (K, 153–55, 166), he keeps relapsing into a more and more psychotic paranoia. As long as he refuses to accept the "dark powers" as his own, he is doomed. During one of his remissions, he recognizes that he has been the victim of a "gruesome illusion . . . the product of his own mind," and that the optician Coppola cannot possibly be "the ghostly double [verfluchter Doppeltgänger] and revenant of the accursed Coppelius" (K, 156; W, 28). But then, picking up one of Coppola's spyglasses, he "involuntarily" peeps at Olimpia. At first she looks lifeless and rigid (for he has momentarily withdrawn anima from the doll and reinvested Klara with it), but as he peeps she is transformed; "moist moonbeams were beginning to shine in Olimpia's eyes." Hoffmann again uses anima signs—water and the moon.[18] But what is more remarkable in this passage is his insight into the

---

16. McGlathery reduces the tale to a comic *conte licencieux* involving sexual panic or "cold feet" (*Part Two*, 58). I do not deny the sexual element in the tale, but I think it is part of a larger whole. Sexuality is only part of Eros.

17. Here I am following the post-Jungian idea (supporting Freud's notion that humans are innately bisexual) that men must have an animus as well as an anima (Hillman, "Anima II," 141–43). Cf. Samuels, *Jung and the Post-Jungians*, 210; Logos and Eros exist within a person of either sex: "The balance and relation between the two separate principles regulate the individual's sense of himself as a sexed and gendered being." One might argue that Coppelius is better seen as a "shadow" than an animus (as Prawer [302] suggests), but as Hillman and Samuels imply, Jung's notion of the shadow developed in the absence of an animus theory in the male. Once dissociated from anima, the animus *becomes* the "shadow."

18. Emma Jung (65–70) reveals how frequently the anima is associated with water. The moon is traditionally viewed as feminine by men, while the sun is supposedly masculine. Icons of the

unconscious process of projection. Nathanael animates Olimpia with "ever-increasing life," imposing on her his feminine ideal. Thus she becomes an angel that "hovered before him in the air," glowing with "divine beauty" (K, 156–57).

When Hoffmann has Nathanael acquire a new set of eyes, the author creates a symbol of what Nathanael has been doing all along—magnifying. Through apotheosis he turns people into archetypes, and through reification he turns archetypes into people. Olimpia, through projection, becomes a real girl, in character the opposite of Klara. Nathanael is the only man at her concert and coming-out party who does not see that she is dull, empty-headed, and inarticulate—a mere machine. When he dances with her, he animates her further, as his "warm life-blood surges through her veins" (K, 159). She merely takes life from him; she has none of her own. She cannot say anything intelligent, and yet he considers her a "magnificent and heavenly woman! You ray shining from the promised land of love! You deep soul, in which my whole being is reflected" ("du tiefes Gemut, in dem sich mein ganzes Sein spiegelt") (K, 159; W, 31).

Although Olimpia reminds him of "the legend of the dead bride" (K, 160), he continues to give life to her.[19] She is the ultimate in feminine passivity and receptivity, infinitely preferable to the more masculine Klara:

> Never before had he had such a splendid listener. . . . She sat for hours on end without moving, staring directly into his eyes, and her gaze grew ever more ardent and animated. . . . It seemed to him as if she expressed thoughts about his work and about all of his poetic gifts from the very depths of his own soul, as though she spoke from within him. (K, 162)

Perceiving her "utter passivity" as a fascination for him and his poetic genius, Nathanael is unable to see the significance of her identity as the "daughter" of the diabolical Spalanzani, even after he sees Spalanzani and Coppola/Coppelius fighting over her. They twist and tug her "this way and that,

---

androgynous archetype have often been presented as fusions of sun and moon (see *Man and His Symbols*, 89, woodcut illustration).

19. The corpse bride (discussed more fully in Chapter 5 below), as Knight and Kent point out in a footnote (K, 160), is an allusion to Goethe's ballad "The Bride of Korinth." In Hoffmann, the necrophilia made explicit in the poem is only hinted at; Goethe's bride is not ambiguous like Olimpia, whose corpselike features are an ironic metaphor for what Nathanael really wants in a woman and for the dead state of Nathanael's soul.

contending furiously for possession of her" (K, 163). For the first time, Nathanael sees that she is a lifeless doll; and worse, her eyes are missing. What he fails to see is the similarity between this scene and the dream that he had (K, 142) in which it was *his* hands and feet that were being twisted. Spalanzani now tells him that the eyes used in the doll had been stolen from Nathanael, at whom he now hurls the bloody things, which hit his breast. The poem comes true; Spalanzani is revealed as yet another doppelgänger of Coppelius, and Nathanael's mind, overwhelmed by this appearance of yet another goblin, is completely shattered by madness.

The dream, the poem, and now this hallucination are all messages from his unconscious that he is unable to decipher, because he takes the symbols literally. Convinced that the male phantoms are gone, he once again "recovers" by reprojecting anima onto Klara: "An angel guided me to the path of light" (K, 166). They prepare to marry, but one day after they have climbed a tower to look at the mountains, Nathanael "automatically" takes Coppola's spyglasses out of his pocket, and looks at Klara through them. Babbling incoherently about a whirling wooden doll and a circle of fire, he tries to hurl Klara from the tower. Lothar saves her, but Nathanael, seeing "the gigantic figure of the lawyer Coppelius" (K, 167) in the crowd below, throws himself to his death. The narrative ends with the assurance that Klara found a husband many years later, along with the "quiet domestic happiness" that "Nathanael, with his lacerated soul [*Innern zerrissene*], could never have provided her" (K, 167; W, 40). Klara here seems like Veronika in "The Golden Pot"—symbol of domesticity, inappropriate mate for an artist, who must be married to his muse. But since no woman can be a muse except in the imagination of the artist, he is better off not imposing upon mortal woman the awesome responsibility of "inspiratrice." At least, he should recognize, as Nathanael never does, that inspiration ultimately comes from within.

Nathanael is but the travesty of an artist. Instead of creating powerful poetic symbols out of the "dark powers" of his mind (as Hoffmann himself is able to do), he creates reifications, pathetic fallacies that take figures too literally—that make out of the archetypes of the soul mere bogeymen and dolls.

Hoffmann shows us that we all have our inner phantoms. We must recognize them as such without merely dismissing them (like Klara) as unreal figments. Nathanael never realizes that Coppelius, Coppola, Spalanzani, and the Sandman are all identical—all go back to his father imago, the child's unconscious image of the father. He is perceived as sinister only after the child notices a conflict with the mother. This split causes a dissociation of sensibility that makes it impossible for him to love Klara as a woman. He can only perceive her in the holy light of the angelic feminine, utterly dissociated from the analytical, scientific, logical masculine. When she fails to live up to this ideal, he withdraws the anima projection and apparently reprojects it onto a more feminine girl. But Olimpia is nothing more than a vacuous and passive receptacle for Nathanael's projections, a symbol of his own femininity. She is an Echo to his Narcissus.[20]

What dooms Nathanael, then, is his unconscious fission of the androgynous archetype—what Jung called "the divine syzygy"[21]—which is split when the child perceives an unresolvable conflict between his parents. Masculine and feminine become polar opposites; then each gets magnified as Nathanael is unable to outgrow his childish deification of the parents.[22] This polarization in turn causes him to reify the dark powers, mistaking inner daemons for external occult influences.[23] He is trapped in a vicious circle of deification and reification—the "circle of fire" through which he finally throws himself.

"The Mines at Falun": "Mighty Elements" of the Psyche

"Die Bergwerke zu Falun," like "Der Sandmann," is a psychological study of conflicts within a young man's troubled psyche. The protagonist, a Swedish

20. Cf. Irving Massey's chapter 6. He comes to a similar conclusion (that Nathanael is narcissistic) by a different route. When Klara refuses to become a projection of Nathanael, "she throws him back upon his . . . nothingness" (118). Cf. also G. R. Thompson, *Romantic Gothic Tales*, 50, and Kamla's article.

21. Jung, *CW* 9.1. 67: "It therefore seems probable that the archetypal form of the divine syzygy first covers up and assimilates the image of the real parents until, with increasing consciousness, the real figures of the parents are perceived—often to the child's disappointment. Nobody knows better than the psychotherapist that the mythologizing of the parents is often pursued far into adulthood and is given up only with the greatest resistance." Nathanael's parents at first fit the archetypal mold, which presents them as a unity.

22. Cf. Schneidermann, 285, who cites Heinz Hartmann's idea that "there is a tendency in the pre-phallic stage to identify the parents as idealized, powerful, magical protectors"—a tendency Jung explains as archetypal.

23. That Hoffmann was somewhat skeptical of occultism seems clear from McGlathery, *Part One*, chapter 9: "Hoffmann's tales are . . . ironic jests about the widespread occultism and spiritualism of his own day" (155).

sailor named Elis Fröbom, scarcely twenty years old, has lost both his parents—first his father and now, more devastatingly, his mother. The tale opens with Elis just returned from sea, in a pub with his riotous companions who mock his melancholy and advise him to get drunk with the rest of them. "Drink, boy, or may the sea-devil, Nack [*der Seeteufel Näcken*], that old troll, take you!" (K, 190; W, 270).

Nack seems to represent a death instinct,[24] for Elis cannot be placated; he is so depressed that he exclaims, "If only I lay buried at the bottom of the sea! There is no one left in this life with whom I can be happy" (K, 191). As a fatherless boy, he had been more than normally attached to his mother (as Lorenz [251], in his early Freudian interpretation, noticed). The resulting rupture when she died, the trauma of separation, the void left in his soul—all remind him of death. He longs for the mother who is dead; he longs, then (in an unconscious leap), for the dead and for death. Eros abounds all around him—a beautiful girl with a "yearning sadness in her dark eyes"—a whore with a heart attempts to rouse his interest. He likes her immediately: "He could see that the girl's sweet whisperings had found an echo in his heart" (K, 191). Her voice resonates, however, in an empty chamber, a void where love for mother once had been (cf. Negus, 110). He gives the girl an Indian handkerchief and some money. Taking the former and refusing the latter, the girl makes it obvious to Elis that he could be special to her (not just another "trick"). But Elis has only death on his mind, not love.

Again, trauma seems to stir up archetypes. An old miner accosts Elis. Described as a "familiar figure" (K, 191), the miner listens to Elis tell the sad tale of the deaths of his father and brothers at sea and war, how he alone supported his mother as a seaman until her death "lacerated" his heart (K, 192). What really lacerates his heart, however, is guilt: "It seemed to him wicked to have gone to sea at all and not stayed home to care for his poor mother" (K, 192). This—along with the Oedipal fixation Lorenz described—is the source of Elis's melancholy. He blames himself for his mother's death; therefore he wants to die. In a striking image of Elis's guilt, Hoffmann describes the young man's sensation that the "arteries in his *breast* were bursting and that he would bleed to death" (K, 192—emphasis added). Such, Elis feels, would be the just deserts of a man who had killed his

---

24. This sea-fairy, a kind of male nixie or Lorelei, was armed with a hook with which he dragged people, usually children, down under the sea (Bassett, 97). But Hoffmann clearly internalizes him—Elis's fellow sailor sees him as being possessed by Nack.

mother: he who had sucked life from her breast must now bleed life out from his.

Such inner turmoil is just the kind of situation that might summon archetypal figures from their unconscious suspended animation, animating them automatically. The old miner seems to be such a figure, but Hoffmann only hints at his uncanniness for now. Instead, Elis reminisces to the miner about his idyllic relationship with his mother, whom he had all to himself. In a bold image, Hoffmann now adds the Oedipal dimension to the story: "I poured my ducats into my mother's lap" ("ich dem Mutterchin die Dukaten in den Schloss geschuttet") (K, 193; W, 273). Elis, totally unconscious of the ejaculatory image, harps on the more innocent pleasure of sitting with the "old lady" (thus asserting her nonsexuality) and telling her of his travels. He resolves never to go to sea again.

The old man then suggests that Elis go to Falun and become a miner, which at first does not appeal to the youth, until the old man paints a romantic picture of the miner as one who "unlocks nature's most secret treasures." As Fass (96) and Daemmrich (83) have shown, this romantic view of the mine is symbolic of the unconscious; a miner in this tale becomes one who explores the depths not only of the earth but also of the psyche. "It may well be that in the deepest tunnel, by the feeble light of the mine lamp, man's eyes see more clearly" (K, 194)—into both Nature and human nature.

The old man's speech, his vivid pictures of the mines, enchants the youth with a "powerful magic" that seems to transport him to the depths with the old miner. But Elis is fraught with ambivalence: the mine in his mind's eye seems at once malevolent and enchanting (K, 194). The tale now becomes (among other things) a parable of youth in crisis:[25] a young man, especially at such a turning point in his life, needs to sort out the pandemonium of his mind—he must confront the daemons, those numinous internal figures that Hoffmann in this story calls "die mächtigen Elemente" (K, 201; W, 283), "mighty elements" that inhabit the depths of the mind.

That night Elis has a dream in which these mighty ones attempt to communicate with him. He dreams he is "drifting on a beautiful ship in full

25. My interpretation, of course, ignores several levels of this rich tale. Fass, for example, uses it to support her thesis regarding the Romantic artist's ambivalence toward the fairy realm of art (although Knight and Kent insist that the fantasy world in Hoffmann is not associated with art [K, 33]). For Fass, the mine is a self-consuming symbol: "to become a miner is paradoxically to commit himself . . . to an existence inimical to his plans for [domestic] commitment. . . . The mine's symbolic function cancels out the literal one" (99). Similarly, the unconscious death wish cancels out the conscious wish.

sail on a crystal clear sea" (195), which metamorphoses into a crystal floor, out of which grow metal plants. "When he looked down deeper and ever deeper, he saw in the depths innumerable charming female forms [*jungfrauliche Gestalten*] who held each other in locked embrace. . . . and from their hearts there sprouted forth those roots and flowers and plants" (K, 195; W, 275–76). When the *Jungfrauen* smile, they impart energy to the plants, giving them strength and joy. The dreaming youth is overcome with both "pain and rapture" as "a world of love, of desire and of passionate longing expanded within him." He throws himself down to the maidens, but the crystal ground dissolves and he finds himself hovering, suspended, just as he is in the waking world. A voice comes to him; he sees the old miner now, who suddenly dissolves, replaced by a "gigantic shape" that slowly forms "the solemn visage" of a mighty woman ("einer mächtigen Frau"). Thus the dream confronts the sleeper with androgynous transformations: the youthful feminine forms, a kind of unconscious reservoir of energy-giving anima figures, dissolve in the more formidable presence of the father imago. He comes with his consort, the other half of the syzygy, the Great Mother.[26]

As "Elis felt the rapture in his breast turn increasingly into crushing fear" (K, 195), the old man identifies his other half as "the Queen." Then Elis thinks he hears his mother's voice coming from the opposite direction, from the "domed sky," which has cracked; through the cleft he can see the stars and, he thinks, his mother. But then he realizes that it is not his mother; it is a "charming young woman who stretched out her hand towards the dome and called his name" (K, 196). The frightening Queen is below, the mother-as-maiden is above. Elis begs the old man to carry him up to the beckoners, away from the mysterious Queen. The *crushing* fear she inspires is a sign of the Nightmare, the Great Mother in her Terrible aspect. The miner, as her consort, admonishes Elis to be faithful to the Queen, to whom he has already given himself. "But as soon as the youth looked down again into the majestic woman's rigid face, he felt his being dissolve into shining minerals. He screamed in nameless fear and awoke from the strange dream, the rapture and horror of which resounded deep within his heart" (K, 196). The dream (which Hoffmann probably wrote under the influence of von Schubert's *Symbolik des Traums*)[27] is a kind of synecdoche of the whole text,

26. The identification of the Queen as the Great Mother is certainly not new. Cf. Heinisch, quoted by McGlathery, *Part Two*, 237: "Stronger than any earthly love is the longing to be subsumed into the All of Nature . . . symbolized here in the image of the Great Mother."
27. Schubert's work, published in 1814, suggested that dreams use a universal language of

beginning as it does with Elis on a ship and ending with his death, in which he does indeed "dissolve into the shining minerals."

How each figure in the dream anticipates the movement of figures in the rest of Elis's unfortunate tale remains to be seen. But the significance of the dream images seems already apparent. The bipolar feminine archetype reveals itself in the ambiguous aspect of a crushing succubus, associated with hell, and the angelic maternal, associated with heaven. The father imago or animus figure is also clear, dominating the dream with his words: as Logos, only he speaks, and his Word is law. But he is not the Jehovah-Urizen type; he is more like Thor or Jove (or Urthona, Earth-owner), whose consort is the Great Mother and whose law is not moral law but the imperatives of instinct, whether erotic or thanatotic. Elis is pulled in two different directions— toward life, where he must fill the void left by his mother's death by finding a girl to take her place, and toward death or degeneration, a dissolving back into the earth. The dream has made his alternatives clear; it has communi- cated to him, using as its language the archetypal daemons: he must either find a girl to help him forget his mother or inflate the memory of his mother so grossly (by making her the Queen of Heaven) that he will languish in her womb, the mines.

Both wishes are present—erotic and thanatotic. The tug of war between the two instinctual forces continues until Elis makes his choice. But none of the choices he makes is conscious. When he "decides" to go to Falun, it is actually "as though an unknown voice were whispering constantly in his ear" (K, 197) for him to go. Trauma has made him an automaton; like Nathanael, he is at the mercy of his own demons.

The day after the dream, he continues to feel unhappy:

> He thought sorrowfully of his deceased mother; then it seemed to him as if he were longing to meet that girl again who had spoken to him yesterday in such a friendly way. And then he feared that if the girl should appear in this or that little street, it would really only be the old miner whom he feared, although he could not say why. (K, 196)

In his psychic upheaval, he now dreams, this time awake, of another androgynous transformation: longing for the absent mother becomes longing

---

symbols, communicating to the dreamer in hieroglyphics that are the same for humans everywhere. See Ellenberger, 205–6.

for the *Jungfrau*, which mysteriously and most uncannily becomes fear of the old man. But this personification of the death instinct has his positive pole: he is also Elis's guide. Like Dante with Virgil, Elis has a male animus figure guide him to the infernal regions: "He was certain that the voice of destiny had spoken to him through the old miner who was now leading him to his true vocation. . . . The old man was standing like a giant in front of him, pointing . . . towards the mist" (K, 197). For years, Elis has been guided by anima, projected upon his mother. Now, with her death, anima is suspended, associated with vague female forms; and animus has become his guide to the unconscious depths he must explore.

Elis knows that he must somehow come to terms with his seething unconscious. But looking down into its depths is like peering into the "jaws of hell." As he gazes into the great entrance to the mine, he sees a "crumbled rocky abyss," a void from which loom shapes that resemble "gigantic petrified animals . . . like human colossi" ("menschlichen Kolossen") (K, 198; W, 279). Again Hoffmann offers striking images richly suggestive of the numinous archetypes later described by Jung.

Peering into his own mind, the youth sees "an immeasurable abyss" that "yawned beneath him so he could see the frightful monsters of the depths in horrible embraces" (K, 198). These seem to be the demonic inversion of the charming female forms that had embraced each other in his dream. Again, Elis is beset by ambivalence: at times the archetypal figures appear benevolent, but they always have a dark negative pole threatening to dominate the youth if he fails to realize that his own anxiety is the source of their malevolence. Once he mistakes an inner daemon for a wholly other external entity, he is (like Nathanael) doomed to submit to its dread power. Elis's failure to see consciously that the mysterious mine is merely a reflection of his own psychic depths is the beginning of his doom. Like Nathanael, he is the victim of reification.

His failures are all failures of consciousness: he dismisses the dream as meaningless at first (then later misinterprets it), he ignores the significance of his daydreams, and he ignores the real reason he chooses to become a miner even after the vision of horror he had at the entrance. The reason involves Ulla Dahlsjö, the daughter of a miner who befriends Elis. She immediately "ignited all the divine joy and all the pain and rapture of love" in his heart (K, 200). Indeed, he decides he now understands the dream—"It was Ulla . . . who had offered him her hand to save him in that fateful dream" (K, 200).

Hoffmann has traced symbolically the same line Jung noticed young men often moving along: in the dream, Elis had first thought that the hand reaching out to pull him up to the "friendly sky" out of the fearful earth was his mother's, but then it turned out to be some vague but charming young woman's. Now the charming young woman is Ulla. Jung would see these transformations in terms of the youth shifting his libido from the mother, through the anima, to the "real" woman.[28] It is a perfectly normal and indeed necessary process. But Elis has had an unusually close relationship with his mother—has indeed lived to support her and lived for her approbation of his manly travels.

The mother archetype dominates him still—her rigid, rocklike colossus makes him a rock, "rigid, incapable of words" (K, 200). The Queen is in fact compared to Medusa's head (K, 209).[29] Hoffmann sees the myth as a symbol for a psychological truth: inability to break the maternal bond makes a man incapable of real movement and progression. The Good Mother becomes Terrible. Elis moves, but "mechanically" like an automaton (as did Alvare, similarly mother-fixated). Refusal to admit his problem leads him to a complete lack of self-knowledge. The real reason he decides to be a miner appears to be so that he can be near Ulla, even though he is quite incapable of telling her that he loves her. But the reason he tells himself (and Pehrson, Ulla's father) is that his "deepest inclinations were for mining" (K, 201). This is true but not in the sense that he means it. His "innermost desire," of which he is still unconscious, his deepest inclination, is to die. Elis Fröbom, then, will go down into the mines, not to explore the depths of his psyche (for unfortunately he will never realize that it is indeed his own psyche he is exploring), but to return to Mother Earth.

When Pehrson Dahlsjö ostensibly warns Elis of the tedium and difficulty of mining, he is warning him against romanticizing, but his admonition has a psychological meaning: "There is an ancient belief among us that the mighty elements [*mächtigen Elemente*] among which the miner boldly

28. See Jung, CW 9.1. 82: "the archetype of the anima . . . invariably appears, at first, mingled with the mother image." Cf. Samuels, *Jung and the Post-Jungians*, 212–13.

29. H. J. Rose (30) points out that the word Medusa means "Queen." He explains (29–30): "The kernel of the myth is that there existed . . . a creature of aspect so terrible that those who saw her turned at once to stone. I am much inclined to think that this tale has a very simple explanation, namely, certain phenomena of dreams. To see, in a nightmare, a face so horrible that the dreamer is reduced to helpless stony terror is not a peculiarity of any age or race." Moreover the Gorgon has a threefold aspect: Medusa's two sisters Sthenno ("the Mighty One") and Euryale ("Wide-leaping") link her with such deities of archetypal femininity as Hera and Hekate. Like them, she is actually bipolar: she is often represented as beautiful rather than ugly.

reigns, will annihilate him unless he exerts his whole self in maintaining his mastery over them" (K, 201). Elis does not heed the warning, however; he will let these "mighty elements" have mastery over him. Their colossal presence petrifies him, preventing him from declaring his love for Ulla. Like a normal youth, he has projected anima onto the girl he loves—"Elis thought of the fair Ulla. He saw her form hovering like a shining angel above him, and he forgot all the horrors of the abyss" (K, 202). But the projection only flickers; it does not last. Ulla is no match for Medusa.

The mighty elements continue to dominate him, as one day while working "in the deepest bore" among "sulphurous fumes," he hears an "uncanny knocking and hammering" (K, 203). "All at once he saw a black shadow beside him . . . he recognized the old miner." The Thor-like apparition speaks harshly to Elis, calling him a cheat because he mocks the "Metal Prince" and pursues the "Refined Prince." These princes seem to be images of Elis's self and persona respectively, since the former is associated with the mine and is therefore unconscious, and the latter is associated with the surface. The old miner is obliquely telling Elis that his true self has made a pledge to the Earth Mother, and therefore "Ulla will never be your wife" (K, 204).

Ulla's father finally has to employ a ruse to get Elis to ask him for her hand. He pretends she is being courted by another man, but instead of rousing Elis out of his pathological shyness, the scam plunges him into deeper despair. He runs back to the abyss and begs the old man to take him down where he will "never more see the light of day" (K, 206). Descending into the shaft, he has a vision of the fateful dream recurring. "He saw the maiden, he saw the lofty face of the majestic Queen. She seized him, pulled him down, pressed him to her breast, and there flashed through his soul a glowing ray—he was conscious of only a feeling of drifting in a blue, transparent, sparkling mist" (K, 207). It is a vision of death.

Pehrson finds Elis still alive but "standing rigid, his face pressed against the cold rock." Again, images of rigidity and stone emphasize the Medusan quality of the Queen. She is in Elis as Elis is in her. She is the inflated imago of his mother, transformed by fixation into the Goddess of Death.

Elis gets one more chance to grow up, however. Explaining that Ulla's suitor was just a fake, Pehrson tells him that he does indeed want him for his son-in-law. At first, the youth is overjoyed, but "in the midst of all his bliss it sometimes seemed to Elis as if an icy hand were gripping his heart and a dark voice were speaking, 'Is this your highest ideal, winning Ulla? You poor fool! Have you not seen the Queen's face?'" (K, 208).[30] The voice is the "ghostly old man's"—the shadow/animus still in the service of the Medusa.

Because Elis does not recognize these figures as the various shards of his "shattered self" (Daemmrich's term), the mine retains an uncanny aspect; just as Freud explained in his essay on "The Sandman," the "un" in "uncanny" signifies repression (399). The youth knows there is something familiar about the old miner, but his identity has been repressed, and Elis cannot recognize his own father imago. He becomes increasingly dissociated from reality, as he succumbs to the fascination of Medusa's head: "It seemed to him that his better, his true being, was climbing down into the center of the earth and was resting in the Queen's arms. . . . When Ulla spoke to him of her love and how they would live together happily, then he began to speak of the splendor of the shaft" (K, 209).

Like Christian in Tieck's "Der Runenberg," another tale of a hag-ridden man overpowered by his own androgynous archetypes, Elis mistakes barren rock for richest gems (K, 209).[31] Shrugging off the young man's lunacy, Pehrson plans to go through with the wedding. On his wedding day, Elis is "pale as death"; he tells Ulla he wants to give her the beautiful red carbuncle he has seen that day in the mine, and in spite of her tearful attempts to dissuade him, he goes to search for it. He feels himself attached to the Queen as to an umbilical cord, "an intertwined . . . marvelous branch . . . growing from the Queen's heart in the center of the earth" (K, 210).

Elis finally succumbs to the death instinct. The mine caves in—his mind implodes—and his body is not discovered until fifty years later, appearing "petrified." The demon has won; Medusa has claimed her victim. But Hoffmann has vividly shown us that Elis Fröbom, like Alvare and Ambrosio and Nathanael and a host of other male protagonists haunted by female demons, is really a victim of his own lack of self-knowledge, his inability to recognize his own feminine daemons, or to understand their language.

Syzygy

Taken as a kind of Gothic diptych, these two tales of E.T.A. Hoffmann suggest the self-destructive outcomes when sensitive young men do not

---

30. Again, McGlathery (*Part Two*, 94) interprets this as rationalizing sexual panic on the wedding day. But Elis's fear is not only of sex; it is of life itself—life without mother.

31. See Fass, chapter 4, and McGlathery, *Part Two*, 238, for Tieck's influence on Hoffmann's tale.

properly master the shadowy forms, the "mighty elements" seething in the cauldron of the human psyche. In Jungian terms, part of growing up is overcoming the awesome numinosity of the archetypes without denying their existence. They are essential psychic entities that can support both erotic and thanatotic instincts. What Jung and Freud would explain in analytical prose, Hoffmann vividly dramatized a century before: that repressing or ignoring the "unheimliche Treiben" will not make them go away. One must recognize them as one's own.

Furthermore, perhaps more vividly than any other Hoffmann tales, "The Sandman" and "The Mines at Falun" give brilliant symbolic expression to inner entities so transpersonal that the young men inhabited by them do not recognize them as personal. In other words, Hoffmann has presented a paradox: what makes archetypes difficult to recognize as parts of us is their very numinosity and autonomy. Archetypes are inner colossi reminding men of truths they often would rather not face: for example, that we do indeed have, as Freud insisted, a death instinct. In archetypal terms, the death instinct is a message we receive from the darker pole of the anima/animus. The message is that death (as Elis unconsciously knows) is really a kind of life in the womb of the Great Mother. Another message from the unconscious is that woman (as Nathanael unconsciously fears) may actually be a kind of man, endowed with her own animus. Both unconscious reminders involve a fusion of opposites, even as Elis and Nathanael try hard consciously to split them. No matter how hard we try to keep life and death polarized, life is attracted to death, merges with it in uncanny images of life-in-death and death-in-life (automatons, animated corpses); and masculine easily becomes feminine in androgynous images of men-in-women (like the "logical" Klara) and women-in-men (Olimpia-Nathanael).

To recognize the archetype is to acknowledge the marriage of opposites, which seems so irrational. But the archetypal syzygies, Hoffmann implies, need not inspire horror or cause madness; they can (as in "The Golden Pot") be a source of inspiration and love.

4

"ANIMATED CORSE"
Archetypal Travesties in Three Gothic Tales

The demonic feminine in Romantic and Modern fiction is often manifest in the gruesome figure of the animated corpse. Even when the apparition is a ghost or an automaton, authors often allude to the idea of an "animated corse" (as M. G. Lewis called his Bleeding Nun) or "the legend of the dead bride" (to whom Hoffmann compared Olimpia). Since the corpse is generally thought to be animated by a demon, if not by the devil himself, it is often vampiric, because (as James Twitchell has shown in *The Living Dead*, 6–9) the vampire was originally defined as a dead sinner (often a suicide) animated by a devil. The next two chapters, then, focus respectively on mid- and late-Romantic treatments of the feminine undead, which the authors used as psychological symbols (Twitchell, *Living Dead*, 38). In these texts, the demon that animates the corpse comes from the hell of the haunted man's unconscious.

Three tales from the first half of the nineteenth century reveal this psychodynamic with an acuity of image and a precocity of psychological insight rarely before achieved in Gothic fiction. Washington Irving's "Adventure of the German Student" (1824), with its unforgettable image of a female corpse's head rolling off, turns out to be much more than merely "explained" or Enlightenment Gothic—when the reader realizes that the corpse's head is not the same gender as its body. Théophile Gautier's "La Morte amoureuse" (1836), in which a priest's unconscious is represented by a God-defying feminine corpse, takes the vampire legend out of folklore and raises it to the level of literary art as only Goethe (in "The Bride of Corinth") and Coleridge (in "Christabel") had done before. And Edgar Allan Poe's "Ligeia" (1838), with the narrator's hallucination of Rowena's corpse into the living Ligeia, describes nympholepsy in what appears to be its most psychopathic form, with the suicidal impulse of E.T.A. Hoffmann's protagonists now transformed into homicide.

Washington Irving's Headless Bride: "The Adventure of the German Student"

Washington Irving was more of a rational satirist and humorist than a Gothic romancer, but one of his stories provides a striking example of the Romantic haunted mind: "The Adventure of the German Student," included in "Strange Stories by a Nervous Gentleman," the first part of *Tales of a Traveller*. Many critics of Irving's tale view it as Enlightenment Gothic: the apparently supernatural event (the possession and animation by a demon of the corpse of a woman guillotined during the Reign of Terror) is explained away by the terrifying revelation that Gottfried Wolfgang is quite mad, hallucinating. He has either carried a corpse back to his room and made love to it (Clendinning, 37–38), or he has hallucinated the whole encounter (Lupack, 399). There may not "really" even be a corpse; in fact, James Devlin (121) has suggested that the action is simply a rather macabre masturbation fantasy.

G. R. Thompson's view of the tale as Ambiguous rather than explained Gothic ("Washington Irving and the American Ghost Story," 28) is much more persuasive. The events cannot be explained away as "mere" hallucinations, even if Irving intended them to be, as Ringe (97) insists. The text leaves matters indeterminant; enigmas remain for readers to puzzle over but never fully solve, as it sets up a "tension between the supernatural and the everyday" (Thompson, 16).[1]

The supernatural in the tale, then, is not a representation of madness so much as it is of mystery. The man with the Haunted Head who tells "The Adventure of the German Student" delights in mystifying his listeners, as he has just done with "The Adventure of My Uncle."[2] If he is pulling their legs, he is also painfully twisting them. The result is a terrifying yet funny tale: the first American masterpiece of the Gothic short story.[3]

The most intriguing aspect of the text is its "ontological ambiguity" (Thompson, 29). Who or what is this animated corpse? Is there a breakdown of boundaries between Wolfgang as self and the dead bride as Other? If she exhibits anima signs, how does the anima affect the psychodynamics of necrophilia? For even if Wolfgang is only masturbating (as Devlin claims), his fantasy involves more than a failed attempt to purge castration anxiety (Devlin's explanation, 122).

Irving seems to have been trying his hand at the kind of psychologically sophisticated tale Tieck and Hoffmann wrote.[4] He emulated their technique of internalizing ghostly apparitions, so that minds, not castles, are haunted. Wolfgang, the Hoffmannesque protagonist, has a "diseased" imagination, and he is paranoid: "He took up a notion . . . that there was an . . . evil genius or spirit seeking to ensnare him and ensure his perdition" (223).[5] His "evil genius," however, is not a childhood bogeyman like Nathanael's; it comes from an overdose of Idealist philosophy. Ringe sees this fact as a clear indication of Irving's intent to debunk German transcendental philosophy in

1. Thompson's article was written primarily to refute Jack Sullivan's contention that J. Sheridan Le Fanu wrote the first "inconclusive ghost stories" in English. Irving is a much stronger candidate for this honor, even if he did not specialize in the genre.

2. This ghost story is the third of the "Strange Tales by a Nervous Gentleman" in *Tales of a Traveller* (*Complete Tales*, 201–10). The best discussion of the story is in Thompson's article (19–22).

3. Hedges (201), for example, sees it as an anticipation of Poe, especially tales like "Berenice." He compares the head plopping to the floor in Irving's story to the teeth being extracted in Poe's—both grotesques are simultaneously funny and horrible.

4. Irving almost certainly read Tieck's märchen and horror tales. He knew Tieck personally during his stay in Germany the year before he wrote "The Adventure of the German Student" (Pochmann, 1170). One wonders whether Irving knew Hoffmann's tale of a German student, "The Sandman." I have not been able to find any mention of the tale in Irving's journals or letters. Nor could Reichart (148) find any evidence of Hoffmann's direct influence.

5. All page references to "The Adventure of the German Student" are to Charles Neider's edition, *The Complete Tales of Washington Irving*.

favor of Scottish Common Sense (97). Ringe forgets that the tale is being told by the ambiguous man with the Haunted Head: he is quite literally two-faced (Irving, 200). Half of him is a smooth rationalist, dismissing the supernatural in his tongue-in-cheek reminder that the only authority for his tale's authenticity is that of a lunatic (227); but the other half of his head looks like "the wing of a house *shut up* and haunted" (200—emphasis added). This is the half he has just revealed in his "Adventure of My Uncle," in which he refused to explain away the mystery; he "shut up" just at the point when his listeners expected him to explain the ghost. When one of them gives a rational explanation, he scoffs, "Bah!" (210). Having revealed the ghastly half of his haunted face, the narrator seems at first to show his normal half in "Adventure of the German Student," which is supposedly rationally explicable in terms of Wolfgang's madness. But ironically, the story is infinitely more ghastly and haunting than the deliberately enigmatic "Adventure of My Uncle." In short, the story with the apparent rational explanation turns out to be more frightening than the one that has no explanation.

Such is the ironic tension between the two tales. "Uncle" is traditional and conventional. A man sees the ghost of a lady, then later sees a portrait of the same lady, a duchess who died in mysterious circumstances, perhaps at the hand of a murderer. In the "German Student," a young man dreams of "a female face of transcendent beauty" (224), which he later "sees" on an animated corpse by the guillotine. In contrast, the ghost "my Uncle" sees is ordinary, a mere Gothic convention—more parapsychological than psychological. Ghosts themselves are somehow less unsettling than animated corpses, perhaps because ghosts preserve boundaries between life and death more firmly than do ghouls and vampires. A restless or retributive spirit lingering after violent death seems both to acknowledge one's sense of order in the universe and to affirm one's faith in the afterlife. But the corpse found in "The Adventure of the German Student" is one from which the spirit has fled and which has been subsequently inhabited and animated by a demon. Such a zombie, with its "motiveless malignity," is formidable not only to superstitious readers, but even to "enlightened" ones who realize that the demon is really Wolfgang's "evil genius" (223). The two-faced teller thus implicitly reminds his listeners that they cannot take comfort in their "enlightened" knowledge. The literal existence of ghosts is not half as frightening as the "evil genius" *inside* men. The psychic reality of the animated corpse is what gives Irving's "Adventure of the German Student" its undeniable power.

This "evil genius" of Wolfgang's is the key to a post-Jungian reading of the tale. Note the ambiguity of the narrator's words, "an evil genius *or* spirit." Spirit could be inner or outer, but "genius" by Irving's time was considered an inner daemon.[6] This genius is associated by the narrator with Wolfgang's reading in transcendentalism; it is a masculine daemon, an animus of the Word that makes Wolfgang into a "literary ghoul, feeding in the charnel house of decayed literature" (223). Wolfgang, having flooded his consciousness with Logos, has completely neglected Eros. Thus the anima is associated with a corpse, and Wolfgang, sexually feeding off that corpse, becomes a *literal* ghoul.

The urgings of Eros and anima are manifest in Wolfgang's "ardent" personality; his repression of anima is clear in his almost pathological shyness. He is "a passionate admirer of female beauty," but is only capable of fantasizing "images of loveliness far surpassing the reality" (224). Finally he has a dream "of a female face of transcendent beauty." This vision of the Ideal Feminine is a direct result of the "sublimated state" of "his mind" (224).[7] The dream reveals an androgynous ideal: anima and animus are one. But the text reveals that this ideal is unattainable in reality. It must remain only a dream, a "fixed idea" that "haunts the mind."

It is significant that Wolfgang dreams only of a face; he has therefore already decapitated the woman, and yoked her head with his genius. Thus the androgyny he envisions is a travesty. When the face uncannily reappears in the waking world (225), this time attached to a body, he thinks he has found the attainment of his ideal. The heady fantasy of the Idealist has been attached now to a "headless" female body. This apparent fusion of opposites, effected by the "evil genius" within Wolfgang, is really an anomalous attachment of sublime ideal to bodily corruption, misogynistically symbolized by a headless female corpse.

For the narrator, Wolfgang's attempt to reconcile the irreconcilable results in a rationalization of premarital sex. Suggesting that Wolfgang has brought a real girl back to his room, the narrator criticizes the couple, who have come "under the sway of the Goddess of Reason." For them, the institution of

6. Originally "in classical pagan belief a tutelary spirit or attendant god allotted to every person at his birth to govern his fortunes," the word *genius* by neoclassical times no longer had this supernatural denotation, but retained the idea of a "character determinant" (*OED* [1933 ed.] 4: 112–13. Cf. Onians, 160–61; Onians, who locates the genius in the head, compares it to the unconscious.

7. The Freudian meaning of "sublimation" is not of course explicitly suggested by Irving. But the sense of "purifying or ennobling" was in wide use by his time (*OED*).

marriage is among "the rubbish of old times" (226). When Reason becomes a goddess, the narrator implies, it degenerates into mere rationalization—for the kind of violence that is going on all around Wolfgang (the Reign of Terror) and for licentious sex, in which he and his rationalized "bride" engage.

But the reader need not accept the narrator's interpretation. Nor is it necessary to go to the opposite extreme of Devlin's masturbation fantasy. The consummation of the "social compact" between the student and the girl is a complex symbolic act, for it is a joining not of two but of three elements: Wolfgang's masculine "genius" with the transcendent Ideal Feminine (anima) with the corrupt female body. Such a mingling, the text suggests, is impossible: the head rolls away from the body (227)—the masculine genius cannot unite with the generative feminine. The text is ultimately misogynistic, for the dead bride symbolizes the corrupt female body, which is headless. Wolfgang's tale, then, is primarily about the refusal of men to accept the possibility that real women actually might have heads *of their own* on their shoulders.

That the head or face is not the woman's own is further suggested in the text:

> What was his astonishment at beholding, by the bright glare of the lightning, the very face which had haunted him in his dreams. . . . Her face was pale, but of a dazzling fairness, set off by a profusion of raven hair that hung clustering about it. Her eyes were large and brilliant, with a singular expression approaching almost to a wildness. As far as her black dress permitted her shape to be seen, it was of perfect symmetry. (225–26)

Her body is deliberately blurred; it is her face that matters. The eyes especially reflect Wolfgang's own madness. And what is in the woman's head seems nothing more than an echo of Wolfgang's own opinions on revolution and sex. "She was evidently an enthusiast like himself, and enthusiasts soon understand each other" (226). Wolfgang notices that she wears around her neck a "broad black band . . . clasped by diamonds" (226), which the reader learns later is binding the head onto the body. Perhaps the diamonds, as rare precious stones, symbolize the "sublimated state" of Wolfgang's mind; and the blackness of the band may suggest his unconsciousness, his unawareness that he has carried back to his room a decapitated corpse.

Wolfgang's "sensitive nature" is "shocked" by "the scenes of blood" in the

Reign of Terror (223). When he comes upon the guillotine, he shrinks back with horror (224). The thought of decapitation so terrifies him that when he sees the decapitated corpse he unconsciously hallucinates its head. He thinks her face is hid in her lap (224). "Her" face is really a combination of *his* feminine sexual ideal and *his* philosophy, which agrees in some ways with that of the Jacobins: "He was captivated by the political and philosophical theories of the day" (223), so captivated that he projects them onto a decapitated body, creating a new head out of his own.[8]

Wolfgang thinks that an evil demon has ensnared him by animating a corpse. Like Nathanael, that other German student, he has confused an inner daemon for an outer demon. And like Nathanael, he is an Idealist, worshiping feminine beauty as a spiritual essence but unable to deal with female bodily existence. Wolfgang's bride, like Nathanael's Olimpia, is a mere reflection of his own beliefs (226). Irving, then, has traced an archetypal pattern: the failure of a young man to integrate the feminine, a failure resulting in madness. The sublime face in Wolfgang's dream is the anima figure in the text. The headless corpse is Irving's gruesome contribution to the myth of the dead bride. She has no head because the ideal feminine dreamed in the man's head does not fit onto a real woman. If the reader is misogynistic like the narrator, the reason is clear: real women cannot think. But the Unconscious archetypes insist that an androgynous ideal is possible and need not result in the travesty of a headless corpse with a head artificially attached. It is the simplistic identification of sublime Logos as masculine and corrupt Eros as feminine that creates the travesty.[9] Washington Irving, quite independent of his "intention," intimates through the imagery of decapitation the need, in a supposedly "enlightened" society, for new definitions of masculinity and femininity.

8. Perhaps an etymological pun on the root prefix *cap* (head), while probably not intended by Irving, supports this subliminal theme.

9. The Word is no more masculine than the Flesh is feminine: Logos and Eros exist within both sexes. "It is the function of Eros to unite what Logos has sundered" (Jung, CW 10: 275). Cf. Hillman, "Anima I," 107. Jung believed that Eros was better developed in women, and Logos in men (CW 9.2: 28), but this view could be simply a result of cultural conditioning (Hillman). A harmonious, androgynous psyche seeks a balance between the two (Samuels, *Jung and the Post-Jungians*, 210).

Théophile Gautier's Defier of the Lord: "La Morte amoureuse"

Théophile Gautier's "La Morte amoureuse"[10] is also in the Hoffmannesque mode, both because of its epistemological ambiguity, its hesitation between the marvelous and *l'étrange*,[11] and because it is primarily a psychological romance. Like Irving, Gautier was not merely imitating Hoffmann (whom he greatly admired);[12] he was, more consciously than Irving, trying to make his own contribution to the new "literary psychology" of the Romantics.

The narrator, Romuald, is a sixty-year-old priest who tells his story in response to a question (asked by someone he calls "brother") whether he had ever loved (274).[13] As a response to such a question, a tale of a vampire is peculiar to say the least; Gautier immediately mingles the mundane and the supernatural. One expects an amorous reminiscence; instead, Gautier delivers a Gothic horror story. It is Ambiguous Gothic, for the narrator is never sure that the supernatural events were dreams ("God grant they were dreams only!"—274). But more important is the ontological ambiguity of the apparition herself (to what extent is she part of Romuald?) and the moral ambiguity of what she represents (both good and evil?) (Cf. Grant, 124).

As a pious priest, Romuald gives his tale a moral before he even tells it: "A single glance, too full of approval, cast upon a woman, nearly cost me the loss of my soul" (274). After the story is told, he returns to this notion, expressing it now as an imperative: "Never look upon a woman, and walk always with your eyes cast on the ground" (306). Apparently, his listener is young (probably a brother of the church), and Romuald gives this advice earnestly,

---

10. The title is not easily translated. It means "The Dead Woman in Love," or more literally "The Amorous Female Corpse." Since *morte* is the noun, "The Dead Lover," is not exactly right, especially since "lover" has inescapable male connotations. True, in her dominance, Clarimonde does take on a masculine role, but that is not implied in Gautier's title, which emphasizes the corpse's femininity. As shall be seen, Clarimonde's masculinity is an unconscious substitution for the masculine religious system she subverts.

11. Much has been written on Gautier's "*Morte amoureuse*" as a fantastic text: Castex, 51–60; Todorov, 52–53; and Albert Smith, 21–36.

12. Hoffmann's influence on Gautier is well documented in Retinger, 60–72, and Castex, 54–55. Like Poe, Hoffmann was highly regarded in France—especially by Gautier and his friends Nodier and Nerval. In 1831, Gautier wrote a youthfully exuberant article expressing his enthusiasm for Hoffmann (Rpt. In Lovenjoul 1: 11–15).

13. All page references to "*La Morte amoureuse*" in English are to "The Dead Lover" in G. R. Thompson's anthology *Romantic Gothic Tales*. Since this is an excellent translation (by F. C. de Sumichrast), I have used it in all quotations except when a connotation lost in translation needs to be brought up. The French edition used is *Spirite, suivi de la morte amoureuse*.

however ridiculous it must sound to any but the most prudish—to say nothing of misogynistic—readers. Behind it is the medieval Catholic view of woman as essentially carnal and corrupt, her very Being a temptation. But the story itself, sandwiched between these two stale moralistic "wafers," has a much spicier flavor.

From the beginning Romuald is confused. He has a difficult time distinguishing waking from sleeping: "When at dawn I awoke, it seemed to me rather that I was going to sleep and dreaming of being a priest" (274–75). This confusion is never cleared up. On the contrary, it is made more and more complicated, as the reader is led into a world of dreams within dreams. Romuald first tells of his youthful desire to be a priest—so strong he would even dream of saying Mass (275). As a seminary student, he was totally unaware of women ("I knew vaguely there was something called a woman"), and hardly ever even saw his mother. Romuald is therefore completely dominated by masculine elements represented in the text by constant references to *Dieu le Père*, Jehovah, *Le Seigneur*, and by his human representative, Father Sérapion. That this denial of feminine influence may also be a denial of anima is first suggested when Romuald describes his feeling on the day he is to be ordained: "It seemed to me that I was borne in the air, or that I had wings on my shoulders; I thought myself an angel" (276). He attributes to the male ego what is rightfully anima's; he has not admitted the existence of the "femme aérienne."[14]

True to form, she appears at a turning point in his life: just when he is about to be ordained. Seeming both near and far (a part of him he thinks an Other), she radiates a "regal magnificence" so powerful that "the bishop, so radiant till now, was suddenly dimmed" (276). She appears as "an angelic revelation," a source of energy (the opposite of a vampire): "she seemed illumined from within, and to give forth light rather than to receive it" (276). To Romuald, the woman standing in the church is Platonic Ideal, Madonna, goddess and queen all rolled into one (277). The archetypal feminine has suddenly flooded his consciousness, and he has projected it upon the first woman he sees: Clarimonde, who he is not yet aware is a courtesan. Clarimonde herself should not be here equated with the anima; she is the "screen woman"[15] on whom Romuald projects the suddenly released anima.

14. This is the term Gautier coined to describe Hoffman's female apparitions. See Gautier's article on Hoffmann in Lovenjoul 1: 14.

15. I am borrowing this term from Shoshona Felman, who uses it in her article "Re-reading Femininity" in a different (non-Jungian) way, applying it to Balzac's Girl with the Golden Eyes.

Another sign of the archetype is in her bipolar aspect: "I know not whether the flame that illumined [Clarimonde's "sea-green eyes"] came from heaven or hell. . . . From time to time she drew up her head with the undulating movement of an adder or of a peacock" (277).[16] Her ambiguity (heavenly bird or earthly, hellish serpent?) is a reflection of his ambivalence; he no longer feels certain about becoming a priest. "I said, 'yes,' however, when I meant to say 'no,' when everything in me was revolting and protesting against the violence my vow was doing to my will" (278). He goes through with the ordination, much to the apparent consternation of Clarimonde (one cannot determine if the screen woman really says anything to him; the anima is trying to communicate to him, but he thinks the woman is talking). Her "tender and caressing" glance becomes "disdainful and dissatisfied" (279). She seems to say, "Unfortunate man, what have you done?" He tries to cry out that he does not really want to become a priest, but he is unable to speak: "I was, although wide awake, in a state similar to that of a nightmare, when one seeks to call out a word on which one's life depends, and yet is unable to do so" (279).

Her look seems to challenge Jehovah (279); it seems to say, "I love you and mean to take you from your God." As in Hoffmann, the archetype attempts to communicate to the man, demanding compensation for the lack of complementarity, demanding equal homage. Romuald has denied Eros— again associated with the anima ("I am beauty and truth and Love," she says)—in favor of Logos, the Word of God the Father. Now she will have her revenge, for she has "breathed her soul into [Romuald] and [he] no longer lived but in her and through her" (281). He has contracted nympholepsy; he is anima-possessed.[17]

But since he has consciously decided to be a priest, he is given to "icy shadows" and wears black as mourning for himself (281). Part of him is dead (ironically, the conscious part), and part very much alive: "Meanwhile I felt life rising within me like an internal lake, swelling and overflowing" (281). Responding to the glance of a woman in the church, he never realizes that he is responding to the call of his own soul. He is in effect *un mort amoureux*:

16. Not only is there bipolarity between the serpent and the bird, but the peacock itself is an ambiguous symbol with reference to Clarimonde. Ferguson (22) reminds us that the peacock was a traditional symbol of immortality, and De Vries writes (360) that it was a symbol of the soul's incorruptibility. Clarimonde's revelation as a vampire is a travesty of both ideas.

17. In Jung's words, "The chief danger is in succumbing to the fascinating influence of the archetypes [which then] escape from conscious control altogether and become completely independent, thus producing the phenomenon of possession" (*CW* 9.1: 39).

"I had myself sealed the stone of my tomb" (282). He goes through the motions of priesthood, sleepwalking through the role, while he continues to long for the world of love.

This world is not only sexual (Freudian interpretations of the tale notwithstanding):[18]

> A young mother was playing with her child on the threshold of a door. She kissed its little rosy lips still pearly with drops of milk, and indulged, as she teased it, in those many divine puerilities which mothers alone can invent. The father, who stood a little way off, was smiling gently at the charming group, and his crossed arms pressed his joy to his heart. (282)

Romuald knows he has sealed himself off in his priestly tomb not only from sexual but also from familial love; it is indeed this latter realization that causes him to start "raging . . . like a wild beast." The abbot Sérapion's first admonition comes, significantly, as a response to Romuald's envious rage: "The evil spirit, angered at your having devoted yourself to the Lord, prowls around you like a ravening wolf" (283). Gautier thus insinuates that Sérapion finds familial love evil. This is the first of several clues that Sérapion is the tale's antagonist (cf. Todorov, 137), an important fact the reader may easily forget if taken in by the old Romuald's pious narration.[19]

When Sérapion escorts Romuald to his new parish, they see Clarimonde's palace in the distance. It seems both near and far (295), as she herself had in the church; and when he sees her in the distance, he has no idea if she is real or illusory. When Sérapion tells him that the palace belongs to Clarimonde the courtesan, Romuald does not respond to this revelation. Her "reality" is unimportant to him, for he has invested her with all the qualities of the goddess of love. Her eyes are "sea-green" (277), and foam is associated with her (284). To his unconscious, she is not a whore; she is Aphrodite, born of sea foam.

18. Of the tale's several Freudian interpretations, Bellemin-Noël's is the best. He sees Clarimonde as the possessive mother, and Sérapion as the jealous father, with Romuald in the throes of an Oedipal conflict. The ending, in this reading, is a happy one because he is delivered from the Oedipus complex. But the archetypal reading shows that he simply goes from one complex to another, with no deliverance at all.

19. Cf. Grant, 124: Sérapion, ostensibly good, is really "harsh, suspicious and domineering." Grant even sees Clarimonde's vampirism as a "metaphor for total love," which I think may be stretching a point.

Romuald finally gets a chance to meet Clarimonde—when she dies. The death of the screen woman allows for the projected anima to attain full autonomy. One day, a servant comes to say his mistress is dying and needs a priest. Romuald does not yet know he is being driven to Clarimonde. In a wild ride to her chateau (anticipating that of Jonathan Harker to Dracula's), he likens himself and the servant to "specters bestriding nightmares" (288) as they traverse the forest, in which the "phosphorescent eyes of wildcats" reflect Romuald's own tigerlike passion (283, 288). When he realizes that the dead woman is Clarimonde, the text begins to unfold like a surrealistic flower into dreams within dreams. The first dream is a wish fulfillment fantasy. When Romuald realizes that Clarimonde is dead, he wants to thank God for delivering him from his painful passion; her name, however, will remain "sanctified" in his prayers (289). In short, the priest feels that the easiest way out of his torturous dilemma (wanting to love both God and Woman) is for the woman to die. But what Romuald does not realize is that, though woman dies, anima does not. So the wish fulfillment gets interrupted. If it had been allowed to continue, he would have given her extreme unction, a Christian burial, and sanctification in his prayers. But the unconscious takes over: "I fell into a revery. . . . The room had in no wise the aspect of a chamber of death. Instead of the fetid and cadaverous air which I was accustomed to breathe during my funeral watches, a langorous vapor . . . a strange amorous odour of woman, floated softly in the warm air" (289).

As Romuald's narrative continues, his mind oscillates between conscious perception of Clarimonde as dead ("a sigh of regret escaped my breast") and unconscious fantasy of Clarimonde as alive ("I thought I heard someone sigh behind me, and I turned involuntarily. It was the echo"—289). Anima signs abound here: the *femme aérienne* is once again represented by breath, air, vapor, and sighs. It is Romuald's breath that animates the corpse; the conscious wish that she is indeed dead is blocked by the unconscious, which slowly turns the corpse into a living creature. "She was covered with a linen veil of dazzling whiteness . . . it was so tenuous that it concealed nothing of the charming form of the body, and allowed me to note the lovely lines, undulating like the neck of the swan, which death itself had been unable to stiffen" (289). The "undulation" now is only of the positive pole—the adder is absent. But this first step in the animation process only produces "an alabaster statue, the work of some clever sculptor." A statue is more alive than a corpse, because it eternally reflects the life of its creator, whereas a corpse rots. But Clarimonde does not remain a statue: "I imagined that she was not really dead. . . . Once indeed I thought I saw her foot move under the white veil" (290). Finally he is carried away in fantasy as he gazes at the corpse, imagining himself "a young husband entering the room of his bride."

These frankly sexual longings that trouble Romuald "more voluptuously than was right" cause an onrush of ambivalence: he is "sunk in grief, mad with joy, shivering with fear and pleasure." In this state he raises the shroud, meanwhile "holding in [his] breath for fear of waking her." It is indeed psyche's breath, his anima, that wakes her. The male god is again suppressed: "Her lovely hands, purer and more diaphanous than the Host, were crossed in an attitude of silent prayer" (291). Romuald imposes the attributes of the masculine deity upon the female, which he does not realize has been killed—that is, repressed—by the male.

In the final stage of the animation process, Romuald, bending his face over Clarimonde's, breathes life into her with a kiss, like the prince into Sleeping Beauty (Grant, 124); "a faint breath mingled with mine, and Clarimonde's lips answered to the pressures of mine" (291). She speaks too, telling him that she is dead but that they are now betrothed. She then says, "Good bye, but not for long" (292), whereupon a "wild gust of wind" bursts into the room, seeming to carry her soul away (292). Romuald finally swoons "on the bosom of the lovely dead." His unconscious has taken over completely.

When he wakes up, he is in his own bed. Has it all been a dream? Or only from the moment he said, "I fell into a revery"? His housekeeper saw the driver bring the unconscious Romuald home, but no one knows of any chateau in the neighborhood (292). He does find out, though, from Father Sérapion, that "the great courtesan Clarimonde died recently, after an orgy that lasted eight days and nights" (293). Did Romuald go to the alleged orgy and then repress the whole thing? Or did he arrive afterwards, see her dead, and hallucinate her alive? A Jungian reading favors the latter possibility, since the death of the screen woman gives the anima complete autonomy. The text, however, remains ambiguous. In fact, it becomes more complicated as Sérapion tells Romuald of Clarimonde's reputation. She is not a mere courtesan; she may even be "a ghoul, a female vampire . . . Beelzebub in person . . . for it is not, I am told, the first time she has died" (293). Another question is raised: has Clarimonde been a vampire all along, or is she just a woman whose shady reputation has been magnified by Catholic superstition? The text supports either possibility, but again, a Jungian reading favors the latter: a real woman has died; she becomes a vampire when Romuald transfers breath and life from him to her.

What ultimately matters is not when she died or whether she is a literal vampire, but the existence in Romuald's mind of the living, loving dead. As in Hoffmann's tales, the grotesque appears as a marriage of contraries, a travesty of true archetypal harmony. Because the young man has been unable to harmonize masculine and feminine archetypes, he perforce creates a perversion of that ideal. The tendency toward the fusion of opposite archetypes appears to be instinctual; repression does not stop it. Repression just turns it from an ideal to a horror.

Like Nathanael and Ellis, Romuald has a "remission"; he appears "cured" after repression of the feminine takes over again when Clarimonde is buried. "I had at last entirely recovered, and had resumed my usual duties," until "one night I dreamed a dream" (294). He sees "the shadow of a woman" standing before him as he sits up in bed. Like Biondetta and the Bleeding Nun, she carries a lamp in her hand: she is Psyche. But she is also Aphrodite—her linen shroud works again on Romuald like lingerie, "which revealed all the contours of her body" (295). She tells him she has come from the grave because "love is stronger than death and overcomes it." Echoing the Song of Songs, she is the archetypal Bride, Romuald's Ideal appearing now as an undead lover.

She makes the demands that anima must make—equal homage. "Oh I am jealous of God, whom you loved, and whom you still love more than me" (296). But he assures her now that he loves her "as much . . . as God" (297). They agree to meet the next day. When she leaves, he sleeps heavily, then seems to wake up convinced it was all a "mere fever of [his] heated brain" (297). Praying to God to drive away evil thoughts and protect his chastity from succubi, he falls back to sleep and his dream continues. God has not answered his prayer, since he has pledged himself to His adversary. She appears now fully dressed, and seems to wake him up (298). He gets out of bed and assumes a completely new persona—that of a nobleman. The French word is *seigneur*, the lower case of the same word used in the text to signify God: *le Seigneur*, the Lord. Gautier even juxtaposes them, to make sure the reader gets the message: "[Par] jour, j'étais un prêtre du Seigneur, chaste, occupé de la prière et des choses saintes; la nuit dès que j'avais fermé les yeux, je devenais un jeune seigneur, fin connaisseur en femmes" ("Morte," 193). Once the Lord is denied, Romuald thinks he has become his own lord. But the archetypal father can no more be denied than the archetypal mother or anima. Romuald is no lord of himself—he alternates between anima possession and Jehovah possession. He cannot find the mean.

For many weeks, Romuald is a priest during the masculine day (*le jour*) and a lordly lover by feminine night (*la nuit*), but he has no idea which is the reality and which the illusion (299). The fission of the archetypal syzygy (God the Father with his consort the Queen of Heaven) has resulted in a fission of the self. Dominated by the Great Father, Romuald is a pious priest who has voluptuous dreams; dominated by the Great Mother, he is a voluptuous nobleman who has nightmares of being a penitent priest (300). Although the sixty-year-old narrating Romuald is convinced he was simply confounded by Satan, the text itself remains ambiguous.[20]

These alternating dominations continue in a seesawing motion until apprehensions planted by Father Sérapion finally tip the scales in the Lord's favor: the animated Clarimonde now begins to grow pale and pine away (300). But when Romuald accidentally cuts himself, she springs from her sick bed like an animal and begins sucking his blood, which revives her. Clarimonde is elated that "a few drops" of Romuald's blood can keep her alive so that she can continue to love him. "My life is in yours," she tells him, "and *all that I am comes from you*" (301—emphasis added). Her vampirism, then, is a symbol for the truth Romuald continues to ignore: her identity derives from him. Never making this crucial realization, he lets her dominate him—he submits to her gruesome feedings (302–3). The seesaw is back on her side, until Father Sérapion steps in again. He takes Romuald to Clarimonde's tomb to prove to him not only that she has died but that she is now undead. When the abbot sees upon her lips a drop of blood (which the narrator likens to a rose), he becomes furious. "Ah! there you are, you demon, you shameless courtesan!" (305). His two accusations serve to acknowledge her ambiguity—which is she? Demonic vampire or shameless woman? To the father, there is no difference: the carnal female is indistinguishable from the female corpse. He sprinkles her body with holy water, causing her "lovely body" to fall into dust. But she is not, as Grant (124) claims, annihilated. Romuald sees her the next night, although now she is no longer a corpse animated by him. She is a disembodied spirit. "Unfortunate man! What have you done? Why did you listen to that foolish priest? . . . All communion between our souls and bodies is henceforth broken.

---

20. The situation is reminiscent of Cazotte's *Diable amoureux*. Gautier was without question familiar with Cazotte's novella, and Clarimonde probably owes much in conception to Biondetta. Both carry lanterns like Psyche, both are creatures of the air, and both are associated with Beelzebub. But I think Clarimonde retains enough individuality to be an anima figure integral to Romuald, whose situation is much different from Alvare's. The latter has problems with his real mother's dominance—totally absent from Romuald.

Farewell, you will regret me" (305). He is no longer anima-possessed, but she has simply retreated to complete unconsciousness. "She vanished in air like a vapor. . . . Alas! she spoke the truth. I have regretted her more than once, and I still regret her. I purchased the peace of my soul very dearly. The love of God was not too much to replace her love" (305). Without realizing how completely his words contradict each other, Romuald ends his narrative. What peace of soul has he found, if he still regrets having denied her? And if he is still regretting, he must still be longing for erotic love.

Gautier's tale is one of war. A battle of the titans rages: God the Father versus the Queen of Heaven.[21] As long as the archetypal masculine defines itself as the negation of the archetypal feminine—Her darkness the absence of His light—the two instinctual elements will vie for dominance in the human mind, creating a lifelong confusion. For the sixty-year-old narrator, despite his pieties, is no less confused than the young priest. Like Cazotte's Alvare, he only *seems* to be saved from the amorous daemon within; like Lewis's Ambrosio, he is in reality damned. He is damned to a half-lived life; or perhaps to no life at all, since his whole life as a priest is lived in constant regret of Eros and anima denied.

Archetypal Projection in "Ligeia"

Poe's "Ligeia" is, like Gautier's "*Morte amoureuse*," a story of extreme anima possession. It seems, however, unlikely that Gautier's story influenced "Ligeia," the psychodynamics of which are quite different because the father archetype is not directly involved in the conflict.[22] Poe does seem to have been somewhat familiar with Hoffmann's tales, however. While "Ligeia" has no immediate source in Hoffmann (as does "The Fall of the House of Usher"),[23] the story is apparently a self-conscious metamorphosis of the love theme from Scott's *Ivanhoe* into a Hoffmannesque tale—at Scott's expense,

21. For more on this conflict, see Paglia, 138: Like Sérapion, "the Church Fathers recognized the Great Mother as the enemy of Christ." Paglia, however, overemphasizes the chthonic, earthy, Terrible aspect of the Great Mother; she fails to account for "*la femme aérienne*," the airy, sylphan, heavenly feminine.

22. In fact it was Poe who would later influence Gautier (Tennant, 82). It was partly through Gautier that Baudelaire first became interested in Poe.

23. "The Fall of the House of Usher" may be indebted to Hoffmann's "Das Majorat" ("The Entail"), but Poe seems to have been more interested in Hoffmann's reputation (via Scott) as a drunken visionary than in the tales themselves. See Lippe's and Pitcher's articles.

since he despised Hoffmann's work.[24] Indeed, "Ligeia" contains many of the elements of "The Sandman": the unreliable narrator, the mixture of burlesque and horror, and above all (for my purposes) the psychological analysis of the haunted male ego.

Critical perceptions of the haunting Ligeia seem at first glance completely contradictory. Is she "primarily sensual" (Basler, 89), "the perfection of erotic dreaming" (Porte, 71)? Or is she the *non*erotic muse, Aphrodite Urania (Bennett), "the personification of intellect and . . . of will," dwelling in "the realm of epistemology, not of sex" (Halliburton, 209, 207)? Is she a bona fide revenant, a real ghost (Lauber, Schroeter, et al.)? Or did she never "really" exist at all except in the narrator's mind (Basler, Gargano, Stovall, et al.)? Is she a psychological vampire/succubus (G. R. Thompson, *Poe's Fiction*, 87; Twitchell)? Or is she just a woman murdered by an insane narrator (Matheson)? But then again she is a siren, ambiguous goddess both of love and of death (D. E. Jones). She is "the corpse of the sublime" (Jay, 163), the embodiment of a frustrated Romantic quest for "the ideally motivated sign" (Williams). She is also Poe's mother, Eliza (Bonaparte). Such critical disagreements suggest that a number of signified concepts underlie the signifier "Ligeia." Critical texts rename her variously as "Lilith," "numen," "muse," "siren," "Eliza"—signifiers that, along with the apparently conflicting interpretations they represent, may be reconciled in one sign: *anima* (cf. Bickman, 78; Knapp, 131; Saliba, 152).

There is no need to say that Bennett and Halliburton (the nonerotic camp) are right while Basler and Porte (the sexual readers) are wrong: anima theory allows for Ligeia to be both muse and siren; Aphrodite Urania and Aphrodite Dionea are not two different goddesses: they are two aspects of the same goddess. Porte did not have to rationalize Ligeia's "ethereality" into a verbal cover-up of her essential sexuality (71). The narrator' marriage to Ligeia creates the kind of marriage of contraries between the spiritual and the bodily that have already been encountered in Cazotte, Lewis, Hoffmann, and Irving. This archetypal harmony is shattered by the narrator's Platonic dualism, which idealizes Spirit and corrupts Body.

Identifying Ligeia as an anima figure, then, helps synthesize various antithetical aspects of the text. But what, precisely, is entailed in the identification? As Bickman points out, the seemingly innocuous phrase "for my soul" in Poe's first sentence relates Ligeia to "the narrator's own psyche" (74). After the lady dies, Poe is more explicit: "Now, then, did my spirit fully

---

24. See Scott's essay, "On the Supernatural in Fictitious Compositions," 467–68.

and freely burn with more than all the fires of her own" (323).[25] Ligeia is "the fierce energy" (315) that animates the narrator's spirit: an energy that manifests itself often in the text in the act of breathing. After the first wife's death, Ligeia still exists as "almost inarticulate breathings" in the tapestries (324); and later, just before the narrator first projects her into Rowena, he finds himself "breathing with greater freedom" (326). As soon as he takes those breaths, "a thousand memories of Ligeia" rush upon him. Only when Ligeia animates the dead Rowena does the narrator feel his own soul to be "awakened within" him (326–27). Ligeia is the narrator's own soul—an inhalation of breath—as well as the projecting force—an exhalation. He hears a sigh (surely his own), and Rowena's corpse is animated once again (327).

When the narrator is finally successful at completely projecting his soul into Rowena, the resultant travesty—an animated corpse—terrifies him; he shrieks aloud. Perhaps he has finally realized what he has done: killed a body so that he can give it the "proper" soul. In any case, the reader does not know what happens to him at the end. He is not frightened to death like Roderick Usher; he lives to tell his tale, though probably, like Wolfgang, from the madhouse. Having suffered memory loss (perhaps as a result of the terrifying vision), he is largely dominated by the unconscious as he writes, reconstructing his first wife, whose name he does not remember, out of archetypal material. He says that her first name was Ligeia, but his memory is "feeble from much suffering" (310). He forgets "topics of deep moment" (321). Ligeia may not even be the real name of his first wife.[26] What he has done is to discover (or perhaps invent) his own soul by giving it a name.

Whoever his first wife "really" was, she exists in the text only as a cipher, a blank screen. The narrator erects, out of his wife, the statue of a goddess ("she placed her marble hand upon my shoulder"—311). She is a colossus, dominating him completely: "a majesty so divine!—the skin rivalling the purest ivory, the commanding extent and repose, the gentle prominence of the regions above the temples" (312). Whatever his wife was in mundane reality,

25. All page references to "Ligeia" are to Mabbott's edition, *The Collected Works of Edgar Allan Poe*, vol. 2.

26. It is the name of a mythological siren. See Rose, 253; D. E. Jones, 34; and Milton's "Comus," line 880. Mabbott (331 n. 1) also realizes that "Ligeia" is not the first wife's real name, but he thinks it is Ligeia herself who does not reveal her real name. It is more likely that the narrator, in mythologizing his wife, represses her real name in favor of the siren's. Perhaps her name was Rebecca, since one of Poe's sources was the story of Rebecca and Rowena in Scott's *Ivanhoe* (Mabbott, 306). "Ligeia" completely erases Rebecca, and then effaces Rowena.

he has now magnified her into the colossal icon of Astarte ("Ashtophet"—311), the Great Goddess, in the shadow of whose "infinite supremacy" he trembles.

Consider what is known about the first wife, after sifting through the narrator's archetypal magnifications. She is apparently a transcendentalist whose wisdom and learning the narrator has hitherto "never known in woman" (315). "The acquisitions of Ligeia were gigantic . . . yet I was sufficiently aware of her infinite supremacy to resign myself with a childlike confidence to her guidance" (316). In spite of a strong will to live, she grows sick and dies. He claims that she loves him almost to the point of idolatry (317), but he does not return her love while she lives. In fact, he is quite ambivalent. His idolatry begins only when she dies. And her so-called idolatry is often "violently a prey to the tumultuous vultures of stern passion" (315)—to which he would become alerted by her eyes, which "delighted and appalled" him. Such ambivalence suggests a mother complex; the narrator's first wife plays a "more than womanly" role (317); she plays a motherly role.[27]

After the narrator tells of her illness and death, he reveals the reason he married his first wife. "I had no lack of what the world calls wealth. Ligeia had brought me more, far more than ordinarily falls to the lot of mortals" (320). At first he does not love the woman herself: her love for him has been "all unworthily bestowed" (317). Implicitly, he never loves her as a wife but as a mother who takes care of him, provides for him both materially and intellectually. This inference does not, however, lead a Jungian reader to Bonaparte's conclusion. Whether or not Ligeia is an image of Poe's own mother is irrelevant to the text. But the imagery does suggest a mother *figure*: when the first wife dies, the narrator, missing her motherly love and catalyzed by opium (320), transforms her into the Great Mother. Ligeia is the narrator's wife viewed with "telescopic scrutiny" (314). Her magnified brightness makes him feel the same sentiments as when he sees a "butterfly, a chrysalis, a stream of running water . . . the ocean, a meteor" (314). The wife, upon reflection and refraction, becomes not only anima but *anima mundi*. As world soul, she is not only soul-bride but Great Mother. As Halliburton brilliantly puts it (218), "She takes up all the breathing space." Indeed it is she, as *anima mundi*, who "breathes fitfully / The music of the spheres" (318).

Ligeia, then, is not only the anima but also the mother archetype (or

27. Similar conclusions were of course also made by Marie Bonaparte, 224–36. But to go from motherly images in the text to Eliza Poe is too big a leap for me.

imago) within the narrator. Poe had, as Shulman suggests, a "genuine understanding of unconscious processes" (245)—processes shared by many men, not just those who (like Poe) lost their mothers at an early age. "Ligeia" traces the unconscious process whereby a man projects upon a woman the qualities not only of his own mother but also of his inherited sense of maternity. The paternal archetype is completely negated in the story. "I have never known," the narrator claims, "the paternal name of her who was my friend and my betrothed" (311). Again, the reader must question this claim, for the narrator has apparently repressed the paternal and elevated the maternal with his hyperbolic language.

Perhaps the tumultuous vultures of Ligeia's "stern passion" become too much for the narrator, and he kills his first wife as Matheson suggests. In any case, her motherly love is withdrawn, and the narrator feels like "a child groping benighted" (316). The only way he can get her back is childishly to deny the reality of death. Her will to live is actually his will to immortalize, to deify. Archetypal images seethe chaotically within him, but now he has no screen, no feminine figure on whom to project them. He has become one of the "mere puppets" in Ligeia's poem: "At bidding of vast formless things" (318). The colossal archetypes are in abeyance until he can find a surrogate for Ligeia. Their existence is implied in the love/death chamber he creates, in the "gigantic sarcophagus," "the lofty walls, gigantic in height," the "arabesque figures," and "the ghastly forms which belong to the superstition of the Norman, or arise in the guilty slumbers of the monk" (322).[28] The "wind behind the draperies" is his soul-breath, waiting to breathe life again, to incarnate Ligeia in a new form, "a hideous and uneasy animation."

He marries the first woman he can. She does not have to look like his wife; she is to be a screen. That he may plan to kill her, as Basler (90) and G. R. Thompson (*Poe's Fiction*, 81) suggest, is implied by his remark about Rowena's relatives: he wonders how they ever could have let her "pass the threshold of an apartment so bedecked" (321). But Rowena's ambiguous, unquiet death should not simply be literalized as a murder. The narrator's first wife has died, and with her death the mother archetype has receded to unconsciousness, where she now exists inside him as "the fierce moodiness of [his] temper" (323) directed at the hapless Rowena. Her identity is progressively denied until she becomes a screen on which he is finally able

---

28. An allusion to Lewis's monk may be intended here—he was certainly the most infamous guilty monk. But Ambrosio's problem bears little resemblance to Poe's narrator's, because the latter does not seem to have a guilt complex.

to project the archetype. She grows into Ligeia, from woman to goddess—just as the first wife did. But the mother goddess in her final form appears now as Medusa: the narrator is "chilled . . . into stone" (329). This time, the negative pole of the archetype appears, the black-eyed Gorgon, to remind the man that by relentlessly projecting his own Ideal of the Feminine onto woman, he is not loving, he is killing; he is erasing her identity, just as his very narration erased the identity of the first wife, replacing it with "Ligeia."[29]

As an anima figure, Ligeia leads the narrator into "a world of mythopoeic experience" (Bickman, 74). Following Erich Neumann, Bickman sees her as a Jungian "transformative" archetype who guides the narrator into "an animistic . . . mythical consciousness" (74). Moreover, Bickman notes that the anima has the "potential for psychic growth" (79); it is the weakness of the male ego that prevents "a creative reintegration" (66) of unconscious anima with consciousness. But what makes the ego so weak? One cannot ignore the elementary/static feminine archetype while examining the transformative. The anima is what animates the mother archetype, making the statue breathe.[30] In the case of a man who has achieved some kind of integration, the transformative anima is completely free of the static mother archetype, but Poe's narrators rarely if ever achieve such a break; their animas are weighted down, as it were, by the primitive monoliths of the Great Mother. Ligeia could be a light and airy sylph, but the narrator's nympholepsy prevents her liberation. With much of Mother Earth in her, she remains a colossal statue.[31] Since she is both anima and mother archetype, she is "double and changeable" (314), like the star in Lyra to which she is compared. She is "bright and burning with fierce energy," but then she is dim, "duller than Saturnian lead" (316).

The narrator's ego disintegration, then, is not, as Bickman argues, a result of his rejection and repression of the anima (78); it is the result of his inability

29. This erasure or preempting of female identity parallels Cynthia Jordan's ideas in "Poe's Re-vision: The Recovery of the Second Story." See especially p. 2: "Poe was . . . prolific in creating images of violently silenced women." My archetypal perspective complements her conclusion: "the loss of 'woman' throughout [Poe's] writings represents a halving of 'man's' soul" (19).

30. In other words, the mother archetype is the first manifestation of femininity in the male psyche. See Jung, *CW* 9.2: 26; Jung makes it clear that the anima is not a mere substitute for the mother imago, but the latter is "dangerously powerful" because it is the boy's first sense of the feminine. Cf. Ellenberger, 708, and Neumann, 33–34.

31. Mabbott (*Works* II, 331 n. 3, and 332 n. 7) calls our attention to other statuary imagery in the description of Ligeia. Poe alludes to a statue of Aphrodite and to the Venus de Medici.

to dissociate mother archetype from anima. In other words, woman is for him a matrix, a mold out of which he casts and shapes—a blank page on which he writes his text, "Ligeia." To love this Great Goddess is to fall back not into the womb of the personal mother but into the ultimate abyss, the pit of Mother Earth.

These three tales of animated corpses seem on the surface to adumbrate the psychopathology of necrophilia. But it is not really a love of the dead per se that afflicts the haunted males. It is a longing for the Ideal Feminine, which in Western culture has always been the static rather than the transformative archetype: either the completely passive bride receptacle which the man animates and which therefore drains him of life (the undead vampire into whom he willingly lets his lifeblood flow), or the maternal womb/tomb, the uroboric "circle that ever returneth in / To the self-same spot" ("Ligeia," 318).[32]

Nor are these tales really dramatizations of extreme pathology. What Hoffmann said of Nathanael may also be said of Wolfgang, Romuald, and even the narrator of "Ligeia"—they are not so abnormal; their obsessions are representative of the male ego as it tries desperately to deal with the "irruption of the other in the self" (Jay, 149). If the man does not recognize the feminine entity as his own unconscious, or if the anima is still burdened with maternal aspects, the closest he can come to true integration is a travesty. Instead of the ego living in acceptance of androgyny and of death, it is overwhelmed by grotesque perversions: dominating corpses of the sublime feminine like Ligeia and Clarimonde.[33]

32. Bickman (77) calls the Conqueror Worm "a uroboric destroyer of consciousness," but he does not relate the image to the mother archetype even though he derives it from Neumann's *The Great Mother*, 18–21.

33. This reading of Ligeia as "corpse of the sublime feminine" is an elaboration on Jay's. Halliburton's phenomenological method leads him to a similar view of Ligeia as one who "takes up all the breathing space," reducing the man "to a position of despair or adoration. He could never, even if he wanted to, be rid of her" (218). "The lady is literally everywhere" (208); she is the matrix in which the narrator creates the travesty of his life.

5

VICTORIAN VAMPS
Archetypes of Sex and Death

Anima as Sigh from the Depths:
Thomas De Quincey's *Suspiria de Profundis*

Carl Jung often cited Rider Haggard's *She* (with its sequel, *Ayesha: The Return of She*) as a good Victorian example of an intuitive tale of anima fascination.[1] But as literature, Haggard's work is far more juvenile and far less compelling than the two greatest Victorian vampire tales, Sheridan Le Fanu's *Carmilla* (1872) and Bram Stoker's *Dracula* (1897). These texts confront the reader with vivid images of the feminine "Un-Dead." Rather

1. For *She* as an anima tale, see Jung, *CW* 9.1: 28, 30. Haggard's *She* (1887) presents the negative pole of the mother archetype still attached to the anima, while *Ayesha* reveals the positive pole.

than viewing them solely in the light of Jungian theory, I will also set them in the context of a Victorian piece that I think brilliantly illustrates the psychodynamics of the archetypal feminine: Thomas De Quincey's *Suspiria de Profundis*.[2] What Bickman says of American Romanticism may also be said of De Quincey's dream visions—they seem to spring from the same "confluence of traditions" (5) that led to Jungian theory. Whether or not De Quincey was artistically illuminating actual dreams, the parallels between figures like "Our Ladies of Sorrow" or "The Dark Interpreter" and Jung's archetypal anima or animus are, I think, striking. Like E.T.A. Hoffmann, De Quincey seems to have come to some of the same conclusions as Carl Jung.

It should not be surprising that De Quincey had a vision of the archetypal feminine, since the major influences in his life were female.[3] His dreams and visions reveal the mechanism of magnification by which men invest women with archetypal power; but unlike Hoffmann's Nathanael, the persona in *Suspiria de Profundis* is that of a true poet, who (after having gone through the "nympholepsy" of the unfortunate Gothic protagonists) has made the archetype conscious and integrated it into his psyche. In De Quincey's *Suspiria* one finds what is either missing or only latent in the Gothic tales examined thus far—the full consciousness of the anima and a realization of its positive aspects. Since, as James Hillman contends ("Anima II," 117), the anima lights the way to the inner caves of the unconscious, to follow her promptings does not necessarily lead to happiness; but neither does she lead necessarily to despair. Instead she may bring wisdom at the price of suffering.

In "The Affliction of Childhood," part 1 of the *Suspiria*, the persona relates how his "infant feelings were molded by the gentlest of sisters, not by horrid pugilistic brothers" (123).[4] But when he was seven, his older sister Elizabeth died. She had been a precocious child, not only his intellectual guide but also the one who taught him how to love. "Hadst thou been an idiot, my sister, not the less I must have loved thee, having that capacious heart overflowing even as mine overflowed, with tenderness, and stung, even as

2. Published in *Blackwood's Edinburgh Magazine* in 1845, De Quincey's work is a far cry from the kind of "Blackwood's articles" common twenty years earlier—e.g., the "predicament" tales that Poe satirized in "A Predicament" and imitated in "The Pit and the Pendulum." In De Quincey, the predicament has become that of the human condition.

3. On De Quincey's life and his "feminine" influences, see Lyon, 17–19 and chapter 1, *passim*. Cf. Lindop, 10–11, 13.

4. All page references to *Suspiria de Profundis* are to *Confessions of an English Opium Eater and Other Writings* (New York: New American Library, 1966): 113–223.

mine was stung, by the necessity of being loved" (127). Elizabeth becomes an introjected spirit of love. Later, when he falls in love with the prostitute Ann, he projects that spirit into her: "I loved her as affectionately as if she had been my sister" (49). The feminine element reinforced by his sister gave De Quincey (or at least his poetic persona) a loving quality reflected both in the *Confessions* and in the *Suspiria*. Although the voice of these works is often that of the tortured opium addict and therefore, as Lyon and Lindop both show, of a man with considerable psychological problems, there is a general movement from the demonic paranoia of "The Pains of Opium" to the daemonic visions of the *Suspiria*: a progression that suggests individuation rather than static psychopathology.[5]

Elizabeth's death transforms her into a saint replete with "tiara of light" and "aureola" (125), and she becomes the paragon to which all other women will be compared. If these women do not encourage him to express his feelings, he will keep them to himself (127–28). Elizabeth is the Feminine Ideal, "the lamp lighted in Paradise . . . kindled for me" (127). This sister within, however, is not only a "pillar of fire . . . to guide and to quicken," she is also the "pillar of darkness . . . that didst too truly shed the shadow of death over my young heart" (126). Staring alone at her corpse, the boy feels a blast of wind (her spirit?) and falls into a trance, seeming to have an out of body experience. "A vault seemed to open in the zenith of the far blue sky, a shaft which ran up forever. I, in spirit, rose as if on billows that also ran up the shaft forever" (132). He seems to be pursuing but never attaining God's throne, until he recovers his "self-possession" and finds himself "standing, as before, close to [his] sister's bed." The identification with Elizabeth is so complete that the boy is unconsciously one with her rising spirit as it searches for God in heaven.

The man writing the *Suspiria*, however, is more conscious, and has come to understand the dangers of anima possession. He has learned from experience that grief over loss, coupled with projection of anima into the girl, leads to

> a languishing which, from its very sweetness, perplexes the mind and is fancied to be very health [*sic*]. Witchcraft has seized upon

5. Lyon (58) goes so far as to consider De Quincey a "psychopath" because of the pleasure he derived from opium. The selfless generosity (e.g., his "loan" to Coleridge when he himself would soon be broke) and the tender sympathies he evinced throughout his life are hardly evidence of psychopathology.

you—nympholepsy has struck you. Now you rave no more. You acquiesce; nay, you are passionately delighted in your condition. Sweet becomes the grave, because you also hope immediately to travel thither. (145)

This passage is the "personal" counterpart of the subsequent "transpersonal" vision of the archetypal *Mater Tenebrarum*, the "molding" that shapes all female demons and vampires.

"Levana and Our Ladies of Sorrow" leads further than "The Affliction of Childhood" into the world of dream and vision. That it is also an archetypal world has already been recognized by critics, although not in a Jungian frame of reference. De Luca, interpreting the three Ladies of Sorrow as representations of three phases of De Quincey's "personal history" (72), considers the dream vision itself a way of restructuring "the diachronic order of personal experience" into a "synchronic pattern" that transcends the realm of biography. And Joel Black (57) relates "Levana" to the scene in *The Confessions* in which De Quincey as a child perceives his nurse as a demonic colossus: "His dream-image of his nurse as a demonic Levana-figure is indicative of an archetype"—which is bipolar: "consolatory-malevolent, ascent-descent oriented, young-old" (59).[6] But whereas the nurse is demonic, Levana is daemonic.

"Oftentimes at Oxford," writes De Quincey, "I saw Levana in my dreams" (172). Levana, he explains, was the Roman tutelary goddess who raised the infant from the ground, and who therefore presided over the education of the child. For Jean-Paul, De Quincey's source for Levana, she is a positive figure; but as Black shows, De Quincey's portrait is "a macabre parody" of Jean-Paul's maternal muse (49–50). For she raises the child up only to let him fall a greater distance. She teaches through suffering, through gravity: "By the education of Levana . . . is meant not the poor machinery that moves by spelling books and grammars, but *by that mighty system of central forces hidden in the deep bosom of human life*, which by passion, by strife, by temptation, by the energies of resistance, works forever upon children" (173—emphasis added). Grief leads De Quincey to new heights of consciousness. As King Lear learned, and as Herman Melville's Ishmael asserts in *Moby Dick*, the most profound knowledge comes from suffering; perception

6. Black (42) relates the feminine archetypes in "Levana" to those in Frye's *Secular Scripture*. Levana is similar to other "mythical prototypes" of feminine guides like Ariadne and Dante's Beatrice. But these figures are not bipolar in the Jungian sense.

of the "invisible spheres" of the universe is terrifying but enlightening. I think there is a world of difference between the demonic "doubling" in De Quincey and that seen in the real romantic ironists, Poe and Hoffmann. The voice of the *Suspiria* is that of a man who has recognized his inner daemons, and rather than cast them off and call them Other, he has used their energies to create his art. The same may be said of Hoffmann and Poe, but not of their narrators. De Quincey is ultimately not an ironist like them.[7] "Levana and Our Ladies of Sorrow" is a poetic effusion in honor of the Daemonic Feminine, a hymn to Demeter and Kore/Persephone, as these goddesses impress the *mysterium tremendum* into his soul.[8]

The goddesses communicate to him through signs, "hieroglyphics written on the tablets of the brain" (175). De Quincey explicitly states what Hoffmann and Poe implied: archetypes are modes of communication between the unconscious and consciousness, but the ego must study to understand the language. "*They* wheeled in mazes; *I* spelled the steps. *They* telegraphed from afar; *I* read the signals. . . . *Theirs* were the symbols; *mine* are the words" (175—emphasis De Quincey's). What are "they"? The diction is suggestive of archetypes: they are "mighty phantoms," "the mighty abstractions that incarnate themselves in all individual sufferings of man's heart" (174). But the visionary mind does not merely reify the abstractions into external demons; instead it recognizes them as powerful feminine forces within.

This femininity is more than the mere "girlish tears" of which his older brother made the young De Quincey feel so ashamed;[9] this is a trinity within, holy to him, but unholy to those who would deny the existence of God's feminine side. The Father, Son, and Holy Ghost, each has his

7. Black (53) sees the "central forces" as an allusion to Newtonian gravitation, working symbolically to cancel out Levana's "levitating" positive pole; moreover, "if the child can rise easily through Levana's agency, it is only because she has thoroughly possessed his soul" (54). Black views De Quincey as a romantic ironist for whom "the ascending movement towards self-recognition [in Frye's *Secular Scripture*] is invariably betrayed by gravity. Ascent proves to be descent, identity is demonically parsed into yet more disparate sections" (59), by which he means the three Ladies of Sorrow. But I think Black ultimately fails to recognize the potentially positive aspects of Levana's "gravity"

8. This term is Rudolf Otto's, in *The Idea of the Holy* (see Varnado, 10). He meant it in the sense of religious dread in the presence of the numinous. Peter Brooks (262) has shown that in the Gothic genre, the *mysterium tremendum* is no longer the Sacred but the unconscious.

9. This brother, William, was raised separately, under more masculine (public school) influence. Thomas, in the *Suspiria*, notes that "young boys torn away from mothers and sisters" at such an early age as William "not infrequently die" (173–74)—at least in spirit—presumably, from the lack of a well-developed feminine side.

feminine counterpart: the Madonna, Our Lady of Sighs, and Our Lady of Darkness. "These Ladies," writes De Quincey, "are the Sorrows, and they are three in number, as the Graces are three . . . the Parcae are three . . . the Furies are three . . . and at once even the Muses were three" (174). The Graces, Fates, and Furies are all aspects of the same triple goddess, the Queen of Heaven, Earth, and the Underworld.[10] De Quincey imprints upon this prototype his own individual melancholy, but it nonetheless retains its archetypal numinosity.

He names the eldest of the three "awful sisters" Our Lady of Tears; she is "Rachel weeping for her children" (175)—or Demeter weeping for the abducted Kore. And she is not only the cherishing, maternal Madonna; she is within man as well. "She, to my knowledge, sat all last summer by the bedside of the blind beggar, him that so often and so gladly I talked with" (175). She is what makes a grown man cry—without shame. The second sister is the spirit of meek submission to ill fortune, to cosmic, social, or political forces over which men have no control. The Lady of Sighs, "humble to abjectness," is a spirit of resignation, but not quite of despair. That is a province of the third and youngest sister, Our Lady of Darkness:

> Her kingdom is not large, or else no flesh should live; but within that kingdom all power is hers. Her head, turreted like that of Cybele, rises almost beyond the reach of sight. . . . She is the defier of God. She is also the mother of lunacies, and the suggestress of suicides. . . . this youngest sister moves with uncalculable motions, bounding, and with a tiger's leaps. (177)

Together, the three sisters in the dream vision seem to conspire against the dreamer. But the writer, years afterward, is no longer paranoid, for their purpose is not, he finally knows, to destroy him. Although the tears he shed, under the influence of *Mater Lachrymarum*, for the deaths of Elizabeth his sister, Ann his friend, Catherine Wordsworth his little protégée, and Margaret his wife, all tended to make him a nympholeptic who "worshipped the worm" (178)—tended indeed to make him a vampire with "languishing desires," to whom the grave was "lovely darkness" and "saintly corruption"—he now realizes that "he shall rise again before he dies," not as the undead but as the regenerated. To achieve such a state, he must be tormented by Our Lady of Darkness, who will tempt him to suicide and

10. See Robert Graves, *The Greek Myths*, 48–49; cf. H. J. Rose, 105, 122.

harass him until he is "accomplished in the furnace," his door of perception cleansed:

> So shall he see the things that ought not to be seen, sights that are abominable, and secrets that are unutterable. So shall he read elder truths, sad truths, grand truths, fearful truths. . . . And so shall our commission be accomplished which from God we had—to plague his heart until we had unfolded the capacities of his spirit. (178)

So the female daemon, Our Lady of Darkness, is not simply the chimera of a possessed or hallucinating mind; she is an elemental force, chthonic as Cybele, who leads men inward and downward to the depths, to Melville's "invisible spheres" that were "formed in fright." De Quincey teaches that cultivation of the feminine within the man means acceptance of the *mysterium tremendum*, the unconscious, over which she reigns.

De Quincey's insights into "nympholepsy"[11] and its transcendence can help us learn more about the nineteenth-century collective obsession with the femme fatale, which Mario Praz first described in *The Romantic Agony*. I don't think it can be completely explained as man's unconscious affirmation of woman's power and superiority (Nina Auerbach's feminist thesis in *Woman and the Demon*). Rather, the female demon leads us to the dark depths of the soul, where surprising revelations about both humanity and divinity are written in the "hieroglyphics" of the archetypes. Few men, writes De Quincey, ever learn the language; most "lack the passion, without which there is no reading of the legend and superscription upon man's brow" (200). Most are deaf to "the deep note that sighs upwards from the Delphic caves of human life." For the vision of the conjunction of opposites is both beautiful and terrifying. "The horror of life" mixes with "the heavenly sweetness of life" in "the confluence of the mighty and terrific discords with the subtle concords. . . . Not by contrast or as reciprocal foils do these elements act, which is the feeble conception of many, but by union. They are the sexual forces in music: 'male and female created he them'; and these mighty antagonists do not put forth their hostilities by repulsion, but by deepest attraction" (200). Notice the key words "mighty" and "elements"

---

11. This word, meaning "a state of rapture supposed to be inspired by nymphs, hence, an ecstasy or frenzy of emotion especially inspired by something unattainable," which then leads to "frustrated idealism," was first used in the 1770s (*OED*, 1933 ed., vol. 7). It might therefore reflect a sort of Enlightenment version of anima psychology. Many of our Gothic protagonists, especially Nathanael and Wolfgang, may be described as nympholeptics.

used once again to connote the archetypes, which seem to get stirred up by traumatic experiences like the death of a beloved sister. They are frightening, uncanny forces capable of overwhelming consciousness, as in Hoffmann, Gautier, and Poe; but De Quincey is quick to point out that the archetypes—whether Our Lady of Darkness or the Dark Interpreter[12]—can broaden and deepen consciousness. De Quincey agreed with Blake's dictum, "Without Contraries is no Progression."

As already seen, if the mind becomes perplexed by the feminine archetypes the result is what De Quincey called nympholepsy and what Jung called anima possession. Such a state usually leads to travesties of archetypal fusion rather than to integration, to the reanimated corpse instead of the regenerated man. But the anima herself is not the culprit; it is the man unable to interpret her language or meet her demands.

"Our Dual Existence": Loving and Dying in Le Fanu's "Carmilla"[13]

The Irish author Joseph Sheridan Le Fanu (1814–73) is known today primarily for his Gothic stories—especially "Green Tea" (1869), which occupies an important place in the British development of the ghost story in the nineteenth and early twentieth centuries,[14] and the novella "Carmilla," which first appeared in the collection *In a Glass Darkly* (1872). Le Fanu wrote of everything from dead lovers to demonic monkeys,[15] but not until near the end of his life did he tackle the female vampire.

James Twitchell claims that "Carmilla" is "a conscious attempt to render

12. The Dark Interpreter appears as an intruder in his dreams (182), a "shadow" (187) who really turns out to be more of an animus figure that aids him in translating the hieroglyphics of his dreams.

13. Reprinted by permission of Greenwood Publishing Group, Inc., Westport, Conn., from *Contours of the Fantastic: Selected Essays from the Eighth International Conference on the Fantastic in the Arts*, edited by Michele K. Langford. Copyright © 1990 by Michele K. Langford.

14. See Jack Sullivan, *Elegant Nightmares*, chapters 1 and 2; and Julia Briggs, *Night Visitors*, 44–51.

15. In "Schalken the Painter" (1839) and "Green Tea" (1869) respectively. In his own time, Le Fanu was known more for his excellent mysteries (e.g., *The House by the Churchyard*, 1863, and *Uncle Silas*, 1864). It was M. R. James's edition of Le Fanu's ghost stories in 1923 that gave him his present reputation as the originator of the British tradition that continued in the works of M. R. James, the Bensons, L. P. Hartley, Oliver Onions, Walter De La Mare, et al.

Coleridge's *Christabel* into prose" (*Living Dead*, 129). But the text is much more than a mere "rendering" of Coleridge. Many of the similarities between the two works may be due to their authors' mutually independent manipulation of the same folklore motifs about the lamia figure. Le Fanu's anxiety is not merely one of influence.

In any case, the most important similarity between the two works is what distinguishes them from all other lamia tales—lesbianism. Why do Geraldine and Carmilla seek female loves? It is, I think, *not* because the male writers wanted to explore "they psychodynamics of perversion" (Twitchell, *Living Dead*, 129). Whether or not lesbianism is viewed as a perversion in these ambiguous texts depends on the reader, not the original writer. The crucial issue is gender signification. Male writers are identifying with female characters. Coleridge reveals that Christabel is his persona when he has her carry Geraldine across the threshold—a male role, after which Christabel/Coleridge assumes a feminine role (cf. Paglia, 334). Likewise in "Carmilla," Le Fanu deliberately avoids mentioning the narrator's name for the first forty pages, inviting confusion between female narrator and male author. He also has her play occasional male roles (Veeder, 207). Since the lamia's victim (usually male) is in a submissive, even masochistic role, which is sociocultually defined as feminine, he may as well have a female name: he is revealed as "Laura." But why, then, are Carmilla and Geraldine not signified by masculine names to correspond to their dominating sadistic roles? Perhaps because they are dominating maternal figures, icons of the Terrible Mother archetype, who is always a dominatrix.[16]

The gender reversals in the vampire tale, moreover, reflect the confusion caused by the tension between archetypal androgyny—the instinctive tendency to fuse the opposites—and stereotypical dualism, the sociocultural tendency to polarize them. If feminine aggressiveness is denied (if woman's role is reduced to one of submission, of suffering and being still), it will reassert itself with the fury of a "writhing fiend"—as Carmilla does.[17] So terrifying is this return of the repressed, that the man succumbs and submits, ironically becoming feminine himself. Again the result is a travesty

16. That Geraldine is a mother figure has often been pointed out. She appears in tandem with Christabel's "good" mother, who allows the demoness her "hour." See for example, Schapiro, *The Romantic Mother*, 73: "As Geraldine embodies both the desired and ideal good mother and the feared and vengeful bad mother, so the mother image is split generally between the good and the bad throughout the poem."

17. This psychodynamic has been explored fully by William Veeder, "Carmilla: The Arts of Repression," and by William Patrick Day, *In the Circles of Fear and Desire*, 86–90.

of androgyny. But "Carmilla" is more than just a tale of terror; it is also a love story in which the instincts are subliminally viewed in a positive light.

The work begins with a prologue in which the author cites one Doctor Hesselius (a "psychic doctor") who considers the story "as involving . . . some of the profoundest arcana of our dual existence" (222).[18] How this phrase is meant exactly the reader is invited to conjecture after reading the tale. But from this announcement of ontological ambiguity, one knows at the outset that "Carmilla" is not going to be another *Varney the Vampire*.

Set in Styria (Austria), the story is narrated by a person revealed much later as Laura. She is addressing her narrative to an unnamed English girl. Her father, she tells this woman, is English, but her mother remains mysterious. All that is known of her at first is that she was a Styrian lady who died in Laura's infancy. Laura lives with her father in a *Schloss*, and she has been brought up by a benign governess "whose care and good nature *in part* supplied to me the loss of my mother" (224—emphasis added.). But only in part—that phrase is crucial, as Laura unconsciously reveals when she describes her "early fright":

> I can't have been more than six years old, when one night I awoke, and looking around the room from my bed, failed to see the nursery-maid. Neither was my nurse there. . . . I was vexed and insulted at finding myself, as I conceived, neglected, and I began to whimper . . . when to my surprise, I saw a solemn, but very pretty face looking at me from the side of the bed. (225)

The apparition is a young woman whose presence causes the child to stop whimpering. "Delightfully soothed" as the lady lies beside her, Laura falls asleep again, only to be "wakened by a sensation as if two needles ran into my breast very deep at the same moment" (225). She cries out, causing the lady to slip down to the floor and hide under the bed. Finally, the child is frightened (anything that hides under the bed has to be scary) and screams.

This first vampiric visitation of Carmilla is remarkable for several reasons. She comes when the child feels neglected and anxious, needing a mother to soothe her to sleep. The cherishing, nourishing, positive pole of the mother archetype is conjured, but she suddenly turns into her opposite, the anti-

---

18. All page references to "Carmilla" are to *In a Glass Darkly* (London: John Lehmann, 1947), 222–88.

mother, she who takes life from the breast.[19] She is the mother in her Terrible aspect, who withdraws the breast as punishment. So traumatic, in other words, is the loss or withdrawal of the mother, that her absence becomes a demonic presence: a devouring antimother. Both the soothing presence and the punishing absence of the mother constitute Carmilla's character. Thus, when she reappears, she will be a pleasure-giving lover-friend and a "writhing fiend."

Laura insists that this "early fright" was not a dream; but in true Ambiguous Gothic form, Le Fanu has given the vampire a hypnagogic origin. It is not surprising, however, when Laura finally meets her dream-mother in waking life. Laura is nineteen now, awaiting the arrival of a prospective friend, whose "visit, and the new acquaintance it promised, had furnished my day dream for many weeks" (227). But the girl, she learns, has died. She was the ward of Laura's father's friend General Spielsdorf, who has written in a letter that she was killed by a "fiend who betrayed our infatuated hospitality" and whom he now is hunting (228). Deprived of a new friend, Laura once again needs soothing. She finds a friend to fulfill those daydreams: the very fiend Spielsdorf hunts.

The scene describing Carmilla's reappearance (229–32) is one of the triumphs of late Gothic fiction. The carriage accident on the horror story level is a sham designed to dupe the unsuspecting mortals into inviting the demon into their house. But the incident is given mythic dimensions when the carriage swerves "to bring the wheel over the projecting roots of . . . a magnificent lime-tree." In Germanic mythology, the lime or linden is sacred to Minne, the goddess of love, and to the Great Goddess (De Vries, 229) who appears in this violent irruption from the unconscious. At first, she is manifest only in the persons of Carmilla and her mother, but Le Fanu seems to have intuited that this vision of archetypal femininity was somehow incomplete. As Blake and De Quincey knew, it is threefold, not twofold.[20] And as Jung explained, her three aspects, corresponding to heaven, earth, and the underworld, evince respectively "cherishing and nourishing good-ness," "emotionality and passion," and the "Stygian depths" (CW 9.1: 82). Carmilla's mother, Mrs. Karnstein, at least in appearance, is the good mother; her daughter is the love goddess, but where is the missing lady to

19. The vampire did not originally go for the jugular vein. In folklore, it often attacked "the chest near the heart," as Ollier puts it euphemistically, like a good Victorian (39). There were even some kinky vampires who went for the toes (Ollier, 39).

20. Of Blake's many examples of the "threefold feminine," see his poem "The Crystal Cabinet," lines 15–20.

complete the trinity—Hekate? The reader only learns later that she was in the carriage all the time. Le Fanu seems to have understood that, although Mrs. Karnstein and Carmilla were the only ones necessary to the narrative's surface structure as a horror story, its deep structure as myth demanded the third figure. One of Laura's companions, Mademoiselle De La Fontaine, claims that she saw "a hideous black woman with a sort of colored turban on her head . . . who was gazing all the time from the carriage window, nodding and grinning derisively towards the ladies, with gleaming eyes and large white eye-balls, and her teeth set as if in fury" (234). Her teeth suggest vampirism, but more important is her terrible aspect—hideous, derisive, angry. She plays no other part in the story but to complete the Unholy Trinity, integral to the conflict that later develops between patriarchal and matriarchal forces.

The apparently injured Carmilla is escorted into the *Schloss*, while her mother goes off on what she calls a mission of life and death. When Carmilla regains consciousness, she asks where "mamma" and "Matska" are (232–33). (The latter name means mud.) She is informed that her mother has had to leave her while she convalesces at the *Schloss* for three months. But no one asks her who Matska is. She remains the mysterious hag in the carriage. Her only other manifestation seems to be in the anecdote Mademoiselle De La Fontaine tells about the full moon's effect on a sailor cousin of hers: one night he fell asleep "with his face full in the light of the moon. . . . [He] had awakened after a dream of an old woman clawing him by the cheek, with his features horribly drawn to one side; and his countenance had never quite recovered its equilibrium" (229). This passage symbolizes what William Veeder has shown to be one of the major themes of "Carmilla": the vicious return of repressed femininity in a patriarchal society.

The mysterious hag, associated with the moon and with earth ("Matska"), is the first of several indications that the demonic feminine in this tale is closely associated with Nature. Although "mamma" and Matska appear to leave Carmilla, they really do not—they are a part of her. Carmilla is herself a mother figure. Her aspect as Nature-Death Goddess becomes more apparent later when she begins her gruesome depredations on Laura.

Laura eventually discovers that Carmilla is the same woman who had appeared to her when she was six (236). Carmilla claims that she had a similar dream, and Le Fanu begins a breakdown of boundaries between the two ("I you and you me"), as Laura becomes inexplicably attracted to and repelled by Carmilla (237). The "ambiguous alternations" of attraction and repulsion have been adequately explained by Veeder and Day in sexual terms. Carmilla is the sexual element Laura has had to repress. But there is a dimension to Carmilla "beyond the pleasure principle": Carmilla is the "suggestress of suicide" (Cf. McCormack, 191: "vampirism seen as a projection of this kind is suicidal in structure"). She is De Quincey's *Mater Tenebrarum*, who makes the grave seem sweet by creating a languor "which, from its very sweetness . . . is fancied to be health. . . . There was an unaccountable fascination in its earlier symptoms. . . . Dim thoughts of death began to open, and an idea that I was slowly sinking took gentle, and somehow, not unwelcome possession of me" (255). The passages evincing Carmilla's sultry sexuality have been quoted by practically every commentator on the tale. Less emphasis has been given to the Carmilla who says "everyone must die; and all are happier when they do. Come home" (242). This death goddess, whose "home lay in the direction of the west," cannot be completely explained in sexual terms. The tapestry opposite the foot of her bed "representing Cleopatra" shows the queen not in the act of vamping, but "with the asps to her bosom"—killing herself (235). Sex is important to Carmilla because it produces a "little death":

> "You are afraid to die?" [Carmilla asks Laura.]
> "Yes, everyone is."
> "But to die as lovers may—to die together, so that they may live together . . ." (246)

She sounds like Gottfried von Strassburg in *Tristan*; her vision is that of *Liebestod*—she seeks a dialectic of love and death. "I live in you; and you would die for me, I love you so" (248). The first clause is a vivid reminder that she is daemon, not demon—an inner spirit. But she is not the transformative anima, an energy source. She is the static, languid spirit of dissolution, whose element is not air but earth.

What makes her so frightening is not only her attractiveness but her ardor. She loves Laura passionately because Laura cannot admit to herself that *she* loves death. Much easier to accept is the notion that death loves her. Her repression, then, is not only of the sex instinct but of the death instinct. She cannot admit the truth about herself—that she finds death romantic (248) and inwardly longs for it like Elis in the mines of Falun. As with Elis, her longing for the dead mother becomes a longing for death itself, personified as a vampiric reincarnation of the dead mother. Carmilla's identity as an image of the dead mother becomes even more obvious when she and Laura are looking at the portrait of Mircalla of Karnstein, a seventeenth-century countess (obviously Carmilla herself). Laura reveals, out of nowhere, that she is maternally descended from the Karnsteins. "Ah!" replies Carmilla languidly, "so am I" (248).

Laura and Carmilla are related through the mother, then. Laura's father later reemphasizes that his daughter's Karnstein connection is purely matrilineal (267); his family is free of vampiric pollution—that is, of suicidal tendencies.[21] Again, the parental archetype is vividly polarized: the patriarchal Logos is the Lord of Light and Spirit, while the matriarchal Eros is the Lady of Darkness and moribund flesh (*Karn*stein; *Car*milla). Is it possible to destroy the polarization so that the two contrary systems can interact progressively in Blake's and De Quincey's sense? To view Carmilla only as a horror to be eradicated by General Spielsdorf and his crew is to keep the contraries apart, maintaining "male hegemony" (Veeder, 205; Day, 88). Laura never wholly subscribes to the masculine view of Carmilla as a monster. Unconsciously, even after the vampire is dispatched, she still listens for Carmilla's "light step . . . at the drawing-room door" (288). Archetypes do not die. Although repulsed by the men's revelation to her of Carmilla's vampirism, Laura is still attracted to Carmilla's beauty, to the beauty of death. Throughout the story, she oscillates through "ambiguous alternations" (288), vividly realized in Carmilla's transformations from beautiful woman, to a black-cat-like beast (252), to a "black palpitating mass" (281).

She is the animal and the muddy earth, reminding us of our tie with Nature. Thus she coldly rejects Spirit. When Laura's father says, "We are in God's hands. Nothing can happen without his permission. . . . He is our faithful creator; he has made us all, and will take care of us," Carmilla scoffs vehemently: "Creator! Nature! . . . And this disease that invades the country is natural. Nature. All things proceed from Nature. . . . All things *in the heaven, in the earth, and under the earth*, act and live as Nature ordains (245—emphasis added). At a funeral, the religious hymns make her ill (242–43), and Laura has never seen her kneel and pray (252). Like Gautier's Clarimonde and De Quincey's Lady of Darkness, she is the "defier of God." Notice that she is careful to place all three provinces—heaven, earth, and the underworld—within the Nature Goddess's realm. She is the voice of the Unholy Trinity who claims that there is no resurrection of spirit after death. She wants Laura to rise again before she dies, to find

21. In folklore, the vampire was often imagined as the animated corpse of a suicide (Twitchell, *Living Dead*, 7–9).

regeneration rather than horror in the vision of death as Nature's way of creating life.

The vampire in Carmilla, then, does not represent, as Twitchell and the men in the text think, the unnatural, "sterile love of homosexuality" (*Living Dead*, 129). She is the natural tendency that makes the snowy woods of death look "lovely, dark, and deep." The beauty of this death goddess becomes the Gorgon's ugliness only when her promptings are ignored. Repressing her does no good; one must try to befriend her without letting her take complete possession. It is a delicate balance, which Laura is not able to attain because the archetypal opposites remain hopelessly split; the sexes and what they represent maintain their "dual existence." A dialectic is never achieved.

In Jungian terms, it now becomes clearer why Sheridan Le Fanu chose to make his haunted protagonist a girl. In most Gothic tales involving a female demon, she haunts a man—as temptress, succubus, or vampire. Le Fanu followed Coleridge's exception to the rule, not because he was fascinated by lesbianism, but because he was concerned about his own death. Shortly before writing the tale, he made out his will, feeling the end to be near. He died only a few months after Carmilla was published (McCormack, 268–70). When a man needs to come to terms with death, he searches the dark side of his soul. Anima comes out of abeyance. In taking the first-person point of view of a fascinated girl, Le Fanu identifies with her—that is, he signifies his own anima as "Laura." She becomes the mediator between the man and the frightening mystery of death, which is signified by "Carmilla," the mother archetype in her aspect as *Mater Tenebrarum*. As a lover of death, she makes death easier to face. The writer, moreover, makes his mediatrix suffer, purging himself, at least while he writes, of the painful anticipation of his own death.

For Le Fanu, to write "Carmilla" was to practice the art of dying.

Dracula's Lamiae: Unholy Circle[22]

Dracula differs from the other texts examined thus far in that it was the originator of a major mythology in popular culture. It (or at least its mythos)

22. Reprinted by permission of Greenwood Publishing Group, Inc., Westport, Conn., from *Selected Essays from the Tenth International Conference on the Fantastic in the Arts*, edited by Lloyd Worley. Copyright © 1992 by Lloyd Worley.

has never been relegated to obscurity, even though as art it is at about the same level as *The Monk*. David Punter considers Dracula "underrated" as literature (256), and Phyllis Roth claims it is a "considerable literary achievement,"[23] but despite some fine isolated passages, most critics tend to agree with James Twitchell's estimation of the novel as worthless in "artistic merit" (*Living Dead*, 134). Nevertheless, as Twitchell maintains, Dracula is a major mythical document. Perhaps one can say correctly of *Dracula* what Harold Bloom says (incorrectly, in my opinion) of Poe's tales—"the tale somehow is stronger than its telling. . . . What survives despite [Stoker's] writing, are the psychological dynamics and the mythic reverberations" (23).[24]

Stoker's novel is also important because it provides, along with *Doctor Jekyll and Mr. Hyde* and *The Picture of Dorian Grey*, the *fin de siècle* consummation of the Gothic genre. Like Stevenson's and Wilde's novels, *Dracula* reflects anxieties about Darwin's discovery of the intrinsic link between men and beasts, and anticipates Freud's discovery of the id by only a few years. These texts are important documents in the decline of the Victorian world picture. Although Wilde was all for that decline, Stevenson and especially Stoker were more ambivalent. It is indeed ambivalence that makes *Dracula*, albeit overtly supernatural, a species of Ambiguous Gothic.

The novel has received an abundance of commentary, especially from psychoanalysts, feminists, and myth critics. The anthropologist Maurice Richardson laid the groundwork in his article "The Psychoanalysis of Ghost Stories" (1959), in which he was the first to suggest that *Dracula* seems to dramatize, in amazing detail, the Primal Crime (described in Freud's *Totem and Taboo*) of the sons in the "Primal Horde" banding together and killing the father, who had been hoarding all the women to himself. Richardson's initial insight has been elaborated by Astle, Twitchell, and others. An even more influential article was published in 1972: C. F. Bentley's "The Monster in the Bedroom." He seems to have been the first publicly to admit what I am sure many readers of the novel before 1972 already knew—that

23. Roth says *Dracula* succeeds because "it realizes a perfect balance between terrifying but desired fantasies and appropriate defense" (*Bram Stoker*, 125). But William Patrick Day thinks Stoker fails because he does not create a consistent vision of Mina (147). And Stephanie Demetrakopoulos claims that *Dracula* fails as art because it never achieves integration of sexuality, which remains monstrous—a questionable criterion for artistic merit (111).

24. If one strips "the telling" from "Ligeia," for example, one is left with a tale of a woman who gets sick and dies in spite of a strong will to live, and then who comes back to possess the body of another woman. It sounds like *Love Story* combined with *The Exorcist*.

vampirism is a trope for sexual activity, which in the book appears in various "perverted" forms from incest to fellatio. Stoker, of course, was not consciously writing pornography; indeed no Victorian novel evinces more fear of sex and "sexual women" than does Dracula (Weissman, 392). Consciously, the book is a male hysterical reaction against the emergence of both the New Woman and "suddenly sexual women" (Phyllis Roth's term) in Victorian society. Stoker wishes to reassert the proper womanly role of angelic, sexless matron.[25] But his unconscious is fighting him on every page. He makes the female vampire very sexy. She does not smell putrescent like Dracula, who always has about him the noisome odor of rotting flesh. Like Gautier's Clarimonde and Le Fanu's Carmilla, the female vampire has a "honey-sweet" breath—"but with a bitter underlying the sweet, a bitter offensiveness, as one smells in blood" (Dracula, 39).[26] Still this blood smell is not as bad as Dracula's stench, which "was composed of all the ills of mortality" (265). The bittersweetness of the lamia's breath is one of scores of images reflecting Stoker's profound ambivalence about sexuality.[27]

The underlying structure of the plot is boldly sexual. A young man (Jonathan Harker) who is engaged to be married to a respectable Victorian girl (Mina Murray) is tempted, while away on a business trip in the mysterious Near East (the borderland between Christendom and the pagan world), by three voluptuous ladies who would like nothing better than to kiss him to death. He is quite ready to submit, for he feels unconsciously that one orgy with these sirens will give him more pleasure than a lifetime with the proper Mina. But Dracula "saves" him from this fate of death-through-orgasm: "Back," he cries to his daughters. "This man belongs to me!" (40). He has other plans for Harker, through whom he wants to spread his satanic dominion into Christendom. Only after Dracula has used Harker to expedite his conquest of the West, will he allow the girls their orgy: "When I am done with him you shall kiss him at your will" (40).

Consciously fearing those "weird sisters" more than the Devil himself, Harker somehow manages to escape—it is never clear precisely how. Nevertheless, his experience has caused a "brain fever," undoubtedly the

25. See Christopher Craft's excellent article, "'Kiss Me with Those Red Lips,'" 121: "Appetite in a woman is a diabolical inversion of the natural order, of the novel's futile hope that maternity and sexuality be divorced."

26. All page references to Dracula are to the Bantam Classic edition (New York, 1981), which is both accurate and easily available.

27. An ambivalence that of course has been well documented. See especially Phyllis Roth, Bram Stoker, chapters 1 and 5.

result of the clash between his unconscious desires and his conscious fears. In any case, Dracula invades England without Harker's help. The demon's presence is felt indirectly through diaries, letters, journal entries, and newspaper accounts in which only the reader knows what is happening: the devil in the form of a dark beast is attacking the Fair Maiden of Victorian England. She is becoming, in other words, more aggressively sexual, more passionate. Lucy Westenra, the angelic Light of the West, is being polluted by the pagan spirit of sexual appetite. Lucy, before her transformation into a vampire, has been blessed with three suitors—indeed three proposals in one day, from John Seward, a doctor who runs an insane asylum; Quincey Morris, a chivalrous Texan and unintentional parody of Americans; and Arthur Holmwood, whom Lucy loves. But she is a "horrid flirt" and wishes she could marry all three men (62). This conscious admission actually hides her unconscious desire—to have sex with all of them. Her three proposals echo the scene with Jonathan Harker and the three sisters in Dracula's castle.

Lucy, a somnambulist, is totally put out of touch with her true feelings, which come out only at night. She is the kind of girl who likes sex, the kind of girl the men in *Dracula* fear and desire the most. She has her polygamous orgy—through the blood transfusions the men give her.[28] This woman, in yielding to the devil, has been wasting away; every orgasm makes her weaker. She languishes in autoerotism (Dracula's bites), and the men should know that sex with them (albeit displaced) is not going to save her. By their own standards, it will only make her more of a vamp. Becoming one of the "Un-Dead," she is finally given the "appropriate" punishment for such a creature—she is staked; that is, raped to death by the man she should have married (cf. Craft, 122).

If this female Lucifer, Lucy as "Bloofer Lady," the sexual woman, is not the True Woman, then who is? Mina, of course, who does not want three men, but only one, whom she marries as soon as he has recovered from his brain fever. The devil tempts her, too, though, and she even begins to feel drawn to the magnet of sexual pleasure. But it is not her fault; unlike Lucy, she did not revel in flirtation and the idea of polygamy. Even this good Christian woman, however, is not immune. The men make the mistake of leaving her to her own devices, placing her outside their protective sphere. She gives in to the temptation of masturbatory sexual fantasies. Ironically, her sexual awakening (again instigated by Dracula's bite) makes her more

28. That the blood transfusions are sexual was first pointed out by C. F. Bentley, 29.

affectionate to her husband (282). But then she goes too far: she even has a fantasy of oral sex. But no, the devil forced her to do it. In the most vivid horror scene in the book, Dracula claws open his own flesh and holds Mina to his breast, forcing her to drink.[29] When she must tell the men all about her experience, she ostensibly takes comfort at Jonathan's breast, unaware that she is really mimicking the "unclean" act she experienced with Dracula (300; 302: "she clasped her husband closer to her and bent her head lower and lower still on his breast").

Mina, however, is too much the matron to succumb completely to such fantasies. Unlike Lucy, she feels guilty; she considers herself "unclean," and she is "tainted," branded, until Dracula (the id) and his daughters (the spirits of female sexual pleasure) are destroyed.

Such is the Freudian interpretation of the novel. Since its mythos is a familiar part of our collective consciousness, perhaps a Jungian reading can further illuminate the text. Archetypal implications abound throughout the novel, especially in Jonathan Harker's dream of Dracula's Daughters.[30] The scene in which he is approached, while in a hypnagogic state, by the three vampire ladies has received much comment, but no one has attempted to answer the question, Why are there *three* of these women? If the scene functions merely as the beginning of the theme of sexual ambivalence in the novel (Harker is beset by "some longing and at the same time some deadly fear"—39), or if the "fair one" of the triad is a vision of his mother, as Roth suggests ("Suddenly Sexual Women," 119), one or two ladies would have served the purpose.

Like Le Fanu, Stoker seems intuitively aware that the feminine, in order to be archetypally complete, must be threefold. And like De Quincey, he knows that "the Graces are three, the Parcae are three, the Furies are three." And the Harpies are also three. Emand Ollier had suggested in 1855 that the Harpies may have been prototypes for vampires (40). Moreover, the Harpies were snatchers of children (Rose, 28), as Stoker's Harpies are: Dracula throws them a sack containing a child (40). But more to the point, the Harpies were bird-women, like the Sirens, with which they were associated (Rose, 28). Harker's dream-women are sirens, for when they

---

29. As has been repeatedly pointed out, this is a nightmare image of oral sex (e.g., Bentley, 30). When Mina tells the men of her experience, she cries, "I must either suffocate or swallow some of the—Oh my God!" (304). Nowhere is Ernst Jones's thesis in *On the Nightmare*, that blood and semen are often equivalent in dreams, made more obvious.

30 Stoker claimed that this scene was based on an actual dream (see Demetrakopoulos, 99), which may help to explain its archetypal power.

laugh, it is "a silvery musical laugh . . . like the tinkling of water glasses" (39)—alluringly beautiful yet inhuman. The Harpies and the Sirens (who were also three) yield the bipolar archetype: they are both attractive and repulsive, like Dracula's daughters. The Harpies are archetypal soul images (Rose, 28), whose allusive presence in the beginning of Dracula gives it both a mythological dimension and an ontological ambiguity: Harker is visited in his sleep by his own phantoms—sirens that become Harpies because he feels guilty for having such sexual fantasies. The Harpies often snatched people up and carried them to the Errinyes—the Furies of guilt (Graves, 128). The passage in which the three weird sisters appear to Jonathan Harker is one of the most artistically successful in the novel because of this archetypal suggestiveness. Perhaps Stoker had Charles Lamb's famous statement in mind: "Gorgons and . . . Chimaeras . . . and the Harpies may reproduce themselves in the brain of superstition—but they were there before. They are transcripts, types—the archetypes are in us, and eternal."[31]

Of the three sisters, one is singled out—the one who is "fair, as fair can be." "I seemed somehow to know her face, and to know it in connection with some dreamy fear" (38). Her sisters urge her on to the dozing Jonathan: "Go on! You are first, and we shall follow; yours is the right to begin" (39). Harker is in "an agony of delightful anticipation" as the fair girl bends over him and he smells her bittersweet breath. Phyllis Roth has identified her as "the mother (almost archetypally presented)" ("Suddenly Sexual Women," 119). I think her qualifier ("almost") can be disregarded, but I would add that the Fair One is an image of the anima with the mother archetype still attached. Represented by breath, moisture, and moonlight, she is the dark side of his soul, allied (like Clarimonde and Carmilla) with the beast: "There was a deliberate voluptuousness which was both thrilling and repulsive, and as she arched her neck she actually licked her lips like an animal, till I could see in the moonlight the moisture shining on the scarlet lips and on the red tongue as it lapped the white sharp teeth" (39). But since the anima is still attached to the mother archetype, she is not an energy source. On the contrary, like Carmilla and Our Lady of Darkness, she produces a "languorous ecstasy" (39). Since Harker's sexual fantasy involves the "static" mother, it must be invaded by the father figure, who enters furiously to interrupt. The price

31. This quotation, from Lamb's essay "Witches and Other Night Fears" (*Works* 2: 114), has often been cited as anticipatory of Jungian archetypal theory. Cf. Penzoldt, 58. Lamb goes on to add, "How else should the recital of that, which we know in a waking sense to be false, come to affect us at all?"

this young man pays for refusing to separate mother from anima is a punishing father complex. The Furies are nothing compared to his rage: "Never did I imagine such wrath and fury, even to the demons of the pit" (40). The father comes in as the image of hate personified ("You yourself never loved; you never love," the fair one tells him—40). Then, in one of the novel's more gruesome moments, Dracula appeases the thirst of the Harpies by throwing them a bag containing "a half-smothered child," which they snatch up and then "fade into the rays of the moonlight" (41). Harker finally lapses into complete unconsciousness. Again one sees how easily the good mother (the fair one) becomes the antimother, the devourer of babies, when a mind is unconscious of its contents, and especially of its projection of anima into the mother imago.

"The three ghostly women" to whom he is "doomed" (47) continue to haunt Jonathan Harker as he seeks escape from the Haunted Castle. "I am alone with these awful women. Faugh! Mina is a woman, and there is nought in common" (55). And that is Harker's problem: he links sexuality with the devouring aspect of the mother archetype, while he attributes all the cherishing, nurturing aspects of the mother to the exalted Mina, who gladly plays that role.

In *Dracula*, polarization of archetypes is complete. Each half of the parental imago is hopelessly split. God (in his avatar, Van Helsing) versus the devil; and the Virgin Mary (Mina) versus Our Lady of Darkness. Dracula's association with the devouring mother is symbolically suggested in his trip to England aboard the *Demeter*—the pagan Mother Earth. Stoker must have wanted to emphasize Dracula's connection with the pagan gods, but he unwittingly chose the cherishing mother. If he had wanted to avoid all positive connotations, he should have named Dracula's ship the *Hekate*. His unconscious continues to fight against him.

Every archetype appears with its opposite. Van Helsing is the positive father archetype, who (especially at the end of the novel) is paired with Mina the mother to destroy Dracula and the weird sisters. Whereas Mina the mother helps Van Helsing destroy the sexual devil, another mother unwittingly helps Dracula sexualize Lucy. Twice Lucy's own sick mother, without realizing it, allows Dracula access to her daughter (141 and 151). When the mother realizes what she has done, her weak heart finally fails her. But actually this dying mother is a double of Lucy herself: "My dear mother gone! It is time that I go too" (152; cf. 154: the tableau of mother and daughter unconscious on the bed). Subliminally, the text keeps insinuating what the men keep denying: that the mother is a sexual being; Lucy dies into a sexual awakening (168–69) and becomes what Jonathan Harker dreamed of in Dracula's castle: a devourer of babies, an antimother (185–87), like the original Lamia.[32] She becomes Our Lady of Darkness, but there is still hope for the world that insists on seeing mothers as asexual creatures; there is still Mina. "There are darknesses in life, and there are lights," Van Helsing tells Mina. "You are one of the lights" (193). And later he adds: "She is one of God's women, fashioned by His own hand to show us men and other women that there is a heaven where we can enter, and its light can be here on earth" (198).

This latter passage reveals especially well the "unconscious cerebration" (Dr. Seward's term—73)[33] in Van Helsing's conscious celebration of Mina. Heaven may be entered through the Ideal Woman, as one enters the dreaded dark place, the vagina. The only way Van Helsing and the rest of his Crew of Light can have intercourse with a woman is by violent entrance, not through the dreaded vagina (mouth of the vampire),[34] but through the transfusions and the staking—gruesome displacements from below upwards. In Van Helsing's vision of Mina, the displacement has gone so far upwards it has become completely spiritual.

Why do these men view sex and sexual women with such horror? Why must they sublimate like Ambrosio, the celibate monk? Because aggressive sexual passion makes a woman less womanly (i.e., motherly) to them. It threatens to emasculate them. They are victims of their own stereotypical codes. Lucy the "Bloofer Lady" is unclean, a black cat (222), with eyes "full of hell-fire" and "unholy light" (223). Her voluptuous smile is "carnal and unspiritual" as she importunes Arthur Holmwood: "My arms are hungry for you. *Come*, and we can rest together. *Come*, my husband *come!*" (223; emphasis added). Arthur cannot resist such enticement—unconsciously, that is. Like Jonathan under the influence of the Sirens, he is in a trance; he opens his arms to her. Van Helsing intervenes, but not quite as Dracula did with the weird sisters. He shoves a crucifix between Lucy and Arthur, and the carnal woman recoils "with baffled malice" (223). Suddenly the beautiful

---

32. For Lamia as child-destroyer, see Graves, 205, and Nethercott, 84: "out of her despair and her envy of the happy mothers of living children, she issued [out of her cave] to prey upon these children . . . seizing them outright from their mothers and killing them by sucking their innocent blood."

33. The term "unconscious cerebration" was coined by Dr. William B. Carpenter in his book *The Unconscious Activity of the Brain* (London, 1866), which Stoker read. See Uwe Böker, 325–33.

34. Cf. Craft, 109: "the vampire mouth is an image of equivocation, luring at first with an inviting orifice, a promise of red softness, but delivering instead a piercing bone."

face turns into the Gorgon's: "the brows were wrinkled as though the folds of the flesh were the coils of Medusa's snakes." She is revealed as the Terrible Mother, who will hold a child to her breast than cast him away, as Lucy has just done (223). The message remains clear: motherhood and sexuality do not mix. Unconsciously, however, the motherhood of the "Bloofer Lady" is revealed, albeit in her Terrible aspect.

The absurd attempt to dissociate the maternal from the carnal parallels the attempt to dissociate man from the beasts as well. But Dracula's subliminal level again reveals that Darwin and Freud were right. Unconsciously we know we are animals like Dracula, that ape with eyebrows grown together and hair in the palms of his hands (18–19): Van Helsing's eyebrows are just as bushy (191), and as the zookeeper reminds us, "there's a deal of the same nature in us as in them theer animiles" (144). Further, Van Helsing is always hissing like a snake (134, 167, *passim*). And finally, even he, avatar of the Christian Father, is lured by the sirens: "Yes, I was moved—I, Van Helsing, with all my purpose and with my motive for hate" (391). When he comes upon the graves of the three sisters, fascination almost overwhelms him, especially when he sees the fair one:

> I find a high great tomb, as if made for one much beloved, that other fair sister which, like Jonathan I had seen to gather herself out of the atoms of the mist. She was . . . so radiantly beautiful, so exquisitely voluptuous, that the very *instinct* of man in me, which calls some of my sex to love and to protect one of hers, *made my head whirl with new emotion*. (392—emphasis added)

She acts as anima to him here, and he almost responds, until he hears the wailing of Mina, the Blessed Mother, sleeping within the Holy Circle he has drawn with the Host. He snaps out of his "enthrallment" and remembers that the vampire's mouth is an unholy circle, a place of pollution, the very dangerous *vagina dentata*.

The circle is in fact the most pervasive archetypal symbol in *Dracula*. The religious circle Van Helsing draws around Mina (387) appears to be a kind of Catholic mandala. Jung has shown that mandala symbolism often involves the fusion of opposites, for example, yin and yang (*CW* 9.1: 358). In the last pages of *Dracula*, the "Holy circle" (388) keeps appearing in opposition to the unholy circling of the vampires. The Unholy Circle has dominated throughout the novel. At the outset, Jonathan Harker views Transylvania as "the center of some sort of imaginative whirlpool" (2), and he is driven by

Dracula in circles (11), as "a ring of wolves" follows them "in a moving circle" (13). Dracula himself often appears "as a whole myriad of little specks . . . wheeling and circling round like a pillar of dust" (151). The geometric progression of vampiric reproduction is also described by Van Helsing in circular imagery: "All that die from the preying of the Un-Dead become themselves Un-Dead. . . . And so the circle goes on ever widening" (226). Toward the end of the book, the snowflakes and the mist circle around Mina and Van Helsing as they head for Dracula's castle (388), but now "these weird figures [that] drew near and circled round" are confronted by the Holy Circle in which Mina stands. The last gasp of the vampire before destruction appears in the windswept snow blowing in "circling eddies" (396). All of Dracula's whirlpools, vortices, and circles within circles are neutralized by Mina's Holy Circle.

What the men in the novel never realize, however, is that Dracula's circle is part of the same archetype. The Weird Sisters form out of the circling mist and beckon Mina, calling her "sister" (388). They want to fuse with their opposite, for they represent the dark side of the mother archetype, and therefore of woman. But the feminine dark is not archetypally evil; it is Van Helsing's *instincts* (with which archetypes always side) that make him appreciate the beauty of the vampire, especially of the Fair One, who should be a contradiction in terms, but instead represents the fusion of opposites. A vamp is supposed to be brunette. Her very existence violates the stereotypical code and asserts the integrity of the archetype. In fact, the very term "Un-Dead," which Van Helsing repeatedly uses to describe the vampire, on the archetypal level means to be truly alive; the ones who are really dead—"God's true Dead," as Van Helsing unwittingly calls them (229)—are the men and women who look upon the Dark Circle of the vampire's mouth in horror. They never understand what Van Helsing unconsciously implied in his description of Mina—the vagina can be a heavenly place.

One might well wonder at this point if there is anything besides sex in the "psychodynamics and mythic reverberations" of Dracula. According to William Patrick Day, Stoker created "a pair of androgynes" in Count Dracula and Mina Harker (143). Vampires, he believes, are "monstrous androgynes" (144) because the "conventional idea of masculine and feminine identity" that the novel espouses can only lead to such grotesque parodies (145). Following Nina Auerbach's notion that Mina is much more powerful than the men, Day points out that by initially excluding her from their vampire-hunting crew and keeping her "in her place," they actually make her more vulnerable to the vampire's attack (cf. Roth, "Suddenly Sexual Women," 118); but when she is allowed to be their equal, "it is she that really plans the pursuit of Dracula; her courage far outstrips that of her comrades" (Day, 145). Van Helsing sees her as an androgyne: she has "a man's brain and a woman's heart" (*Dracula*, 248). But, Day believes, Stoker fails to make Mina a convincing mythic androgyne because he overspiritualizes her (especially with what she herself calls "the mother-spirit"—243) and gives the novel's last words to Jonathan Harker who sees her seven years later as the woman whom the men chivalrously defended, "not the woman who led men in her own defense" (Day, 147). Mina sleeping in the Holy Circle is a perfect image of the passive, spiritualized ideal.

Day concludes that the Androgynous Ideal is really just a fantasy. The phrase "man's brain and woman's heart" reflects dualistic thinking and "deadly opposition." It should be, Day asserts, woman's brain, woman's heart. Van Helsing's masculine brain/feminine heart is indeed a vision of stereotypes, not of archetypes. But I think it is wrong to conclude that androgyny is as impossible as the unicorn (Day, 148). Archetypal androgyny involves qualities linked with anatomy: enclosure and darkness are unconsciously considered feminine; emission and light are perceived as masculine. No hierarchy is involved, but once these ideas are moralized, bivalent polarization occurs, and the progression that can result from the perception of sexual difference is destroyed. Androgyny is indeed an ideal, but not just a fantasy. It simply means the progressive interaction of opposites seen as equals, not as superior or inferior.

In *Dracula*, androgyny works on two levels. On the conventional, pious level, the more "masculine" New Woman is satirized (94–95), and the proper "spheres" of men and women are asserted. Auerbach's feminist thesis notwithstanding, Mina's "power" is passive—she is hypnotized when she leads the men to Dracula, and she sleeps within the Holy Circle. Nevertheless, on the novel's subversive, subliminal level, archetypal androgyny is affirmed in the vampire itself, especially in its mouth (cf. Craft, 109). In *Dracula*, the vampire is not the travesty or grotesque parody of the androgyne; it is the archetypal vision itself, always working instinctively to abrogate conventional gender codes (cf. Craft, 116).

A Jungian reading of *Dracula*, then, reinforces the Freudian readings by revealing what may be called the archetypal counterpoint in this ambiguous text. While Stoker continually asserts the spirituality of the mother through Mina, he makes the Lamia very attractive through the Fair One and through Lucy. All the horror surrounding them is conscious male hysteria masking unconscious desire. Perhaps the real reason *Dracula* remains compelling even in the twentieth century is not, as Twitchell maintains, because it upholds the incest taboo (*Dreadful Pleasures*, 137), but because on an archetypal level the novel provides a vision of Thomas De Quincey's "mighty antagonists the sexual forces . . . putting forth their hostilities . . . by deepest attraction." The female vampire is especially attractive because she is able to do what Our Lady of Darkness compels De Quincey to do: "rise again before he dies." As an alternative to resurrection through the transcendence of the carnal, the Lamia offers a vision of resurrection *through* the flesh. While religious consciousness declares the feminine darkness unholy, the instinctual archetypes keep insisting that it is only through darkness that light has meaning. And it is only through flesh that spirit lives.

6

FEMININE OBSESSION IN TWO
EARLY TALES OF HENRY JAMES

In his introduction to *The Ghostly Tales of Henry James*, Leon Edel explains that the author of the greatest ghost story in English ("The Turn of the Screw") did not write about haunted castles, houses, or chambers. He wrote from the first about the haunted mind, about men and women "haunted by phantoms . . . of their own creation" (xxvi), about "victims of unconscious obsession." Edel therefore dissociates James's ghostly tales from the Gothic tradition of Horace Walpole and Anne Radcliffe; he considers the Jamesian ghost story more closely related to Defoe's "True Relation of the Apparition of One Mrs. Veal," even though James would have rejected Defoe's tale "as too closely resembling a case history of psychic research" (xxvii). If Defoe started a tradition, it was that of the parapsychological ghost story, not the psychological ghost story.

Actually, James's brand of Ambiguous Gothic is closer to the tradition begun by E.T.A. Hoffmann, who initiated the tale featuring the intrusion of the ghostly into the familiar, *heimlich* world. While usually avoiding Hoffmann's sense of the grotesque, James often creates the same effect of the uncanny: "the strange and sinister embroidered on the very type of the normal and easy" (James quoted by Edel, *Tales*, xxviii). James was not, however, actually influenced by Hoffmann; it was Nathaniel Hawthorne who more likely showed him how richly symbolic a tale of the Uncanny can be.[1] Works like "The Artist of the Beautiful," "Egotism: The Bosom Serpent," "Rappaccini's Daughter," and *The Marble Faun* stimulated James to try his hand at the *Kunstmärchen*.[2]

Two of James's early tales about men haunted by a female daemon are especially precocious in their psychological insight, richly suggestive of the archetypal patterns I have been tracing: "The Madonna of the Future" (1873) and "The Last of the Valerii" (1874). Both involve men incapacitated by obsession with a feminine ideal. In the first story, the ending is almost tragic; in the second it is apparently happy but somewhat pathetic. Together the texts form an excellent Jamesian diptych—both "panels" of which display a female goddess worshiped by a *puer eternum*, a man who remains a boy.

The Muse as Medusa: "Madonna of the Future"

"The Madonna of the Future," though not ghostly enough in Edel's view for inclusion in his anthology,[3] is unquestionably about a man with a haunted mind. He is an idealistic American artist named Theobald who lives in Florence, where he wanders by day through the Uffizi and Pitti galleries musing over the masters, to whose greatness he aspires, hoping to paint the ultimate Madonna—a modern epitome of all the others. As his story is told by a narrator identified as H——, who meets Theobald outside the Uffizi,

1. For more about Hawthorne's influence on James's ghost stories, see Briggs, 118.
2. That James's ghost stories are artistic fairy tales (*Kunstmärchen*) is clear from Edel, *Tales*, xxviii. Cf. Martha Banta, 51. Even some of James's "mainstream" novels (esp. *The Golden Bowl*) have been compared to märchen (e.g., by Philip Sicker, 146–49).
3. It remains unclear to me how "Maud-Evelyn" or "The Beast in the Jungle"—both included in *The Ghostly Tales of Henry James* (1948)—are any more "ghostly" than "The Madonna of the Future." In "Maud-Evelyn," Marmaduke loves a girl long dead whom he has never even met—but she is only a ghost psychologically. John Marcher in "The Beast" is stalked by a gnawing creature of the mind. Edel even includes these stories in his reedition, *Henry James: Stories of the Supernatural* (1970)—an unwise change of title, in my view.

the reader learns that the artist is a hopeless dawdler. H. sees one of his pieces: an excellent sketch of the *bambino* for his Madonna. Theobald spends much of his time visiting a woman, the supposed model for his painting, whom he considers the most beautiful in Italy, but as H. discovers, she is actually an old lady. When he informs Theobald of this fact, the artist is shattered. When H. visits him in his room, he sees the "masterpiece" in progress—a blank, cracking canvas. Theobald apparently contracts a "brain fever" and dies a disillusioned man, never able to recover from the revelation that his "Serafina" is really a crone. From this synopsis one sees that Theobald, a would-be artist, appears to be another nympholeptic idealist like Hoffmann's Nathanael, a would-be poet. Their unfortunate careers follow some of the same archetypal patterns, especially those involving anima possession and androgyny.[4]

Just before H. begins his narrative, he tells his companions (who have been discussing painters who produced only a single masterpiece) that he once knew an artist who "painted his one masterpiece, and . . . he didn't even paint that" (11).[5] He begins, then, with a paradox: How could a man have both painted and not painted a picture? One other question is raised in the reader's mind by the prologue. As H. begins his story, the hostess of the gathering comes in among the cigar-smoking men and listens "graciously" in spite of the cigars. At the "catastrophe," she glances at the implied author

4. To my knowledge, no Jungian readings of "The Madonna of the Future" have yet been offered. Critics of differing persuasions have discussed it, however. One would have thought such an impressive early tale would have had a prominent place in James Kraft's *The Early Tales of Henry James*, but he dismisses it as having only biographical interest. Kraft thinks the story is about nothing more than James's own fear "that he will not be able to continue to write effectively, that he has the vision of his art only in his mind and will not be able to execute" it (78). While not denying this aspect, I cannot accept Kraft's belief that the story has been "consistently overestimated." On the contrary, it remains underrated, many of its riches yet untapped. Most of the work on the story has been on its sources in Balzac and Browning (e.g., Kelley and Ross). Other analyses include those of Charles Feidelson, who finds an unsolved enigma in James's view of art, which seems to multiply rather than solve "the problems latent in itself" (55); Carl Maves, who finds Theobald in the throes of "the terminal stage of the romantic agony, romanticism refined to a theory and completely detached from action" (28); Krishna Vaid, who sees the narrator as a dynamic character whose attitude toward Theobald changes from "amused disapproval" to "sympathetic understanding" (26), but who also feels that James ruined the story with "unnecessary scenes" toward the end; and Philip Sicker, who is closest to a Jungian perspective: "James suggests that love, like art, is doomed to failure if it exists only as an *idée fixe*. . . . To define oneself as a fixed image reflected in the fixed image of a loved one is . . . to seek death itself" (31).

5. All page references to "The Madonna of the Future" are to Leon Edel's compilation *The Complete Tales of Henry James* 3: 11–52. Edel uses James's final version of a tale revised three times (Aziz, 202). For variants, see Aziz's edition, 505–24.

(who is among H.'s audience) and shows him "a tender tear in each of her beautiful eyes" (11). One wonders why James included this scene in his prologue. Of what importance is it that a female listener shares a sentimental moment with the authorial "I"? Perhaps he is simply saying that the reader should be sympathetic to Theobald. But the hostess is not merely crying; she shares her tears only with the authorial persona. She is not a character in the story; she exists only as a feminine force breaking into the male circle, dropping a tear amid the cigar smoke. The author seems to be confiding that perhaps he shares something special with this "hostess." Taken together, she and the authorial persona appear as an androgynous ideal reader of the text. In other words, what makes one shed a tear for Theobald (himself possessed by a feminine element) is a feminine element, gracious and sympathetic, which may be cultivated without becoming possessed by it.

That archetypal androgyny is important in the text itself becomes apparent through James's illusions to art works. H. describes Michelangelo's *David* as "a magnificent colossus shining through the dusky air like some embodied Defiance" (12). Then he turns from this image of "sinister strength" to "a slender figure in bronze . . . a figure supremely shapely and graceful; gentle almost"—which turns out to be Cellini's *Perseus*. Considering David masculine and Perseus feminine, H. is glancing back and forth from one sculpture to the other when he first sees Theobald, who is therefore associated with androgyny. With what colossal Gorgon, I wonder, must Theobald be contending?[6]

It is a magical moonlit night that makes Theobald feel "as if the ghosts of her [Florence's] past were abroad in the empty streets. The present is sleeping; the past hovers about us like a dream made visible" (13). Both haunted and inspired by these ghosts, he seems to expect some sort of uncanny revelation from "the moonlit air," which appears "charged with the secrets of the masters." When H. meets Theobald, the painter is in a rapturous state—"I dream waking," he says (15). In other words, his mind is

---

6. Although H. considers Cellini's Perseus feminine, the hero's "masculinity" is clearly on display (even if it is smaller than David's). Perseus is himself androgynous. He is holding a sword in one hand and Medusa's head in the other. She is not at all ugly. At his feet is her twisted but shapely body, with its beautiful breasts a prominent feature. What makes her almost impossible to look at without feeling revulsion, however, are the exposed innards of her severed neck, graphically depicted. In short, it is not the Medusa herself that is ugly, but Perseus's decapitation of her. The attempt to repress the feminine element is what makes her a monster: Medusa's head lives on. Theobald is Perseus: he turns the beautiful Mrs. Coventry into an ugly hag—a Gorgon (27).

haunted precisely in Hawthorne's sense.[7] Out of the moonlight, which (as in Hawthorne) is a symbol of psychic energy, Theobald forms his dream vision of Florence as an Eternal Woman: "It's the fashion to talk of all cities as feminine . . . but as a rule, it's a monstrous mistake. Is Florence of the same sex as New York, as Chicago? She's the sole true woman of them all; one feels towards her as a lad in his teens feels to some beautiful older woman with a 'history'" (23–24). H. is not sure whether Theobald's rhapsodic effusions are the mark of lunacy or of genius. Whichever they are, it is clear that Theobald has a vision of the Feminine; it appears that the ghosts of the past he sees in Florence are female ghosts. But are the Gorgons? Is the statue of Perseus an icon of Theobald's fight with an inner female daemon, a Medusa? He does have a tendency to feminize—not only the city of Florence but also art: "If we work for her, we must often pause. She can wait!" (16). But that is common enough, and does not necessarily involve the kind of turmoil over the female daemon seen in Nathanael. Still, Theobald seems to have an overabundance of femininity (or rather, it has him), which he projects as "moonlight" on everything he sees. H. therefore finds him "a shade too sentimental" (18).

Theobald's "Gorgon" soon reveals itself. He is obsessed with Madonnas, and hopes to create one as perfect as Raphael's "Madonna of the Chair," of which masterpiece he says, "This is Raphael himself." He is talking about both the Madonna and the painting. After completing it, moreover, Raphael "could do nothing but die" (20). Theobald explains to H. that Raphael probably had "some pretty young woman" as a model, but she was only a hint: "Meanwhile, the painter's idea had taken wings. . . . he saw the fair form made perfect . . . he communed with it face to face. . . . That's what they call idealism" (20). "An idealist," H. then remarks in jest, "is a gentleman who says to Nature in the person of a beautiful girl, 'Go to, you're all wrong. . . . This is the way you should've done it!'" (21).

Theobald tries to explain himself more fully despite his new friend's "irreverent mockery." When he paints his Madonna, the beautiful eyes of "the fair woman of flesh and blood . . . shall be half my masterpiece" (21). From this passage it becomes clear that there is nothing really "lunatic" at all in Theobald's idealism; it is rather this tendency to identify the artist's life too

7. In the sketch called "The Haunted Mind" (from *Twice Told Tales*), Hawthorne describes this hypnagogic state (to which Melville also referred in "The Counterpane" chapter of *Moby Dick*). It is a state between consciousness and sleep, a kind of "midnight consciousness" that makes abstractions like Sorrow and Fatality seem like phantoms and demons so real you forget "the fiends were anywhere but in your haunted mind" (307).

completely with the painting (after which "he could do nothing but die") that forebodes his doom.

Out of the pretty girl of flesh and blood, Theobald wishes to create an archetypal image of maternity. When H. is skeptical about the demand for Blessed Virgins in the secular nineteenth century, Theobald disagrees: he thinks "there is always a demand" for the Madonna because she is an image of an archetypal need: "That ineffable type," he says, "is one of the eternal needs of man's heart. . . . Think of the great story you compress into that simple theme! Think, above all, of the mother's face and its ineffable suggestiveness" (22). The Madonna is an icon of man's eternal need to see the mother as cherishing, nurturing, and protecting the naked *bambino*; the painting is of an archetype that communicates the Ideal of maternity; it tells the "great story" of selfless love. Perhaps this is why Thomas De Quincey named Our Lady of Tears "the Madonna" (*Suspiria*, 176).

Impressed by Theobald's eloquence, H. concludes that the visionary painter must have a Madonna of his own well in progress—one that will transform the old into the new: "The Madonna of the Future" (23). What Theobald means, however, is a Madonna beyond time—one that fulfills human needs at any time, in any place or culture. It is not this archetypal vision that makes him a "monomaniac" (24); it is not idealism that prevents him from painting his masterpiece. What dooms him to inaction and failure is an unconscious identification of real woman and Madonna. He says that she (the flesh-and-blood model) will only be half his masterpiece, but actually he considers her The Real Thing. Theobald cannot paint the Madonna because he has already unconsciously created her; the image on the canvas would be redundant. He thinks an aging widow is the Feminine Ideal, the eternally youthful mother.

To clarify this picture, James creates a foil for Theobald's "Madonna Serafina": Mrs. Coventry. She is an American lady who once sat for Theobald when she thought he might really be another Raphael—until she saw what "a horrible creature," what a "fright" he had made of her on canvas (27). Since he had already identified the widow with the Madonna, he could do nothing but turn Mrs. Coventry into a hag, a fiend. She thinks he considers her "a horribly ugly old woman who has vowed his destruction" (28). In contrast to this Gorgon, he wants H. to meet "the most beautiful woman in Italy," a "beauty with a soul" (his, if he only knew). H. learns that Theobald, in a "Platonic ecstasy," has transformed a "coarse" (33), "aging beauty" (31) into an ideal; this "stately needlewoman" has become his Fate. She is like his vision of Florence: a beautiful older woman with a history.

She shows H. Theobald's drawing in red chalk of a *bambino*. "The drawing represented a very young child, entirely naked, half nestling back against the mother's gown, but with two little arms outstretched, as if in the act of benediction" (34). The drawing, as it turns out, is of her own baby that she lost; but in its worshipful attitude, it seems also to be an image of the artist's puerile soul, worshiping Woman. When H. sees Theobald again, the artist asks him what he thinks of "the divine Serafina" (35a). The artist reminisces about seeing her when she was young, with her baby before it died: "I met this apparition at the city gate. The woman held out her hand. I hardly knew whether to say, 'What do you want?' or fall down and worship. . . . She might have stepped out of the stable of Bethlehem. . . . She, too, was a maiden mother, and she had been turned out into the world in her shame . . . here was my subject marvellously *realized*" (35—emphasis added).

In this revealing passage, several aspects of Theobald's character converge. He sees the girl as an apparition, as something not quite real at first. Then she seems both ordinary ("What do you want?") and goddesslike, both real and more than real. Her reality is that she is an unwed mother, and therefore a pariah the world has shamed. But Theobald's idealism transforms the unwed mother into the Blessed Virgin, an act that would be sheer genius on canvas—it would indeed be the Madonna of the Future: the redemption of the unwed mother as the "Image of Divine Maternity," like the adulteress Hester Prynne. But he has already "realized" his subject. The unfortunate girl with her bastard *bambino* is really just a screen woman for his projection of the Feminine Ideal. The projection should be on the blank canvas, not on the woman. H. is amazed when he learns that, after all these years, she has never even sat for Theobald. "My poor friend, . . . you've dawdled! She's an old, old woman—for a Madonna!" (36).

Theobald reacts as though H. has brutally beaten him. Realizing "the immensity of the illusion" (37), H. tries to placate him by assuring him that "Serafina" has "*de beaux restes*" of her former beauty, which Theobald with his imagination could still capture. After "the poor fellow's sense of wasted time, of vanished opportunity" seems to overwhelm him, he rallies momentarily: "'I'll finish it in a month! After all, I have it here!' And he tapped his forehead. 'Of course she's old! Why, sir, she shall be eternal!'" (38).

But the "ripe enchantress" of his own projected soul has him in thrall. The Madonna is not in his head; he has cast her out and identified her as Serafina. When H. goes to pay this woman another visit, he encounters a vivid tableau of her reality: "Her attitude as I entered was not that of an enchantress. With one hand she held in her lap [instead of a *bambino*] a plate of smoking maccaroni; with the other she had lifted high in the air one of the pendulous filaments of this succulent compound, and was in the act of slipping it gently down her throat." (39). Moreover, she has a lover—a sculptor of vulgar statuettes. Theobald, in fact, has not been her lover, for he is, she tells H., celibate: "You may almost call him a man of holy life" (41). His celibacy (or impotence) should not come as a surprise, for he has in an earlier scene "turned his back on the Venus" (17) in favor of the Uffizi triptych by Mantegna. Such a gesture may not at first seem symbolic, until one realizes that the Blessed Virgin is the central figure in all three panels.[8] So strong is his Mariolatry that women become for Theobald dualized into either celestial Madonnas or Mona Lisas "tinged with . . . sinister irony" (48), like Mrs. Coventry. He projects the bipolar anima: a "coarse" and perfectly ordinary woman becomes "The Madonna Serafina"; an intelligent, witty American woman becomes a Gorgon. I have already shown why the former woman has become the Blessed Virgin: the image Theobald saw of her with the baby transfigured her. But why is Mrs. Coventry the Gorgon? Perhaps because she did not encourage his attempted identification of her as a Madonna the way Serafina did (42). Once she refused to play the role of the Good Mother, she became the Terrible.

Theobald is a *puer eternus*. He is a naked bambino who needs a Madonna to nourish and protect him. When H. finally visits him in his room it is described as "naked" and "haunted," like Theobald himself. Seeing the blank, cracked, and discolored canvas, H. finds Theobald in despair, still insisting that he has his masterpiece "here": "he tapped his forehead with that mystic confidence which had marked the gesture before" (47). As a counterpoint to Theobald's forehead tapping, James describes three other instances of the gesture: Madame Serafina does it twice: first to signify that Theobald is crazy (33), then to indicate that he is a genius (34); and H. does it once ambiguously to signify that Theobald is ultimately a mystery (41–42). The gestures reveal that Theobald's problem is in his head: his belief that the masterpiece is in his head is a delusion, for he has projected the archetypal feminine out of it—he has, in other words, mistaken the model for the muse (21). The muse is the feminine element in the artist's creativity; to project her completely upon a woman of flesh and blood is to lose her.

8. See *The Complete Paintings of Mantegna*, plates xxxiii–xxxv; or any book of the Uffizi collection. The three panels, "The Adoration of the Magi," "The Circumcision," and the "Ascension," are unified by the central presence of the Blessed Virgin Mary.

Theobald thinks he is "the half of a genius" and wonders where his "other half" could be: "Lodged perhaps in the vulgar soul, the cunning, ready fingers of some dull . . . trivial artisan" (48). As Feidelson (52) and Maves (32) both note, he is describing the sculptor, Serafina's lover. This "jaunty Juvenal of the chimney-piece" (44) creates statuettes of cats and monkeys "fantastically draped, in some preposterously sentimental conjunction" (44). The animals appear as "little couples," satirically suggestive of "natural men and women" in the "different phases of what, in delicate terms, may be called gallantry and coquetry." The sculptor, caressing the vaguely obscene pieces "with an amorous eye," reminds H. of an "intelligent ape" (45). As Carl Maves puts it, the sculptor's work is "the aesthetic opposite of Theobald's idealism, human characteristics debased instead of exalted, reduced to their lowest animalistic level" (32). But Feidelson sees "something positive" in "the values of the monkey and the cat, the sculptor and his mistress . . . repellent as they seem to the high-minded narrator" (53).

What is needed, of course, is a synthesis of Theobald's idealism and the sculptor's "naturalism." To turn one's back on Venus is to deny the erotic element in creation; just as the artist cannot completely project lest his muse escape him, he cannot totally sublimate lest his Madonna become an abstraction, angelicized out of nature, existing only as a heavenly Idea ("Serafina") imposed on an earthy woman.

Theobald, then, both paints and does not paint his masterpiece: by painting it on the screen woman, he fails to get it on the canvas where it belongs. Frustrated by his inability to reintegrate his muse, he contracts a "brain fever" (De Quincey would call it nympholepsy) and dies a "deplorable failure." As Raphael's "Madonna of the Chair" was Raphael himself, so Theobald's Madonna Serafina is really a projection of himself. And as Raphael supposedly "could do nothing but die" after painting his masterpiece, Theobald also has to die, for he has spent himself on the delusive masterpiece he has made of the widow.

His death is not horrific like those of Ambrosio and Nathanael; it is in fact almost tragic, for he has had a great vision—of the unwed mother redeemed through sympathy into the modern Madonna (still a long way from our *post*modern Madonna, who fuses [auto-]eroticism and virginity in "Like a Virgin"). But the vision was misplaced; his *hamartia* is literally a "missing of the mark": he kept the vision fastened on the woman who inspired it, instead of directing it to the canvas. Although H. shatters his illusion, Theobald brings his downfall on himself by never admitting his problem, by still thinking he has the paintings "in his head" (49). Since he never achieves self-knowledge, he is not quite a tragic figure. He comes very close, however—close enough for the sensitive reader (the "hostess") to shed some tears for him. His ideals make him noble, but his deification of woman and his reification of the muse (mistaking the spiritual archetype for the flesh-and-blood woman) make him impotent as both an artist and a man.

James lets the vulgar sculptor have the last word in the story: "Cats and monkeys, monkeys and cats; all human life is there!" (52). In a sense, he is right: his statuettes are travesties of natural androgyny (the cats are feminine; the monkeys are masculine). What is missing in his vulgar worldview, however, is a vision of spiritual androgyny—something more than mere hermaphroditism. It is present in the Jamesian ideal reader; it is potentially present in the artist of the ideal, Theobald. But when he projects his muse, he loses his vital feminine soul. It becomes the Medusa's head, turning him—and his canvas—to stone.

Fetish vs. Wife: The Juno Archetype in "The Last of the Valerii"

One of Henry James's first literary efforts (in 1861) was a translation of Prosper Mérimée's *conte fantastique* "La Vénus d'Ille" (1837). In this tale, a young man who is about to be married makes the mistake of placing his engagement ring, which is bothering him while he is playing tennis, on a finger of a recently excavated statue of Venus. Forgetting the ring, he returns to the statue later only to find that it has clenched its fist, preventing him from extricating the ring. He manages to find another one for his wedding, but on his wedding night he is found dead, crushed by the stony goddess who has come to claim her groom.[9]

When James read this tale, he found himself "fluttering deliciously—quite as if with a sacred terror" (quoted in Edel, *Life*, 54). It is not surprising, then, that he would later not only translate Mérimée's work (an effort he failed to get published) but also write his own version of a man haunted by a goddess. The similarities between "The Last of the Valerii" and "La Vénus d'Ille" are superficial, however; [10] James turns a cautionary fable about the exacting

9. See *The Venus of Ille*, 1–32. For more about Mérimée's story as a Romantic retelling of the old Venus-ring legend, see Fass (chapter 7) and Ziolkowski (chapter 2).

10. See P. R. Grover's article on Mérimée's influence on James, and Ziolkowski, 61–65.

demands of erotic passion on a "crass modern civilization" (Ziolkowski, 63) into a "precious psychological study" ("Last of the Valerii," 93).[11] Mérimée's protagonist, Alphonse, does not fall in love with the statue; it simply comes to claim him. James's Italian count, on the other hand, worships a newly excavated statue of the goddess Juno, neglecting his new American wife, Martha, in the process—until she intervenes and has the thing reburied, whereupon the couple presumably live happily ever after.[12]

Most critics of the tale agree that the ending, though happy, is somewhat ambiguous because the count retains the hand of the statue—suggesting "some doubt about the value of [his] 'rehabilitation'" (Fass, 146; cf. Berkson, 86). Moreover, if the statue is an archetypal image, the ending is clearly problematic, because it suggests that the anima has been repressed again (reburied in the unconscious) instead of being integrated into consciousness. Another possibility, however, is that the count has successfully projected the Juno into his wife and may have therefore begun a necessary process whereby he would eventually withdraw the projection and make the feminine element part of his own consciousness.[13] Projection is a dangerous process when it remains completely unconscious, but no projection at all is even more dangerous because the anima, in that case, never becomes available as a guide either to loving or to learning how to die.

This archetypal ambiguity makes the story more complex, I think, than critics have supposed. Moreover, no one has adequately explained in mythological terms why James changed Mérimée's (and the original legend's) Venus into Juno. Nor has the importance of the narrator's conscious-

11. All page references to "The Last of the Valerii" are to Edel's *Henry James: Stories of the Supernatural*, 69–102.

12. The tale has been variously interpreted. "What [James] seems to be saying," Edel remarked (*Stories*, 70), "was that the past is best left buried—that it is dangerous to exhume dormant primeval things—and that civilized man does well to keep the primitive side of his nature properly interred." Philip Sicker (40) sees psychic vampirism in the tale, while Lisa Appignanesi (25) considers it "perhaps the clearest example of James's rejection of [overly masculine] ritualistic . . . states of mind and being" that prevent "critical self-scrutiny." Barbara Fass sees the story mainly in terms of neo-Hellenism, but she mistakes the role of the narrator (145). Dorothy Berkson gives a feminist interpretation especially relevant to the reading offered here, but she underemphasizes the narrator's role as foil and keeps calling Martha a passionate woman, for which description she offers little evidence. Carl Maves thinks Valerio survives his delusion, while Theobald does not, because "his [the count's] romanticism, unlike Theobald's, is instinctive rather than voluntary" (38). But since Theobald's projections are unconscious, they must also involve instincts.

13. See Jung, *CW* 9.1: 84—"Our task is not . . . to deny the archetype but to dissolve the projections, in order to restore their contents to the individual who has involuntarily lost them by projecting them outside himself." Cf. Samuels, *Jung and the Post-Jungians*, 213.

ness been sufficiently emphasized. As Martha's godfather, he is more than a detached observer; and as a painter, he has an aesthetic sensibility that allows him to respond also to the Juno, suggesting that the count's fascination, though peculiarly atavistic because of his racial inheritance, is not merely anomalous.

For Mérimée, Venus is a symbol of primitive erotic passion unadulterated by "the sterility of modern civilization"; she "exemplifies the power of pure passion . . . indignant at the bourgeois commercialization of love in 19th century France" (Ziolkowski, 53). When the statue is melted down and converted into a church bell, Mérimée is satirizing both utilitarianism and the Judeo-Christian annihilation of the pagan gods, which like many Romantics he considered daemons within men. Venus, he well knew from the Venus-ring and Tannhäuser myths, was in bitter competition with the Church and the Blessed Virgin for domination of men's souls.

In this story, however, James is not interested in myths associated with the goddess of love. Perhaps he chose Juno for no better reason than that he had recently seen a neglected statue of her in a garden house in Rome (Edel, *Stories*, 69). Or perhaps Carl Maves has the answer: "The change from Venus to Juno . . . indicates an emphasis on the past as a coherent alternative to the present rather than just a dark primal force impinging on it" (158 n. 22). On the archetypal level, however, the past is eternally present in the form of primeval forces. Both Juno and Venus must represent primal forces, needs, and fears. Venus is no more "primal" than Juno, who was originally an Etruscan goddess (Iuno, etymologically related to uni-verse)[14] and who was no more a mere copy of Hera than Venus was of Aphrodite. Juno and Hera were later identified, of course; but Juno, like Venus, was an ancient primal goddess.

Theodore Ziolkowski may be on the right track when he explains James's choice: "The statue is no longer an avenging goddess of love. . . . [It] represents the pagan past . . . as culture, not as eroticism" (63). But culture comprises many aspects: religious mores, ethnic characteristics, familial relations—to name just a few relevant to James's story. Juno cannot be involved in all of them. Furthermore, eroticism does play a part in the story, as will be seen, and Juno has an erotic aspect. Granted, one does not immediately think of love and sex when Juno is mentioned; James simply does what he would often do with sexuality—he clothes it in symbols the way

14. See Barbara Walker, 484: Juno derived from the "Etruscan Uni, the three-in-one deity cognate with *yoni* and *uni*-verse." Cf. Bloch, 179–80.

Hawthorne did. When the narrator first sees the Juno, he notices that "she was amply draped, so that [he] saw that she was not a Venus. 'She's a Juno,' said the expert . . . and she seemed indeed the embodiment of celestial supremacy" (82). Juno is more decorous than Venus, more heavenly and more supreme. She is the Queen of Heaven, and with Jupiter is part of an archetypal pair. Venus blatantly represents the *mons Veneris* and man's desire for it. Juno, on the other hand, is the goddess of the whole woman, including her sexuality.

Furthermore, Juno was a tutelary spirit presiding over the life of women and their marriages.[15] James, then, could not have made his story more ironic when he chose Juno as the goddess of Valerio's worship. The young Italian almost ruins his marriage when he kneels to the goddess of marriage. On one level, of course, the irony is simply explained as part of Valerio's atavism. He ignores his modern Christian wife in favor of an ancient pagan symbol of the archetypal Wife. But if the Juno is a psychological archetype, the story is not merely about neopaganism or neo-Hellenism.

She does seem to have the necessary numinosity (inspiring "sacred terror") to be a Jungian archetype: "She seemed to me [the narrator] almost colossal, though I afterwards perceived that she was only of the proportions of a woman exceptionally tall. *My pulses began to throb*, for I felt that she was something great" (82—emphasis added). She is a numinous source of energy, even for the narrator, who does not share Count Valerio's paganism. Her archetypal power is further revealed in a key passage most critics ignore. As in "The Madonna of the Future," James uses the Hawthornean technique of bathing a scene in moonlight, which represents transformative psychic energy. "The night was magnificent, and full-charged with the breath of the early Roman spring. The moon was rising fast and flinging her silvery checkers into the heavy masses of shadows" (94). The narrator is an artist who cannot help but be affected by the beautiful spring night. But it is more than beautiful; "breath" and "early" have double meanings here: the atmosphere, the soul of early Roman civilization, is in the air. Though not an atavist like Valerio, the painter-narrator cannot help but feel "the grandeur that was Rome." He, too, projects soul into the statue, which in the moonlight seems to undergo a "transfiguration." Deeply affected by her

15. Some of the surnames under which she was worshiped reveal her functions: as *Juno Pronuba* (e.g., in Virgil's *Aeneid*), marriage was sacred to her; as *Juno Viriplaca*, she restored peace to arguing husbands and wives; as *Juno Cinxia*, she untied the wife's girdle on the wedding night (thus evincing an erotic function); as *Juno Lucino*, she presided over childbirth and gave the baby its first view of the light. See Robert E. Bell, 157, 314; and Guirand, 217.

"purity," he finds her "convincingly divine." "The effect was almost terrible; beauty so expressive could hardly be inanimate" (95). She inspires him. He does not lose his soul to her; on the contrary, she fills it with a sense of the Burkean sublime. In contrast to the narrator's poetic rapture, the count lies flat, prostrate before the goddess, face completely blanched by the moonlight, "sunk down at her feet in a stupid sleep" (95).

James's genius in choosing Juno over Venus is especially clear in this moonlit scene. Juno was associated with the moon because she represented Woman in all three "phases": Maid, Wife, and Widow (Hebe, Hera, Hekate).[16] The count is ready to worship woman in all her roles.[17] His wife cannot be all three at once unless he makes her so, which he effectively does by turning from her to the statue. He no longer makes love to her—she must be as pure as Hebe. That makes her wife in name only, like Hera to Zeus. And with Valerio sleeping most of the time, Martha may as well be a widow.

The count's fascination with the excavated statue is immediate; he does not need moonlight to feel its power. As soon as he sees it, he is "pale" and gives "no response as his wife affectionately clasped his arm" (83). The narrator has noticed that Valerio spends a lot of time sleeping; he has "an invincible tendency to go to sleep—a failing his wife never attempted to palliate" even as he lay "statuesquely snoring" (76)—dreaming of a statue. Before Juno appears, he dreams of her placing "her marble hand" on his (82). As a man more accustomed to "unconscious cerebration"[18] than the narrator, Valerio is a prime candidate for possession. James is therefore presenting two opposite types of men. The narrator is a highly civilized man genuinely concerned with his goddaughter's welfare; he is also an artist, with a highly developed aesthetic sensibility manifest when he is moved by the Juno. In other words, his reaction to the statue reveals that he has (unlike Theobald) an active muse. Valerio, on the other hand, has no aesthetic sense (71). He is, moreover, "a little dense"; he is "nothing but senses, appetites. . . . I often wondered whether he had anything that could properly be termed a

16. These three aspects of Hera/Juno are mentioned by H. J. Rose, 105; cf. Graves, 52: "Hera . . . symbolized by the new, full and old moon . . . was worshipped as Child, Bride, and Widow."

17. Dorothy Berkson in her article makes a similar point, but she explains Valerio's worship in terms of the "Magdalen/Mary" (whore/madonna) dualism that she sees as part of the "sexual malaise of the nineteenth century" (86). An archetypal reading suggests that this bipolarity is not peculiar to the Victorian age, or, at least, that the madonna/whore complex is a nineteenth-century manifestation of archetypal bipolarity.

18. See Uwe Böker's article "Wilkie Collins, Henry James, und Dr. Carpenters 'Unconscious Cerebration,'" 325–33. James was familiar with Carpenter's work through his brother William.

soul. . . . He's the natural man!" (77). He also has an overabundance of masculinity: "a manly constancy" (71), with a "powerful, . . . masculine" nose and mouth, neither of which is "delicate." In short, any feminine soul in him is totally unconscious. It is only while dreaming that his anima comes to him.

So when the statue is excavated, he unconsciously projects his feminine soul into it. There is none left for Martha. He never projected it into her in the first place, because he never really loved her. He may even have married the American heiress for her money (all he has to his name is his house). The narrator, at any rate, has misgivings about the marriage from the start. Although they look nice together "from a pictorial point of view" (70), he considers the Italian too much of a shallow sensualist, lacking in intellect and soul, ever to be capable of the kind of love the narrator feels his goddaughter merits—one that includes respect. Latin lovers, he feels, "do not really respect the women they pretend to love" (78).

But does Valerio perhaps learn how to love in the course of the tale? His projection may be a necessary step toward individuation—he has at least freed his feminine soul from its unconscious dungeon. True, he misdirects it (like Theobald), but he may have made it more available for integration. First, however, he must be allowed to act out what should have been acted out in childhood—deification of women. It is perfectly normal for a boy to worship women. Emotionally, the count is still a boy. James makes this clear when he describes Valerio playing "catch-and-toss" with a collection of precious antique fragments (77). The fetishism he evinces would be perfectly normal in a boy, but in a man it too easily becomes a substitute for the real woman. It is not too late, however, for the count to get the fetish out of his system; this is what the narrator hopes has finally happened when he sees that a blood sacrifice has been made to Juno (99). But since the blood is a product of "unconscious cerebration" (the count "sleeping or swooning" at Juno's feet), perhaps it is, as in *Dracula*, a trope for semen. Thus, Valerio's sacrifice is not castration, as Philip Sicker argues,[19] but a kind of orgasm in the presence of his fetish.[20]

19. *Love and the Quest for Identity*, 40. Sicker sees the Juno as a Diana or Cybele figure demanding not only chastity but even castration of its worshiper. Juno is not Diana, however. He is basing his idea on James's original text, in which the moonlight is described as "Juno visited by Diana." James later revised it (wisely, in my view) to "a transfiguration." (See the "Textual Variants" in Aziz's edition, vol. 2: 531 and 277.)

20. Cf. Berkson, 84: The count's "rituals and libations are unmistakably erotic." James makes the blood ambiguous when he has the narrator first assure Martha that it probably came from

Count Valerio's possession first draws him away from people; the anima introverts him—takes him into himself, making him love for the first time in his life—even though what he loves is a narcissistic image of his own deep feminine soul projected onto the statue. He also stares at "a mouldy Hermes" in his garden—what the narrator thinks is a "senseless pagan block," but what is really, for Valerio, his phallus. (Perhaps that is why the narrator wants to knock off Hermes' nose—89–90.)[21] The image, in any case, is autoerotic. Valerio's worship of Hermes and Juno is really an act of narcissism, but as his first attempt at love, it is better than no love at all—if he can successfully transfer it to Martha.

Although at first completely rejecting his wife's affection—even shuddering when she offers it (87)—the count soon gives her "a vaguely imploring look" and kisses her "with an almost brutal violence" (97). The narrator thinks he is asking Martha to help him break the spell, for the goddess is too demanding. But perhaps Valerio is just beginning to reproject, to seek Juno in his wife. She in turn has begun to emulate the goddess, which the narrator notices to his consternation (96). To mold herself after Valerio's ideal is not to be true to herself. She finally finds her own *iuno*,[22] however, and is able to take charge of the situation: as the excavator says, "Sweet-voiced as she is, she knows how to make her orders understood" (100). Martha feels that her husband "will not be himself so long as [the statue] is above ground. To cut the knot we must bury her!" (101). Her metaphor suggests that he is both married to the statue and attached to it like a fetus. He still needs a mother, not a wife with her own *iuno*. But her solution is misguided, because the count has not yet completely withdrawn his projection. He has started to, but he is "not yet" ready to relate to his wife as a wife (100).

When he reappears after the burial, "his eyes were brilliant, but not angry. He had missed the Juno—and drawn a long breath" (102). When James revised this story, he added this line about Valerio's breath. He

---

an animal but then later express himself more equivocally: "The blood drops on the altar, I mused, were the last instalment of his debt. . . . They had been a happy necessity, for he was after all too generous a creature not to hate himself for *having shed them*" (99—emphasis added).

21. In Athens, Hermes was usually represented by herms, "square pillars . . . crowned with a human head, and having a phallos part-way up the front" (Rose 146). In *Lysistrata*, Aristophanes alludes to the castration of the statues of Hermes by unknown vandals.

22. The ancient Romans believed that every woman had a *iuno*, a tutelary spirit corresponding to a man's *genius*. It was her vitality, "her individuality" (Downing, 72). Cf. Kerenyi, 230–31. Like the *genius*, the *iuno* was internalized as a daemon in the head.

originally wrote, "He had missed the Juno—and rejoiced!" (Aziz 2: 283). His change (see Aziz, "Textual Variants" 2: 533) was, I believe, a brilliant one that ties the scene together with the "breath of early Roman spring" at the beginning of the story, making it quite clear that by "breath" James means soul, psyche, anima. But where will Valerio exhale this indrawn psyche? He watches Martha at her embroidery—she becomes his new Fate. "The image seemed to fascinate him," until after watching her for a long time, he "strode forward, fell on his two knees, and buried his head in her lap" (102).

Because he is not allowed to work through the fascination for himself, he simply "trades one Juno for another" (Maves, 39). That is, he reprojects anima into his wife—which is certainly better than ignoring her—but now he is going to worship her uxoriously on his knees. That he never quite grows up is made even clearer when he retains the Juno's marble hand as a fetish, the regressive nature of which is emphasized by his reference to it as Greek rather than Roman—therefore older, more primitive.

On an archetypal level, then, atavism and primitivism in "The Last of the Valerii" are metaphors for regression to a boyish state. The count was just beginning to work out his problem, but his wife, fearing that she would remain a "fiction" while the statue remained "the reality" (97), took away his fetish before he had the chance to get it out of his system. Now she is the goddess; and he, unfortunately, remains a man-child. If he is as impotent as he looks at the end, he will indeed be "The Last of the Valerii."

Here is the final irony. Martha, beginning to assert her own *iuno*, inadvertently prevents her husband from respecting her for it, because she did not let him assert his own *genius*, which was just beginning to manifest itself. The "dense," "stupid" Valerio was actually becoming "witty" as a result of the liberation of his unconscious through the statue (85). But the statue was buried too soon, and now, burying his head, Valerio still seeks to worship the buried goddess in his wife, rather than loving her for her own *genius*, her *iuno*.

7

FROM FIEND TO FRIEND
The Daemonic Feminine in Modern Gothic

The male hysterical reaction to fiends in women's garments continues well into the twentieth century, during which the Gothic mode has flourished in the ghost story and the weird tale. Many of these texts display vivid anima signs. Oliver Onions's "Beckoning Fair One" (1911) is a famous example: a novelist's fictional heroine haunts him as a ghost and rivals the woman whom he should be loving;[1] equally popular is Walter De La Mare's "Seaton's Aunt" (1923), a brilliant portrait of a possessed young man whose anima remains

---

1. See *Widdershins*, 1–68. Many readers who are not fans of "The Turn of the Screw" consider "The Beckoning Fair One" the greatest English ghost story. (See Fraser and Wise's introduction to the story in their anthology *Great Tales of Terror and the Supernatural*.) Sullivan (in Tymn, ed., 261) calls the piece one of the most beautifully written ghost stories in English.

fixated on the Terrible Mother;[2] less well known but almost as effective is Clark Ashton Smith's "Disinterment of Venus" (1934), which continues the Heine/Mérimée/James tradition of digging up "exiled gods" from the earth, from the unconscious.

Moving into the twentieth century, however, one must assume authorial familiarity with Jungian theory. While such an assumption does not preclude the possibility of illuminating a modern text with Jung's concepts, works written merely to illustrate them are by necessity less compelling than those that anticipate Jung. As Jung explained in "Psychology and Literature," "visionary" literature evokes a convincing illusion of "genuine primordial experience" (162). If, on the other hand, an author is consciously deriving his plot from archetypal patterns, the result is a mere expository, almost mechanical device rather than a spontaneous mythos. Such is surely the case with Fritz Leiber's novel *Our Lady of Darkness* (1977).

The protagonist is a writer and widower. Since his wife has died, he needs to reproject anima and eventually manages to do so, but not before experiencing several horrifying encounters with a numinous female entity called Our Lady of Darkness (from *Suspiria de Profundis*, which Leiber quotes). He also makes out, from the papers strewn on his bed, a female form whom he calls his "scholar's mistress": "He unconsciously arranged them into a female form with long long legs . . . a secret playmate, a dashing but studious call-girl, a slim incestuous sister, eternal comrade of his writing work" (5). Before he finally overcomes his autoerotic nympholepsy by loving the heroine Cal, Franz projects female forms onto everything, including a sinister TV tower; he is haunted by his "anima's shadow" (18); there are a White Goddess and a Black Goddess; allusions to Robert Graves and Carl Jung abound. All of it is interesting but not compelling. It is all too self-conscious to create that "sacred terror" Henry James spoke of, that numinous sense of primal dread Rudolf Otto identified, that *mysterium tremendum* of the unconscious (Peter Brooks), or Jung's "genuine primordial experience."

Peter Straub also attempts to create such an experience in *Ghost Story* (1979). Instead of consciously manipulating Jungian theory or illustrating De Quincey as Leiber does, Straub goes back to Hawthorne and James and tries

2. See *The Riddle and Other Stories*, 97–143. Several of De La Mare's tales, including the nonfantastic "The Almond Tree," concern anima possession. In "Out of the Deep," a bedridden dissolute young man summons various ghostly parts of his psyche, including the anima, by pulling a bellrope. See Penzoldt, 214–18.

to synthesize the Ambiguous Gothic tradition with the H. P. Lovecraft "Cthulhu mythos." The latter grew out of the "Weird Tale" tradition, which comprises unabashedly supernatural texts. They assert that the demon is literally real, external to the haunted mind. Lovecraft envisioned a cosmic conspiracy of exiled god-monsters, "lurkers at the threshold" of our space-time continuum, who wait for the interface between dimensions, that door into our precarious world where they can wreak their unspeakable havoc. Straub's novel can be read on this Lovecraftean level, but he also suggests that this worldview is a mere reflection of our own darkness within.[3] The text is filled with mirrors—indeed there are too many of them; the symbolism gets heavy-handed, though not as much as Leiber's. When Don Wanderley, the protagonist, asks the demoness who she really is, she bluntly replies, "I am you" (26). And before he suspects the ghastly identity of his lover Alma Mobley, she tells him that *he* is a ghost. A major theme of the novel seems to be that modern man has indeed become a ghost, deadened by the moral insensitivity that ensues from polarization of the sexes. Straub's principal ghost, then, must be a woman, for she is the revenge on men of their exiled femininity.

John Irvin's movie version of *Ghost Story* turns this ambiguous allegory of cosmic evil into a conventional story of the retributive spirit—the ghost of a woman wreaks her revenge on her killers; she is able to do this because she was never properly buried. The young men, afraid of a scandal even though her death was an accident, put her body in a car that they dump into a lake. In the novel, however, the reader learns that Eva Galli was never human in the first place; she escapes from that sinking car and changes into a lynx. She is a shapeshifter, a manitou. If she is killed, she returns in animal form, becomes a child, then finally grows back into "La Belle Dame sans Merci" (245). She says of her kind, "We could have poisoned your civilization ages ago, but voluntarily lived on its edges" (469). This is pure Lovecraft. She and her subservient male ghouls are embodiments of chaos and of motiveless malice, imps of the cosmic perverse, living proofs that Melville was right—"the invisible spheres were formed in fright." And Hawthorne too—Straub's epigraph is from *The Marble Faun*: "The pit of blackness lies beneath us, everywhere." Both beneath and within.

3. Lovecraft's demons tend for example to reflect his own very conscious prejudice and xenophobia. His fear of miscegenation, for example, is clear in the horrific mingling of man and monster in "The Dunwich Horror." See Punter, 281–84, for an excellent discussion of this overrated writer.

Straub suggests that this shapeshifting monster, whose true form is so hideously Medusan that when she reveals it the sight causes men to jump out of windows or die of fright, is the origin of all vampire and werewolf tales. When she seems, late in the novel, to be utterly alien, the reader need only remember the passage earlier in the text, when she is associated with a young man's (Sears James's) feminine ideal (49–50). As an aging bachelor lawyer (who with his partner Ricky Hawthorne has been haunted for decades—without realizing it—by Eva Galli), James recalls a crucial moment from his adolescence when he used to babysit for the children of "the most desirable woman young Sears had ever seen"—Viola Frederickson (49). After the children were asleep, he would explore their mother's bedroom, where he saw "a photograph of her—she looked impossibly inviting, exotic and warm, *an icon of the unknowable half of the species*" (emphasis added). Fascinated especially by Viola's breasts and the way "they pushed out the fabric of her blouse," he finds one of her blouses, imagining the woman's breasts beneath it. The blouse becomes a metonymic sign for the breasts he worships; masturbating with the blouse he makes love to Viola's breasts. Afterward he feels such intense shame that he tosses the blouse into the river.

Perhaps it is this latter action that triggers the association with Eva Galli, whose body he helped dump into the water; he dimly makes "a connection . . . between her and the ridiculous scene he remembered" (50). Young Sears's infatuation with the beautiful older woman Viola, who became for him the icon (frozen image) of womanhood, a goddess both maternal and sexual, fades as he grows up, of course, but he is never able to have a long-term relationship with a woman. The "unknowable half of the species" becomes the "horror of the half-known life" as he is never able to liberate anima. The only other woman he ever loves is Eva Galli, who is no woman at all, but a Medusan mirror reflecting male dread of the feminine. Adolescent fascination with the feminine degenerates into adult fear and loathing if anima is never recognized as part of self and soul, if she is instead perceived only as other. Other becomes alien, alien becomes monster. Moreover, like some grotesque hybrid of the celibate monk Ambrosio and the goddess-worshiping Valerio, Sears James is never able to overcome breast fixation and fetishism. His wish is to displace the female sex from below upward, to spiritualize it, to turn it into a ghost. But Eva Galli is neither ghost nor spirit. Her true form looks something like an oil slick (540), and when she is killed she comes back as an animal. She is the chthonic feminine devoid of spirit.

Further, with all her avatars' initials being A. M.—Amy Monckton, Alice Montgomery, Alma Mobley, Anna Mostyn–she is revealed as *Anima Mundi*, the soul of a world deadened and corrupted by polarized masculinity. Fission of the "divine syzygy" breeds animated corpses and other monsters more frightening than anything in Lovecraft. The horror of *Ghost Story* is the horror of the half-known life—of men unable to integrate the inner feminine, to accept it as an integral part of the whole self. Instead it remains the "unknowable half."

In Lovecraft, exiled god-monsters are almost always masculine. Straub has restored their proper gender. In Lovecraft, the daemonic is literalized and reified into the demonic. Straub restores its numinosity and psychic reality. With his powerful portrayal of Medusa in the mirror, Straub is more successful than Leiber in creating a "primal numinous dread."

Peter Straub has recognized that "Robert Aickman at his best was this century's most profound writer of . . . horror stories . . . [what] he, with greater accuracy, preferred to call strange stories" (Aickman, *The Wine-Dark Sea*, 7). Ramsey Campbell (1) and Gahan Wilson (61) agree that Aickman is an undeservedly obscure master of the macabre, who creates psychologically sophisticated and richly ambiguous tales without being self-consciously Freudian or Jungian. Like Henry James and Walter De La Mare, he develops a subtle sense of "sacred terror" in his tales, which often involve the daemonic feminine.[4] Perhaps most relevant to my discussion is the strange story "Ravissante" (1968), about a failed English artist's lifelong haunting by a mysterious old Belgian woman. Like Sears James in *Ghost Story*, he is never able to overcome the fascination of a fetishistic encounter he had as a young man.

The text is framed with the traditional Gothic prologue explaining how a mysterious manuscript got into the narrator's possession. He implies that the manuscript may throw some light on why the artist, a symbolist painter of grotesque and mystical works, never found success, married a woman who despised his work, and made his living editing the kind of coffee-table art

4. Aickman, well known only among ghost story and weird tale enthusiasts, remains in the "genre ghetto" in spite of several excellent collections (e.g., *Powers of Darkness* [1966] and *Sub Rosa* [1968], which contain many tales that revitalize the hackneyed motif of the femme fatale). See especially "The Stains" (Campbell, 1–57), "The View," (*Painted Devils*, 57–85), "The Wine-Dark Sea" (*Powers of Darkness*, 205–53; rpt. in Peter Straub's compilation of Aickman, *The Wine-Dark Sea*, 11–42), and "No Stronger than a Flower" (*Sub Rosa*, 180–92), which is reminiscent of Hawthorne's "The Birthmark." These are modern fables, not horror hackworks.

books that he detested (Aickman, *Painted Devils*, 1, 10). Moreover, the narrator cannot understand how a man who had created such sublime art—which though "demented" on the surface had somehow "broken through to a deep and terrible order" (2)—could be such an insipidly dull and boring person.

After the aging artist dies of unknown causes, the narrator manages to save one painting and the artist's papers from the flames to which his widow is eager to consign them. Among the papers is the strange manuscript, a personal narrative composed by the painter, describing a trip he took to Brussels when he was in his twenties, before he met his wife. He went to Belgium to see some paintings by a deceased *symboliste* he calls A. The paintings are in the elderly widow's possession. Madame A. has answered his querying letter; she will gladly let him see her husband's works.

But Madame A., the reader soon learns, is not at all interested in showing the painter her husband's art. Like his own future wife, she despises it. What she is interested in is a strange kind of vicarious sex act with the painter, who is simultaneously repulsed and enchanted by her. Indeed, he begins to transform the encounter into one of his grotesque paintings: a ridiculous old woman trying to seduce a young man becomes the archetypal hag; attempting to be Venus, she becomes "Venus" of Willendorf—her head resembles "an old brown egg" (15), and attention is constantly drawn to her bosom. She tells him of her beautiful "adopted daughter" Chrysothème, who is out on a date "with some creature" but with whom he still may have a kind of metonymic intercourse through her clothes, rich with her scent. Madame A. forces the man to kneel and bury his face in one of her daughter's dresses. "I did so. It was a wonderful sensation. I felt myself enveloped in a complex silky nebula. The owner, the wearer of that elegant garment, began . . . to be much more present to me than Madame A." (22–23). It is the scent that makes the absent girl present. Once again, anima is evoked through breath. The painter kisses the dress, never realizing he is making love to himself at the request of a dominating mother figure who does not want him to encounter a real woman.

Next, Madame A. makes him sink his arms and face into a trunk filled with Chrysothème's lingerie (24). Intoxicated by the scent, he obeys Madame A.'s commands. "Love them, tear them, possess them," she says. While making love to the "soft underclothes," he notices for the first time that the only painting in the room is one of his own. Clearly, the dead Belgian artist is but a trope for the living English one whose art is moribund. He does not describe the painting beyond mentioning that "the central figure, which I

might have painted as an angel, had somehow become more like a clown"
(25). As Madame A. insults the painting, the painter's enchantment dissolves; feeling nausea, he flees, chased by Madame A. with a pair of scissors.
The next day he realizes that there probably was "no picture over the bed,
and . . . no adopted daughter" (26).

From angel to clown—the image in the painting is a perfect description of
what happens when anima is not made conscious, not made available as an
energizing force, a spirit or angel. Instead, she solidifies into an icon: the
only other work of art in Madame A.'s house is a statue of a woman giving
birth to a succubus (14). That "the general coloration" of the house "had
something in common with my own works" reveals that the house is actually
the painter's mind, and Madame A. is the mother archetype, Chrysothème
the anima. The statue giving birth to the succubus echoes Madame A.'s
conjuring of Chrysothème. As seen here over and over again (from *Le Diable
amoureux* to "Ligeia"), angelic anima becomes devilish fiend when she
remains attached to the mother archetype. And the man becomes either a
madman or a fool, a clown.

Chrysothème's dresser is likened to an altar (21); her whole room
resembles a chapel (22), in which the painter actually kneels. With Madame
A. and Chrysothème, he is like a primitive priest, humbled in the presence
of the Great Goddess and her daughter—Demeter and Persephone. Since
he is unable to stop projecting the godlike powers of the mother archetype
onto women, he is never able to perceive women as human beings (cf.
Mattoon, 212–15). Chrysothème never materializes; she remains a wraith of
scented lingerie. The painter marries a woman with hair "the color of old
wheat" (2)—a woman in the image of Demeter. But the fertility goddess has
become Hekate.

Like Theobald in "The Madonna of the Future," this artist cannot keep his
projections on the canvas where they belong. Unlike Theobald, however, he
is able to paint, but his work never fulfills its promise. His muse remains the
Terrible Mother. He seems indeed to represent the most decadent side of
the symbolist school—artists like Edvard Munch (painter of "Madonna" and
"Vampyr") and, especially, Felicien Rops (one of the painter's favorites), who
was so obsessed with the demonic feminine that his art ultimately failed. In
fact, if the English painter, while in Belgium, had used his "golden Themis"
("Chrysothème") to do what Themis does best—weigh the merits of two
opposing forces—he would have realized that the conflict in his art was
typified by the tension between two Belgian painters—the stagnant nympholepsy of Felicien Rops and the transcendent achievement of Fernand

Khnopff, who worked his way through the Salomé fixation to create some magnificent paintings. Aickman's painter chooses the wrong role model— Rops, in whom the fear of Salomé, the dangerous castrating female, is never overcome. If the woman within the man is never acknowledged or liberated from the static mother archetype or from her unconscious dungeon, the man's Idea of Woman remains the Medusa, the sphinx, Salomé, or Madame A., who is Atropos with her scissors. That is his fate: fatal enchantment—he is *ravissante*: ravished by his own feminine soul. But if she is given her rightful place in man's consciousness, she becomes the muse who inspires rather than the medusa who destroys. This transformation from terror to beauty is readily apparent in the paintings of Fernand Khnoppf, who transmutes the depredations of the Sphinx into "caresses" (Delevoy, 133).

By 1984, Thomas Disch perhaps realized that the theme of the revenge of repressed femininity had been rather overdone, was indeed rather hackneyed. So he doesn't dwell on it in *The Businessman: A Tale of Terror*, and he evokes it in a new way. This is the story of a man who rapes and murders his estranged wife, who then comes back from the dead to haunt him. At first Giselle seems like just another revenging revenant, a restless retributive spirit who haunts until she can rest in peace after justice is done. But she has no idea why she is being forced by some unseen agency to haunt her murderous husband, and she soon discovers that, even though she is dead, she is pregnant from the rape. In one of the most grotesque scenes in contemporary fiction, she gives birth to a demonic monstrosity that goes on a murderous rampage, eliminating everyone it deems a threat to its "Daddy."

This title character, Robert Glandier, represents the cigar-smoking extreme of phallocentric masculinity untempered by any feminine element. He is all business, no art; all head, no heart; all aggression, no receptivity. When his masculinity is threatened, he loses control. But the rape and murder are not merely crimes of passion, they are the inevitable acts of a man who is sexually excited by violence. His favorite writer, whom he uses as a masturbatory aid, is John Norman, author of *The Slave Girl of Gor* and a myriad of other sadistic fantasies. His unconscious desire for dead women has deadened his soul. Death lurks in his language about sex: he "gets his ashes hauled" (3) by a prostitute at the beginning of the novel—an ironic foreshadowing of his actual death when he is incinerated to ashes in an unsuccessful attempt to burn his wife's remains, hoping to end the haunting. The last thing he sees is the "fiend in women's garments" lying down by his side, as "her grinning fleshless mouth rose toward his to seal their union with a final kiss" (276).

The Businessman is a "tale of terror" only to Bob Glandier; Giselle is a demonic figure only to him. To the reader, the novel is a grotesque comedy, a clever fusion of humor and horror, and perhaps (with *Ghost Story*) the most vivid contemporary illustration of what Melville in another context called "the horror of the half-known life." Glandier is a grotesque because he is only half a human being. To Giselle's ghost he is "a blast of corruption like the stench that explodes from an icebox of rotted groceries" (93). But though his untempered masculinity makes him a monster, Giselle does not inhabit him to balance out his psyche. She is not his cast-out soul trying to find her way back. She invades his brain and lodges in his corpus callosum—the bridge between the two hemispheres of the brain—but she finds herself helpless there; this psyche is beyond help.

The gruesome child produced by the rape is called a "halfling" (180): sexually bipolarity has created this horror of the half-known life. Giselle had been too passive and submissive throughout her marriage to Bob, and he of course too aggressive. When she asserts her independence, he explodes, becoming all phallus and creating the monster.

In the end, Glandier is the victim of poetic justice.[5] His ghost must haunt the bathroom of his gay brother-in-law, Bing, the ghost of whose mother has placed Glandier there hoping that some of Bing's excessive femininity will rub off on him, presumably preparing him for his next incarnation. She also seems to hope that some of his excessive masculinity will "seep into" Bing's effeminate character. The bathroom Glandier must haunt is decorated with decadent wallpaper: Beardsley's Salomé reminds him that *la femme* has definitely become *fatale* to him; he is the prisoner of what Bing calls "the Oscar Wilde memorial bathroom."

Disch doesn't end on this comic note of cosmic irony, however. The last few paragraphs follow Giselle, who is about to enter a higher plane of existence. The "fiend in women's garments" has become a spirit again: "There are moments when a soul released from this cave of flesh will speed toward a mortal mind as it lies entranced in sleep, will curl across its surface frothing, like waves across a beach, touching its tenderest parts and causing

---

5. In fact, one of the ghosts partly responsible for it is a poet, John Berryman, whose bloody apparition has been haunting the general vicinity of the Minneapolis bridge from which he jumped. He and Giselle become friends, and he acts as midwife to her, having claimed that he had learned something about obstetrics from William Carlos Williams. Berryman ends up having to perform a grisly cesarean.

dreams to rise from its depths, like the bubbles of burrowing clams" (292). She becomes the foam-born spirit of love, "and we awake, knowing we have been touched by something beautiful, whose beauty we shall never understand."

Disch transforms the feminine back from the demonic corpse created by polarized masculinity to a sylphlike spirit. The anima's proper symbol is breath, her elements air and water, not earth and fire. Giselle started in the earth, inhabited a willow tree, then was finally released in the air, disembodied, an animating soul. When the demon is spirit again, the mind is no longer haunted.

CONCLUSION
Archetypal Dialectics

"Archetypes are the psychic instincts of the human species," writes Edward Edinger. "An archetype is to the psyche what an instinct is to the body." (12). In literature, they tend therefore to cluster around themes of love, sex, and death, all of which involve instincts both of soma and of psyche. Since Gothic fiction is usually (and simultaneously) obsessed with all three of these concerns, it is especially vivid in its imagination of archetypal figures.[1] And since the anima, in particular, manifests herself as a numinous demanding

1. Here I am in disagreement with Leslie Fiedler's contention that the Gothic *substitutes* terror for love as the subject of the novel (115). The Gothic tends through terror and horror toward either a love of death or a dialectic between love and death. I am more in agreement with Camille Paglia's contention that the Gothic is "sexually archaic" (265), therefore evoking the mingling of terror and love one might call the sublime, and that the uncanny and the grotesque tend to evoke images of "extreme antiquity" (46)—i.e., archetypes.

goddess, inspiring "sacred terror," her presence is perhaps most strongly felt in the Gothic genre.

This study has therefore largely been restricted to the pursuit of anima in Gothic fiction. But as I hope Chapter 6 has implied, an archetypal perspective may be applied to less horrific texts as well. "The Madonna of the Future" is not quite Gothic. Theobald does not hurl himself through a circle of fire like Nathanael in "The Sandman." His psychological problem, however, is almost identical to Nathanael's. This intertextual parallel is most clearly illustrated through archetypal analysis—through the study of the dynamics of anima projection.

Jungian archetypal criticism need not limit itself, then, to fantastic modes of discourse. Even though some of the most successful Jungian studies (Marie-Louise von Franz on fairy tales, for example, or Aniela Jaffé on Hoffmann's märchen) tend to focus on fantasy, the Jungian approach has also been successfully applied to poetry (see Bickman's chapters on Whitman and Dickinson, and Christine Gallant's book on Blake). If one focuses on the feminine archetype as I have, one finds "Our Lady of Darkness" flaunting herself in the Gothic, but she may be discerned, draped less fantastically, in realistic fiction as well. Joyce's *Ulysses* comes most readily to mind, with his visions of Dublin women as Nausikaas and Circes, nymphs and enchantresses. Whenever human characters are given mythological dimensions in a text, regardless of its genre, archetypal psychodynamics can shed light on it by distinguishing synchronic from diachronic elements.

Intertextual patterns also become clearer with an archetypal perspective. When Alvare hides under the bed unable to breathe, when Romuald breathes life into Clarimonde, when Count Valerio draws in his breath, the bodily instinct of breathing is a trope for a psychic instinct. Obviously breath is not always a sign of anima presence, but if a female daemon is clearly associated with a man's breath, then she may be identified as the anima. Hers are the deepest breaths of psyche, the *suspiria de profundis*.

The female demon in Gothic fiction, then, is often an image of the archetypal feminine, with which men must struggle in their attempts to define themselves and their relation to the female Other. Jacques Cazotte's Biondetta, the prototype appearing in the urtext of Ambiguous Gothic, was perhaps the first demoness in narrative fiction clearly to become a daemon, an inner phantom, part of a man's haunted mind. Inspired by a similar vision, Matthew Lewis in *The Monk* polarized the feminine into two daemons, revealing the disintegration of a male psyche that never becomes conscious of the archetype. E.T.A. Hoffmann was more intuitively aware than either Cazotte or Lewis of uncanny drives working in the human mind—forces felt as human colossi, capable either of integrating or disintegrating the self. Which pole dominates is a complex problem: one must project anima, but without overdoing it like Nathanael;[2] one may sublimate Eros, but not, like Ambrosio, to such excess.

The male ego tends to split and moralize the bipolar archetype, which, however, instinctively seeks fusion. The resultant friction between these opposing forces of ego and instinct often results in grotesque travesties of the marriage of contraries—in the "zombified" rather than the regenerated psyche—as in the animated corpse-brides of Irving, Gautier, and Poe. De Quincey, however, had a vision of life-in-death that suggests the possibility of harmony with the deep feminine soul of man. "Life-in-Death" is only a "nightmare" (as Coleridge imagines her in "The Rime of the Ancient Mariner") to men who have lost their souls. All the female demons have their positive aspects—Lamia and Medusa are beautiful as well as ugly.[3] Le Fanu in "Carmilla" and Stoker in *Dracula* luridly illustrate this bipolarity, revealing the ambivalence men feel toward sex and death, both of which they fear and desire. *Dracula* is an especially ambiguous text, which contains a complete subtext, dictated as it were by the unconscious, counterpointing the Christian pieties of its epistolary voices.

But the master of ambiguity was Henry James, who explored the psychodynamics of feminine obsession in "The Madonna of the Future" and "The Last of the Valerii," identifying men's creative and procreative impotence as the inability to integrate the feminine archetype, whether muse or ideal mate. All of the texts above play a part in what Lisa Appignanesi has called "the myth of femininity" (2). Her idea that the feminine appears in James as a tendency to internalize can be seen in all the stories: the demon is a daemon, offering herself as a guide first to love, then to death.[4] As De Quincey averred, however, she speaks a language many men never bother to learn.

2. Cf. Samuels, *Jung and the Post-Jungians*, 212–13: "Via projection, men and women recognize and are attracted to each other. . . . Projection is normal and healthy up to a point. A man will see in a woman parts of himself of which he was not yet conscious and yet which he needs. However, excessive projection is problematic and the recipient may not be able to [incarnate] the idealized projection." Individuation involves finding "a midway position between insensate projection and no projection at all."

3. See Nethercott, 84–85, on Lamia's transformations from beautiful to ugly to beautiful. For "The Beauty of the Medusa," see Jerome J. McGann's article on the femme fatale in Romantic poetry.

4. For anima as death goddess, see Hillman, "Anima I," 111–12; and *The Dream*, 33. Cf. Christine Downing, 12–13.

"We only know archetypes," Eric Gould writes, "as language events" (30). "An archetype must create some kind of code and enter some kind of dialectic with a perceiving mind, and not merely be a vague memory from the mists of time" (31). Like a dream image, the anima is never vague (Hillman, *The Dream*, 82)—her form, whether of the Madonna or of the Medusa, is sharp and clear. She makes her demands, however, in the code De Quincey called "the hieroglyphics of the brain." To read her, as Hoffmann and James suggested, a man must be less of a literalist and more of a visionary. It takes imagination to become androgynous.

Androgyny, of course, is more than mere hermaphroditism. To admit the anima to consciousness is not necessarily to become effeminate, although that is one way some men accomplish it. Thomas De Quincey and Henry James were both, in their unique ways, androgynous without being Sacher-Masochs.[5] Anima consciousness, as "The Mines of Falun" and "Carmilla" especially reveal, invokes not only eros but also—and, as a man grows older, more importantly—thanatos. Anima possession (as opposed to integration) may result in a domination of the death instinct, manifest in murderous aggression toward either the self (Elis, Nathanael) or the Other (Ambrosio). If neither possession nor integration occurs, then a man will simply remain pusillanimously frightened of death. Anima consciousness, however, need not be a nightmarish vision of death-in-life; it can be ecstatic, like that of the androgynous Walt Whitman in *Song of Myself* and "Out of the Cradle, Endlessly Rocking."

Anima is the psyche's deepest erotic and thanatotic instinct. As Jung pointed out, "Archetypes are among the inalienable assets of every psyche. They form 'the treasure in the realm of shadowy thoughts' of which Kant spoke" (*CW* 9.1: 84). As a treasure, the anima may teach us how to love and how to die; Psyche's lamp illuminates both the bedchamber and the charnel house—as Poe knew so well. But Poe's characters, so often possessed, rarely achieve a love-death dialectic. The male hysteric Roderick Usher buries his twin-sister soul alive; then she returns, an animated corpse, to claim him. A visionary synthesis, on the other hand, of anima's two poles—of the Madonna (daemon of love) and the Medusa (daemon of death)—does not lead to the morbidity of necrophilia, which is but a travesty of the *Liebestod* conjunction. Affirmation of the syzygy of light and dark, of yang and yin, may lead rather to a profound truth, expressed obliquely by the dying Sheridan

5. On De Quincey's androgyny, see Lindop, 13–14; on Henry James's, see Edel, *Life*, 234, 245–46.

Le Fanu in "Carmilla"—but realized unequivocally by Wallace Stevens in "Sunday Morning": "Death is the mother of beauty; hence from her, / Alone, shall come fulfillment to our dreams / And our desires" (lines 3–5). Coleridge's nightmarish "Spectre-Woman and her Death-mate" becomes Stevens's dream-fulfilling "mother of beauty." That ancient mariner, man's ego, may be redeemed "By grace of the Holy Mother" ("Rime" v), through a vision that only anima, as the dark core of our soul, can bring. She reveals herself in the Gothic as not only the Queen of Heaven but also Hades' bride, who transforms this god of death into Pluto—wealth, riches, "the treasure in the realm of shadowy thoughts."[6] So the daemon "in women's garments" need not be a "fiend." When she comes to haunt our minds and lie down by our sides we may welcome her as a friend. Gothic and horror literature at its best may shock us into a recognition of these Ladies of Darkness as embodiments of our own lost souls.

---

6. Cf. Hillman, *The Dream*, 28, and especially 53: "Hades is also Pluto . . . a richness and nourishment" for the soul.

APPENDIX A

Recognizing Anima

Morton Kaplan and Robert Kloss complained that *animae* tend to proliferate like weeds in Jungian analyses: every female character must be the anima or the *magna mater* (184). But as James Hillman says, "All that is female is not necessarily anima. . . . Every woman who comes streetwalking into our dreams" is not necessarily an archetype of our deepest soul ("Anima ɪ" 106). Nor is every female ghost or demon who haunts our fictions. I have selected my texts only after examining many literary *femmes fatales* for signs of the primordial in their structure and behavior. As I hope I have shown, in order for a female character to be a possible anima figure, she must have the numinosity to make her a "mighty Element" in the psyche. She must indeed be Psyche, the feminine half of the unconscious whose proper consort is not only Eros but also the Logos-Animus, from which she is often severed. She must be not only a haunting female but a demanding feminine force within the male, often felt as an *unheimliche Treib*, and usually personified as a goddess/angel, a devil, or a fiendish revenant.

Discerning her existence in literature is not easy because she is often dressed in conventional garb that may have little or nothing to do with psychic instincts. Certain recurring images and behavior patterns associated with the demonic feminine, in other words, may be diachronic—the "madonna/whore complex," for example, is primarily indicative of nineteenth- and early twentieth-century male attitudes and tendencies. But the *basis* for the complex is a synchronic bipolarity manifest also in Eve and Lilith, or Hebe and Hekate—the Fair. vs. the Dark Lady. The archetype affects not only the man's attitude toward woman, but also—more fundamentally—his attitude toward himself. Attempting to distinguish synchronic from diachronic elements in female characters, then, is not a mere mechanical exercise in labeling, as Kaplan and Kloss aver, but an endeavor to understand the primordial elements of the mind.

Several texts that seemed at first promising in this regard had to be dismissed either as completely diachronic or indeterminate. Tales of revenant ghosts, for example, like the lady in Irving's "Adventure of My Uncle," tend to be mere embodiments of thematic or moral elements consciously manipulated by the author. Kipling's "Phantom 'Rickshaw" (1888) also contains this type of ghost—a man's callous treatment of his mistress results in a severe haunting after she dies of a broken heart; the text offers no indication that he is repressing his own feminine element.

In some texts (like "Ligeia" and "La Morte amoureuse"), the anima is overdetermined—she is conspicuous by her signs: intense numinosity; origination in the haunted man's mind; association with soul, air, and breath; and bipolar function as a guide to both heaven and hell. In many texts, however, she is underdetermined—one cannot make a strong case for her significance in the text. Wilkie Collins's "The Dream Woman" (1855), for example, seems to fall somewhere between the complete absence of anima imagery of "The Phantom 'Rickshaw" and the archetypal abundance of "Ligeia."

"The Dream Woman" opens with an enigma. The narrator is a doctor who stops at an inn where he becomes interested in an ostler named Isaac, who has the peculiar habit of always sleeping during the day. He also has nightmares in which he repeatedly murmurs incoherently: "Light grey eyes . . . and a droop in the left eyelid; flaxen hair, with a gold-yellow streak in it—all right mother—fair white arms, with a down on them—little lady's hand, with a reddish look under the finger-nails. The knife—always the cursed knife . . ." (3) The reader is as intrigued and puzzled as the narrator by these suggestive words. The innkeeper then tells the narrator how Isaac ended up having these daily nightmares. As the flashback narrative unfolds, one finds very few archetypal suggestions, even though the initial dream description, with its connection between the mother and some mysteriously dangerous woman with a knife, invites Jungian (and of course Freudian) interpretation. One may be tempted to suggest that this is yet another tale of the return of repressed anima. When almost forty Isaac had a fateful dream of a woman with a knife who tried to stab him in his bed. Could the dream-woman be the anima demanding her due homage? After all, Isaac has never even had a relationship with a woman (4). But he does not seem to have a mother complex, which would have forced the anima along with it into some kind of manifestation. Perhaps it has just been in abeyance all these years, until the dream. But none of the imagery associated with the dream-woman seems archetypal. The grey eyes, with some other Gorgon signifier, might suggest Medusa, but not by themselves. The down suggests a bird, and the bird suggests the soul, but it is by itself not enough. As for her effect on Isaac, she does "clear his mental percep-tions" (7), and when she leaves, that "preternatural sharpness" is gone (8). But she is never an energy source, nor does she seem to have a positive pole at all.

Furthermore, Isaac does not seem to be projecting the dreamed woman onto a real woman. His mother, and not Isaac himself, first notices the resemblance in his description of the dream-woman to Rebecca Murdoch, the woman he meets after the dream and whom he marries—and who later tries to stab him, fulfilling the dream. He does seem unconsciously to recognize her as the dream-woman when he first meets her (12), and she quickly exerts a mysterious influence on him "which utterly confused his ideas and almost deprived him of his powers of speech." He is clearly a victim of fascination, but not necessarily of anima possession. Rebecca turns out to be no more than a sullen woman incapable of love. She has nothing of the goddess, nothing of the daemon, and only a little of the fiend in her. Collins's story is more parapsychological than psychological: it is about a precognitive dream and a thoroughly human *femme fatale*; it may have something to do with anima psychology, but the anima remains underde-termined in the text.

Rather than jumping to the conclusion, then, that every fictive female apparition is archetypal, one must examine the text for signs of anima. And if they are present, one may trace the dynamics of her interaction with male consciousness. In so doing, one is inductively making a case for archetypalism in the text.

APPENDIX B

Post-Jungian Polemics

The post-Jungian critic does not begin with the premise or axiom that posits the collective unconscious as noumenon or center (cf. Hillman, "Anima II," 136–37); rather, one creates a critical text using Jungian signifiers to illuminate a primary text in which primordial, archaic, or archetypal signs seem to cluster or abound. This method thus avoids the reductionism and faulty deductions of which Jungian critics have often been accused.

Jungian criticism was held in especially low regard by psychoanalytical critics of the mid-sixties and early seventies, after the publication of Edward Glover's *Freud or Jung?* in 1965. Glover was supposed (by Kaplan and Kloss, for example—294) to have exposed Jung's "anti-Semitism," which has since been shown to be an unfounded allegation (Ellenberger, 675–78). Kaplan and Kloss attempted to complete Glover's "devastation" of "the Jungian peril" by purporting to show that Jung's analytical psychology is "deficient at base" (294). This assertion, however, is based on a premise poststructuralist Freudians—especially Lacan and his followers—no longer accept: that neo-Freudian ego psychology has an empirical foundation. "Lacan . . . in fundamental disagreement with the whole of ego psychology . . . held that the ego or *moi* is fundamentally an illusory identity" (Lee, 32). Jung also said, "I don't believe such a center [as the ego] exists" (quoted in Miller, 326). In this regard, "Jung was postmodern before the times. He knew unknowing before Derrida's version of Heidegger's insight that the most crucial moment is the deconstructive one" (Miller, 326).

If one deconstructs Kaplan and Kloss's argument, its speciousness becomes noticeable especially in its diction. In their discussion of Maud Bodkin, they first reject her ideas because she begs the question of whether "racial archetypes exist in the first place." Their existence cannot be proven empirically. But can the existence of the ego be empirically proven? It too is a tenuous image, not a solid icon, a self-representation based perhaps (according to Lacan) on one's mirror image (Lee, 18).

Kaplan and Kloss continue their attack: "Ultimately, one must say of archetypal criticism that everything which it explains *mystically* in terms of racial inheritance, psychoanalysis can explain *empirically* in terms of individual learning and *adaptation*" (184—emphasis added). This statement is, as my italics reveal, extremely leading and question-begging in itself. First, Kaplan and Kloss consider archetypal criticism to be mystical. Certain of its practitioners may well be, and Jung himself made excursions into mysticism, but the basic postulates of analytical psychology are not mystical: the idea that part of the unconscious mind has a hereditary element, or that it may be generated from still-functioning primitive brain strata, is not mysticism; it is an inference drawn from empirical evidence—as evolution itself is. That the various mother goddesses from world mythology have certain common characteristics because they may be images of a primordial archetype is no more mystical a notion than explaining such characteristics in terms of structuralist linguistics. As Anthony Stevens states (16–28), archetypes are not mystical concepts but "neuropsychic entities" that may have evolved through natural selection. The collective unconscious as some sort of group mind is a simple misconception; one can support its possible existence, as Stevens and Samuels show, through ethology and sociobiology just as convincingly as one can support ego psychology through behavioral models.

The second loaded word is "empirically." Here and in their direct attack on Jung (294–99), Kaplan and Kloss assume that Freudian and especially neo-Freudian concepts have all been empirically proven—as though signifiers like "ego," "id," and "superego" are linked to actual substantial entities, solid concepts. Materialistic positivism is being used here to support Freud and refute Jung. First, one should be reminded that a strict materialism calls into question the reality of such concepts even as *mind, psyche,* and *psychic apparatus;* a strict materialism asserts the reality only of brain, of electro-chemical reactions among neurons, and of resultant behavior. It makes no sense to claim that ego is real and anima is not; there is no more of a demonstrable link between ego and brain than there is between anima and brain. Indeed there is probably less, since the anima may at least in part result from traces of female hormones in the male body, for all Kaplan and Kloss know to the contrary.

The last loaded word is "adaptation." It sounds so scientific, so Darwinian. But it merely reveals a bias toward ego psychology, which is largely concerned with the struggle of the ego to adapt to its environment. Kaplan and Kloss simply assume that ego psychology is right. After Lacan and Derrida deconstructed this sort of egocentrism, Kaplan and Kloss's method seems more dated now than post-Jungian archetypalism. Ego psychology, with its emphasis on learning, defense mechanisms, and adaptation, happened to be fashionable when *The Unspoken Motive* was written.

Finally, Kaplan and Kloss commit the either/or fallacy—either Freud or Jung is right. Basing their argument on Glover's assertion (19) that Freudian and Jungian interpretations of literature are mutually exclusive, they do not think it is possible for character and behavior to be determined by both personal and transpersonal complexes, both environment and heredity. Glover's lengthy denial notwithstanding, there is clearly room for both Freudian and Jungian ideas to flourish. No one school has the answer to everything. Jung himself gave credit to the Freudian school for showing "the importance of personal factors influencing the poet's choice and use of his material" ("Psychology and Literature," 167). But he insists that art cannot be completely "accounted for" by personal factors. To recognize phyloge-netic as well as (rather than instead of) ontogenetic determinants in human behavior is the goal of a Jungian perspective. Such a perspective might modify a Freudian one, but it would never supplant it.

For Kaplan and Kloss, the postulates of ego psychology are absolute givens. So Jungian terminology seems extremely "jargonistic" to them (185), though they never explain precisely how terms like "ego" and "superego" are any less jargonistic than "anima" and "shadow." The terms most important to Jung, in any case, were not these but rather "spirit" and "soul." Although Kaplan and Kloss would not consider these jargonistic, doubtless they would reject them as mystical and empirically unverifiable. Ironically, Kaplan and Kloss end their groundless "egocentric" attack on Jung with a statement with which Jung (as any reader of "Psychology and Literature" can see) would have been the first to agree: "A work of art is a highly elaborate, extremely complex manifestation of mind and feeling, not to be explained simply" (298).

Eric Gould offers more of a challenge to the traditional Jungian critic than do Glover or Kaplan and Kloss, but not, I think, to the post-Jungian. Armed with semiotics and structuralist linguistics, he argues against the notion of what Jung called the "archetype an sich" (Jung, CW 8: 213). One of the more troublesome postulates of Jungian theory is a distinction between the archetype "as such" and its representation, expression, or manifestation. The former is a genetically inherited predisposition toward a certain pattern of behavior, while the latter is an image or utterance (CW 9.1: 75–76; cf. Stevens, 16–18; Neumann, 6; Ellenberger, 706). Gould rejects Jung's distinction between "image and concept" (20), which he says leads to the problem that Jungian archetypes are ultimately unknowable, since language is the only way we can know anything (22). He argues from the start that "it is the nature of language that determines myth and not the reverse" (12); "myth is a function of language and interpretation" (14). Gould does not summarily reject archetypes, however; he rejects the distinction between "the archetype [an sich] and its discursive extension" (32).

In sum, Gould applies Lacan's famous idea that "the unconscious is structured as a language" to the collective unconscious, concluding that if its archetypes do indeed exist, they are linguistic patterns, not transcendent Platonic Ideas or Kantean noumena. Fine, but if one distinguishes between deep structures and surface structures in grammar, and between signifiers and signifieds in semiotics, why not distinguish between images and concepts? How many images that come to us in dreams have anything to do with concepts? To interpret a dream is to conceptualize an image or series of images, but not all dreams remain open to interpretation, for the simple reason that we forget too much of them. The mere existence of a dream refutes Gould's claim that image and concept are indistinguishable.

Gould declares further "that it is . . . in whatever common characteristics we can determine for language and the act of interpretation that one can locate a more accurate sense of myth and archetype in literature" (28–29). For him, archetypal meaning is created through "the play of signs . . . incorporating the tension between . . . signifying and . . . signified" (32). But what is the "signified" in a mythical text? The classical

Jungian (as opposed to the post-Jungian, of whom Gould is unaware) would claim the "archetype an sich" is the signified concept, a prelinguistic structure that is, granted, verbally unknowable, but which may yet be sensed or felt by a reader. Gould considers this a "superstitious worship of the hidden side" of an archetype (69). The post-Jungian critic may avoid this problem, however, by focusing first on archetypal images, and then carefully and skeptically speculating about what concepts may be connected to those images.

Since Jung asserted the primacy of image over word, he did not fare well with post-Feudian or Lacanian psychoanalytical critics. "Psyche is image," Jung declared (Casey, 319). But for Jung, an image was not "a mere 'copy of an impression,' as Hume put it," not merely, in other words, "the psychic reflection of an external object" (CW 8: 325). The psyche comprises both image and word (Casey, 323); image patterns no less than sentence patterns are surface structures generated from deep structures. The latter may well lie in an unreachable abyss, which is why images are never mere "copies"— and why symbols are never mere allegories.

A post-Jungian critical approach, then, considers archetypal images as signifiers interacting with each other to create patterns the way words create sentences and atoms create molecules; archetypes are not "absolute or transcendent or unchanging" concepts frozen forever (Lauter and Rupprecht, 13). Linguistic patterns as well as common motifs may be used, then, to suggest the signification of archetypes in and among texts, regardless of one's opinion of the *ultimate* nature of the archetype.

For more information on the compatibility of post-Jungian analytical psychology with contemporary thought, see Anthony Stevens, especially chapters 1 and 2; Andrew Samuels, *Jung and the Post-Jungians*, 35–40; and Papadopoulos, chapters 14 and 17. More recently, Barnaby and D'Acierno (xxiv–xxv) also point out several similarities between Jung's thought and poststructuralists'. For example, Jung's conception of the psyche as an "energic system . . . dependent on the tension of opposites" that become hopelessly polarized if perceived hierarchically is similar to Jonathan Culler's discussion in *On Deconstruction* (93) and to Jacques Derrida's concept of "violent hierarchy."

Like Freud, then, Jung remains relevant to contemporary literary studies. Though some aspects of analytical psychology, like some aspects of psychoanalysis, do not hold up, both systems are still basically sound. But Freud is taken more seriously than Jung, perhaps because Jungian theory has never fully recovered from the attacks of the ego psychologists. In any event, Jung gets neglected even in contexts that beg for his aid. For example, in her recent book *Sexual Personae*, Camille Paglia, announcing her "ambition . . . to fuse Frazer with Freud" (xiii), only mentions Jung in passing. It seems to me that a mixture of Frazer and Freud requires more than a mere dash of Jung. Moreover, Paglia is more Jungian than she acknowledges, as she explores "our ancestral memory of earth-cult" (286) and describes "Dionysian liquidity" as a primordial feminine archetype (91). For Paglia, the return of the repressed femme fatale is a recurring symbol of pagan, chthonian nature asserting itself after having been beaten back by civilization (13). Unfortunately, she overemphasizes the Terrible aspect of the Great Mother. For her, nature is all appetite, depredation, cruelty; femininity is essentially a Melvillean Tartarus of Maids, reminiscent of blood and slime (335). But the feminine darkness, as described in the present book, is not merely the "chthonian swamp of female nature" (434); Mother Nature (and therefore the feminine half of human nature) is—as Jung could have reminded Paglia—a threefold goddess: creatrix, preserver, destroyer. Paglia focuses only on the latter aspect. More important to me is that cave of Psyche that protects and preserves.

WORKS CITED

Aickman, Robert. *Powers of Darkness*. London: Collins, 1966.
————. "Ravissante" (1968). Rpt. in *Painted Devils*, 1–26. New York: Scribner, 1979.
————. *Sub Rosa: Strange Tales*. London: Gollancz, 1968.
————. *The Wine-Dark Sea*. Ed. Peter Straub. New York: William Morrow (Arbor House), 1988.
Allen, Virginia M. *The Femme Fatale: Erotic Icon*. Troy, N.Y.: Whitston, 1983.
Appignanesi, Lisa. *Femininity and the Creative Imagination*. New York: Harper & Row, 1973.
Apter, T. E. *Fantasy Literature: An Approach to Reality*. Bloomington: Indiana University Press, 1982.
Astle, Richard. "Dracula as Totemic Monster: Lacan, Freud, Oedipus and History." *Sub-Stance* 25 (1980): 98–105.
Auerbach, Nina. *Woman and the Demon: The Life of a Victorian Myth*. Cambridge, Mass.: Harvard University Press, 1982.
Aziz, Maqbool, ed. *The Tales of Henry James*. Vol. 2. Oxford: Clarendon Press, 1978.
Banta, Martha. *Henry James and the Occult: The Great Extension*. Bloomington: Indiana University Press, 1972.
Barnaby, Karin, and Pellegrino D'Acierno, eds. "Preface." *C. G. Jung and the Humanities: Toward a Hermeneutics of Culture*, xv–xxix. Princeton: Princeton University Press, 1990.
Barthes, Roland. *S/Z*. Trans. Richard Miller. New York: Hill & Wang, 1974.
Basler, Roy P. "The Interpretation of 'Ligeia.'" 1944. Rpt. in *Critics on Poe*, ed. David B. Kesterson, 85–95. Coral Gables, Fla.: University of Miami Press, 1973.
Bassett, Fletcher. *Sea Phantoms, or Legends and Superstitions of the Sea and Sailors*. Chicago: Morrill & Higgins, 1892.
Baughman, Ernest W. *Type and Motif Index of the Folktales of England and North America*. The Hague: Mouton & Co., 1966.

Bell, Robert E. *Dictionary of Classical Mythology*. Oxford: Clio Press, 1982.

Bellemin-Noël, Jean. "Notes sur le fantastique (textes de Théophile Gautier)." *Littérature* (December 1972): 3–23.

Bennett, Maurice J. "The Madness of Art: Poe's 'Ligeia' as Metafiction." *Poe Studies* 14.1 (1981): 1–8.

Bentley, C. F. "The Monster in the Bedroom: Sexual Symbolism in Dracula." *Literature and Psychology* 22 (1972): 27–34.

Berkson, Dorothy. "Tender-Minded Idealism and Erotic Repression in James's 'Madame de Mauves' and 'The Last of the Valerii.'" *Henry James Review* 2 (1980): 78–86.

Bickman, Martin. *The Unsounded Centre: Jungian Studies in American Romanticism*. Chapel Hill: University of North Carolina Press, 1980.

Birkhead, Edith. *The Tale of Terror*. 1921. Rpt. New York: Russell & Russell, 1963.

Black, Joel D. "Levana: Levitation in Jean-Paul and Thomas De Quincey." *Comparative Literature* 32 (1980): 42–62.

Blinderman, Charles. "Vampurella: Darwin and Count Dracula." *The Massachusetts Review* 21 (1980): 411–28.

Bloch, Raymond. *The Ancient Civilization of the Etruscans*. Trans. James Hogarth. New York: Cowles, 1969.

Bloom, Harold. "Inescapable Poe." *New York Review of Books* 31 (11 October 1984): 23–26, 35–37.

Böker, Uwe. "Wilkie Collins, Henry James, and Dr. Carpenters 'Unconscious Cerebration.'" *Germanisch-Romanische Monatschrift* 34 (1984): 323–36.

Bonaparte, Marie. *The Life and Works of Edgar Allan Poe: A Psychoanalytical Interpretation*. London: Imago Publ., 1949.

Bradway, Katherine. "Gender Identity and Gender Roles: Their Place in Analytic Practice." *Jungian Analysis*, ed. Murray Stein, 275–93. La Salle: Open Court, 1982.

Briggs, Julia. *Night Visitors: The Rise and Fall of the English Ghost Story*. London: Faber, 1917.

Brooke-Rose, Christine. *A Rhetoric of the Unreal*. Cambridge: Cambridge University Press, 1981.

Brooks, Peter. "Virtue and Terror: The Monk." *ELH* 40 (1973): 249–63.

Busst, A.J.L. "The Image of the Androgyne in the Nineteenth Century." *Romantic Mythologies*, ed. Ian Fletcher, 1–95. London: Routledge & Paul, 1967.

Campbell, Ramsey, ed. *New Terrors*. New York: Pocket Books, 1980.

Casey, Edward S., et al. "Jung and Postmodernism Symposium." *C. G. Jung and the Humanities*, ed. Karin Barnaby and Pellegrino D'Acierno, 331-40. Princeton: Princeton University Press, 1990.

———. "Jung and the Postmodern Condition." *C. G. Jung and the Humanities*, ed. Karin Barnaby and Pellegrino D'Acierno, 319–24. Princeton: Princeton University Press, 1990.

Castex, Pierre-Georges. *La Conte fantastique en France de Nodier à Maupassant*. Paris: Corti, 1951.

Cazotte, Jacques. *Le Diable amoureux. Romanciers du XVIIIe siècle*, ed. Marguerite du Cheyron, vol. 2, 311–78. Paris: Gallimard, 1960–65.

Clendinning, John. "Irving and the Gothic Tradition." *Bucknell Review* 12.2 (May 1964): 90–98.

Cohen, Hubert I. "Hoffmann's 'The Sandman': A Possible Source for 'Rappaccini's Daughter.'" *ESQ* 68 (1972): 148–55.

Collins, W. Wilkie. "The Dream Woman." *Tales of Terror and the Supernatural*, ed. Hubert van Thal, 1–23. New York: Dover, 1972.

Conger, Syndy M. "Matthew G. Lewis, Charles Robert Maturin, and the Germans: An Interpretative Study of the Influence of German Literature on Two Gothic Novels." Dissertation: Universität Salzburg, 1977.

Craft, Christopher. "'Kiss Me with Those Red Lips': Gender and Inversion in Bram Stoker's *Dracula*." *Representations* 8 (Fall 1984): 107–33.

Culler, Jonathan. *On Deconstruction: Theory and Criticism after Structuralism*. Ithaca: Cornell University Press, 1982.

Daemmrich, Horst S. *The Shattered Self: E.T.A. Hoffmann's Tragic Vision*. Detroit: Wayne State University Press, 1973.

Day, William Patrick. *In the Circles of Fear and Desire: A Study of Gothic Fantasy*. Chicago: University of Chicago Press, 1985.

De La Mare, Walter. "Seaton's Aunt." *The Riddle and Other Stories*, 97–143. London: Faber & Gwyer, 1928.

De Luca, V. A. *Thomas De Quincey: The Prose of Vision*. Toronto: University of Toronto Press, 1980.

Demetrakopoulos, Stephanie. "Feminism, Sex Role Exchanges, and other Subliminal Fantasies in Bram Stoker's *Dracula*." *Frontiers* 2.3 (Fall 1977): 104–13.

De Quincey, Thomas. *Suspiria de Profundis. Confessions of an English Opium Eater and Other Writings*, 113–223. New York: New American Library, 1966.

Devlin, James E. "Irving's 'Adventure of the German Student.'" *Studies in American Fiction* 7 (1979): 92–95.

De Vries, Ad. *Dictionary of Symbols and Imagery*. Amsterdam: North-Holland Publ., 1974.

Disch, Thomas M. *The Businessman: A Tale of Terror*. New York: Harper & Row, 1984.

Downing, Christine. *The Goddess. Mythological Images of the Feminine*. New York: Crossroad, 1981.

Edel, Leon. *Henry James: A Life*. New York: Harper & Row, 1985.

———. "Introduction." *The Ghostly Tales of Henry James*, i–xxxii. New Brunswick, N.J.: Rutgers University Press, 1948.

———. "Introduction." *Henry James: Stories of the Supernatural*, i–xvi. New York: Taplinger, 1970.

Edinger, Edward. "An Outline of Analytical Psychology." *Quadrant* (Spring 1968): 1–20.

Elardo, Ronald Joseph. "The Chthonic Woman in the Novellas and Fairy Tales of E.T.A. Hoffmann." *DAI* 40 (1979): 2704A.

Ellenberger, Henri F. *The Discovery of the Unconscious*. New York: Basic Books, 1970.

Fass, Barbara. *La Belle Dame sans Merci and the Aesthetics of Romanticism*. Detroit: Wayne State University Press, 1974.

Feidelson, Charles. "Art as Problem in 'The Figure in the Carpet' and 'The Madonna of the Future.'" *Twentieth Century Interpretations of 'The Turn of the Screw' and Other Tales*, ed. Jane P. Tompkins, 47–55. Englewood Cliffs, N.J.: Prentice Hall, 1970.

Felman, Shoshona. "Re-reading Femininity." *Yale French Studies* 62 (1981): 19–44.

Ferguson, George. *Signs and Symbols in Christian Art*. New York: Oxford University Press, 1954.

Fiedler, Leslie. *Love and Death in the American Novel*. New York: Stein & Day, 1966.

Fleurant, Kenneth J. "Mysticism in the Age of Reason: Jacques Cazotte and the Demons." *French Review* 49 (1975): 68–75.

Forrester, John. *Language and the Origins of Psychoanalysis*. New York: Columbia University Press, 1980.

Frank, Frederick S. "The Gothic Romance—1762–1820." *Horror Literature: A Core Collection and Reference Guide*, ed. Marshall Tymn, 3–175. New York: Bowker, 1981.

Franz, Marie-Louise von. *Problems of the Feminine in Fairy Tales*. New York: Spring Publications, 1976.

Fraser, Phyllis, and Herbert Wise, eds. *Great Tales of Terror and the Supernatural*. New York: Modern Library, 1944.

Freud, Sigmund. "The Uncanny." 1919. Rpt. in *Collected Papers*, vol. 4, trans. Joan Riviere, 368–407. New York: Basic Books, 1959.

Frye, Northrop. *Anatomy of Criticism*. Princeton: Princeton University Press, 1957.

———. *Fables of Identity: Studies in Poetic Mythology*. New York: Harcourt, Brace & World, 1963.

Frye, Northrop, Sheridan Baker, and George Perkins. *The Harper Handbook to Literature*. New York: Harper & Row, 1985.

Gallant, Christine. *Blake and the Assimilation of Chaos*. Princeton: Princeton University Press, 1978.

Gargano, James W. "Poe's 'Ligeia': Dream and Destruction." *College English* 23 (1962): 335–42.

Gautier, Théophile. "The Dead Lover." Trans. F. C. de Sumichrast. *Romantic Gothic Tales*, ed. G. R. Thompson, 274–306. New York: Harper & Row, 1979.

———. "La Morte amoureuse." *Spirite, suivi de la morte amoureuse*. Paris: Flammarion, 1970.

Glover, Edward. *Freud or Jung?* Cleveland: World, 1965.

Goethe, Johann Wolfgang. "Die Braut von Korinth" ("The Bride of Corinth"). *Selected Poems*, ed. Christopher Middleton, 133–43. Boston: Suhrkamp/Insel Publ., 1983.

Gould, Eric. *Mythical Intentions in Modern Literature*. Princeton: Princeton University Press, 1981.

Grant, Richard B. *Théophile Gautier*. Boston: G. K. Hall, 1975.

Graves, Robert. *The Greek Myths*. New York: Braziller, 1955.

Grover, P. R. "Mérimée's Influence on Henry James." *Modern Language Review* 63 (1968): 810–17.

Grudin, Peter. "*The Monk*: Matilda and the Rhetoric of Deceit." *Journal of Narrative Technique* 5 (1975): 136–46.

Guirand, F., and A.-V. Pierre. "Roman Mythology." *Larousse Encyclopedia of Mythology*, 213–33. London: Batchworth Press, 1959.

Halliburton, David. *Edgar Allan Poe: A Phenomenological View*. Princeton: Princeton University Press, 1973.

Hartmann, Franz. *The Life and the Doctrines of Paracelsus*. New York: Theosophical Publ. Co., 1918.

Hawthorne, Nathaniel. "The Haunted Mind." *Twice-Told Tales*. Vol. 9 of *The Centenary Edition of the Works of Nathaniel Hawthorne*, 304–9. Columbus: Ohio University Press, 1974.

Hedges, William L. *Washington Irving: An American Study, 1802–1832*. Baltimore: Johns Hopkins University Press, 1965.

Hennelly, Mark M. "Dracula: The Gnostic Quest and Victorian Wasteland." *English Literature in Transition* 20.1 (1977): 13–26.

Hertz, Neil. "Freud and the Sandman." *Textual Strategies*, ed. Josue Harari, 296–321. Ithaca: Cornell University Press, 1979.

Hewett-Thayer, Harvey W. *Hoffmann: Author of the Tales*. Princeton: Princeton University Press, 1948.

Hillman, James. "Anima I." *Spring: An Annual of Archetypal Psychology and Jungian Thought* (1973): 97–132.

———. "Anima II." *Spring* (1974): 113–46.

———. *The Dream and the Underworld*. New York: Harper & Row, 1979.

Hoffmann, Ernst Theodor Amadeus. *Selected Writings of E.T.A. Hoffmann. Volume One: The Tales*. Ed. and trans. Elizabeth C. Knight and Leonard J. Kent. Chicago: University of Chicago Press, 1969.

———. *Werke. Vol. 2*. Ed. Herbert Kraft and Mandred Wacker. Frankfurt: Insel Verlag, 1967.

Hume, Robert D. "Gothic vs. Romantic: A Revaluation of the Gothic Novel." *PMLA* 84 (1969): 282–90.

Irving, Washington. "Adventure of the German Student." *The Complete Tales of Washington Irving*, ed. Charles Neider, 223–27. Garden City, N.Y.: Doubleday, 1975.

Jackson, Rosemary. *Fantasy: The Literature of Subversion*. New York: Methuen, 1981.

Jacobi, Jolande. *The Psychology of C. G. Jung*. New Haven: Yale University Press, 1973.

Jaffé, Aniela. *Bilder und Symbole aus E.T.A. Hoffmanns Märchen "Der goldne Topf."* *Gestaltungen des Unbewussten*. Ed. C. G. Jung. Vol. 7. Zurich: 1950.

James, Henry. "The Last of the Valerii." *Henry James: Stories of the Supernatural*, ed. Leon Edel, 69–102. New York: Taplinger, 1970.

———. "The Madonna of the Future." *The Complete Tales of Henry James*, ed. Leon Edel, vol. 3, 11–52. Philadelphia: Lippincott, 1962.

Jay, Gregory S. "Poe: Writing and the Unconscious." *Bucknell Review* 28.1 (1983): 144–69.

Johnson, Barbara. *The Critical Difference: Essays in the Contemporary Rhetoric of Reading*. Baltimore: Johns Hopkins University Press, 1980.

Jones, Daryle E. "Poe's Siren: Character and Meaning in 'Ligeia.'" *Studies in Short Fiction* 20 (1983): 33–37.

Jones, Ernst. *On the Nightmare*. 1931. Rpt. New York: Liveright Publ. 1971.

Jordan, Cynthia. "Poe's Re-vision: The Recovery of the Second Story." *American Literature* 59 (March 1987): 1–19.

Jung, Carl Gustav. *The Collected Works of C. G. Jung*. [CW] Trans. R. F. C. Hull. 20 vols. Princeton: Princeton University Press, 1953–79.

———. "Psychology and Literature." *Modern Man in Search of a Soul*, trans. W. S. Dell and Cary F. Baynes, 152–72. New York: Harcourt Brace Jovanovich, 1933.

———, ed. *Man and His Symbols*. Garden City, N.Y.: Doubleday, 1964.

Jung, Emma. *Animus and Anima*. Dallas: Spring Publ., 1981.

Kamla, Thomas A. "E.T.A. Hoffmann's 'Der Sandmann': Narcissistic Poet as Romantic Solipsist." *Germanic Review* 63.2 (Spring 1988): 94–102.

Kaplan, Morton, and Robert Kloss. *The Unspoken Motive: A Guide to Psychoanalytic Literary Criticism*. New York: Free Press, 1973.

Kelley, Cornelia Pulsifer. *The Early Development of Henry James*. Urbana: University of Illinois Press, 1930.

Kerenyi, Carl. *The Religion of the Greeks and Romans*. New York: E. P. Dutton, 1962.

Kiely, Robert. *The Romantic Novel in England*. Cambridge, Mass.: Harvard University Press, 1972.

Kiernan, James G. "An Ataxic Paranoia of Genius: A Study of E.T.A. Hoffmann." *The Alienist and Neurologist* 17 (1896): 295–310.

Kiessling, Nicolas. *The Incubus in English Literature: Provenance and Progeny*. Pullman: Washington State University Press, 1977.

Kipling, Rudyard. "The Phantom 'Rickshaw." *The Phantom 'Rickshaw and Other Stories*. New York: Standard Classics, 1930.

Knapp, Bettina L. *Dream and Image*. Troy, N.Y.: Whitston, 1977.

———. *Edgar Allan Poe*. New York: Ungar, 1984.

Knight, Elizabeth C., and Leonard J. Kent. "Introduction." *Selected Writings of E.T.A. Hoffmann. Volume One: The Tales*, 9–45. Chicago: University of Chicago Press, 1969.

Kraft, James. *The Early Tales of Henry James*. Carbondale: Southern Illinois University Press, 1969.

Kugler, Paul. "The Unconscious in a Postmodern Depth Psychology." *C. G. Jung and the Humanities*, ed. Karin Barnaby and Pellegrino D'Acierno, 307–18. Princeton: Princeton University Press, 1990.

Lamb, Charles. "Witches and Other Night Fears." *The Works of Charles Lamb*, 108–17. New York: A. C. Armstrong, n.d.

Langton, Edward. *Satan: A Portrait*. London: Skeffington, 1946.

Lauber, John. "'Ligeia' and Its Critics: A Plea for Literalism." *Studies in Short Fiction* 4 (1966–67): 28–32.

Lauter, Estelle, and Carol Schreier Rupprecht, eds. *Feminist Archetypal Theory: Interdisciplinary Re-Visions of Jungian Thought*. Knoxville: University of Tennessee Press, 1985.

Lee, Jonathan Scott. *Jacques Lacan*. Boston: G. K. Hall, 1990.

Le Fanu, Joseph Sheridan. "Carmilla." *In a Glass Darkly*, 222–88. London: John Lehmann, 1947.

Leiber, Fritz. *Our Lady of Darkness*. New York: Putnam, 1977.

Lever, Karen M. "De Quincey as Gothic Hero." *Texas Studies in Literature and Language* 21 (1908): 332–46.

Lewis, Matthew Gregory. *The Monk*. Ed. Louis Peck. New York: Grove Press, 1952.

Lindop, Grevel. *The Opium-Eater: A Life of Thomas De Quincey*. New York: Taplinger, 1981.

Lippe, George B. "Beyond the House of Usher: The Figure of E.T.A. Hoffmann in the Works of Poe." *Modern Language Studies* 9.1 (1978–79): 33–41.

Lorenz, Emil Franz. "Die Geschichte des Bergmanns von Falun bei Hoffmann, Wagner, and Hoffmannsthal." *Imago* 3 (1914): 250–301.

Lovenjoul, Spoelberch de. *Histoire des oeuvres de Théophile Gautier*. 2 vols. 1887. Geneva: Slatkine Reprints, 1968.

Lupack, Barbara T. "Irving's German Student." *Studies in Short Fiction* 21.4 (Fall 1984): 398–400.

Lydenberg, Robin. "Ghostly Rhetoric: Ambivalence in M. G. Lewis's *The Monk*." *Ariel: A Review of International English Literature* 10.2 (1979): 65–79.

Lyon, Judson S. *Thomas De Quincey*. New York: Twayne, 1969.

McCormack, W. J. *Sheridan Le Fanu and Victorian Ireland*. Oxford: Clarendon Press, 1980.

McGann, Jerome J. "The Beauty of the Medusa: A Study in Romantic Literary Iconology." *Studies in Romanticism* 11 (1972): 3–25.

McGlathery, James M. *Mysticism and Sexuality: E.T.A. Hoffmann. Part One: Hoffmann and His Sources*. Las Vegas: Peter Lang, 1981.

———. *Mysticism and Sexuality: E.T.A. Hoffmann. Part Two: Interpretation of the Tales*. Las Vegas: Peter Lang, 1985.

Mahlendorf, Ursula R. "E.T.A. Hoffmann's 'The Sandman': The Fictional Psycho-Biography of a Romantic Poet." *American Imago* 32 (1975): 217–39.

Massey, Irving. *The Gaping Pig: Literature and Metamorphosis*. Berkley and Los Angeles: University of California Press, 1976.

Matheson, Terence J. "The Multiple Murders in 'Ligeia': A New Look at Poe's Narrator." *Canadian Review of American Studies* 13.3 (Winter 1982): 279–89.

Mattoon, Mary Ann. *Jungian Psychology in Perspective*. New York: Macmillan, 1981.

Maves, Carl. *Sensuous Pessimism: Italy in the Work of Henry James*. Bloomington: Indiana University Press, 1973.

Mehlman, Jeffrey. "The Floating Signifier: From Lévi-Strauss to Lacan." *Yale French Studies* 48 (1972): 10–37.

Mérimée, Prosper. "The Venus of Ille." *The Venus of Ille and Other Stories*, trans. Jean Kimber, 1–32. London: Oxford University Press, 1966.

Miller, David L. "An Other Jung and An Other . . ." *C. G. Jung and the Humanities*, ed. Karin Barnaby and Pellegrino D'Acierno, 325–30. Princeton: Princeton University Press, 1990.

Milner, Max. *Le Diable dans la littérature française de Cazotte à Baudelaire, 1772–1861*. 2 vols. Paris: Librairie Corti, 1960.

Negus, Kenneth. *E.T.A. Hoffmann's Other World: The Romantic Author and His New Mythology*. Philadelphia: University of Pennsylvania Press, 1965.

Nethercott, Arthur H. *The Road to Tryermaine: A Study of the History, Background, and Purposes of Coleridge's "Christabel."* 1939. Rpt. New York: Russell & Russell, 1978.

Neumann, Erich. *The Great Mother*. Trans. Ralph Manheim. 2d ed. Princeton: Princeton University Press, 1963.

Ollier, Emand. "Vampyres." *Household Words* 11.255 (10 February 1855): 39–43.

Onians, Richard B. *The Origins of European Thought*. Cambridge: Cambridge University Press, 1951.

Onions, Oliver. "The Beckoning Fair One." *Widdershins: The First Book of Ghost Stories*, 1–68. 1911. Rpt. New York: Dover, 1978.

O'Reilly, Robert F. "Cazotte's *Le Diable amoureux* and the Structure of Romance." *Symposium* 31 (1977): 231–42.

Paglia, Camille. *Sexual Personae: Art and Decadence from Nefertiti to Emily Dickinson*. New Haven: Yale University Press, 1990.

Papadopoulos, R., and G. Saayman, eds. *Jung in Modern Perspective*. London: Wildwood House, 1984.

Peck, Louis. *A Life of Matthew Gregory Lewis*. Cambridge, Mass.: Harvard University Press, 1961.

———. "*The Monk* and *Le Diable amoureux*." *Modern Language Notes* 68 (1953): 406–8.

————. *"The Monk* and Musaeus' 'Die Entführung.'" *Philological Quarterly* 32 (1953): 346–48.

Penzoldt, Peter. *The Supernatural in Fiction.* 1952. Rpt. New York: Humanities Press, 1965.

Peters, Diana S. "The Dream as Bridge in the Works of E. T. A. Hoffmann." *Oxford German Studies* 8 (1973): 60–85.

Pitcher, Edward W. "From Hoffmann's 'Das Majorat' to Poe's 'Usher' via 'The Robber's Tower': Poe's Borrowings Reconsidered." *American Transcendental Quarterly* 39 (1978): 231–36.

Pochmann, Henry A. "Irving's German Tour and His Tales." *PMLA* 45 (1930): 1150–87.

Poe, Edgar Allan. "Ligeia." *Collected Works of Edgar Allan Poe. Volume 2: Tales and Sketches,* ed. Thomas Ollive Mabbott, 311–34. Cambridge, Mass.: Belknap Press of Harvard University Press, 1978.

Porte, Joel. "In the Hands of an Angry God: Religious Terror in Gothic Fiction." *The Gothic Imagination: Essays in Dark Romanticism,* ed. G. R. Thompson, 42–64. Pullman, Wash.: Washington State University Press, 1974.

————. *The Romance in America: Studies in Cooper, Poe, Hawthorne, and James.* Middleton, Conn.: Wesleyan University Press, 1969.

Porter, Laurence M. "The Seductive Satan of Cazotte's *Le Diable amoureux.*" *L'Esprit Créateur* 18.2 (1978): 3–12.

Pratt, Annis V. "Spinning among Fields: Jung, Frye, Lévi-Strauss, and Feminist Archetypal Theory." *Feminist Archetypal Theory: Interdisciplinary Re-Visions of Jungian Thought,* ed. Estella Lauter and Carol Schreier Rupprecht, 93–136. Knoxville: University of Tennessee Press, 1985.

Prawer, S. J. "Hoffmann's Uncanny Guest: A Reading of 'Der Sandmann.'" *German Life and Letters* 18 (1965): 297–308.

Praz, Mario. *The Romantic Agony.* Trans. Angus Davidson. London: Oxford University Press, 1951.

Punter, David. *The Literature of Terror: A History of Gothic Fictions from 1765 to the Present.* London: Longman, 1980.

Rabkin, Eric S. *The Fantastic in Literature.* Princeton: Princeton University Press, 1976.

Railo, Eino. *The Haunted Castle: A Study of the Elements of English Romanticism.* New York: Dutton, 1927.

Reichart, Walter A. *Washington Irving and Germany.* Ann Arbor: University of Michigan Press, 1957.

Retinger, Joseph. *Le Conte fantastique dans le romantisme français.* 1908. Rpt. Geneva: Slatkine Reprints, 1973.

Richardson, Maurice. "The Psychoanalysis of Ghost Stories." *Twentieth Century* 166 (1959): 419–31.

Ringe, Donald A. *American Gothic: Imagination and Reason in Nineteenth Century Fiction.* Lexington: University Press of Kentucky, 1982.

Robbins, Rossell Hope. *The Encyclopedia of Witchcraft and Demonology.* New York: Crown, 1960.

Rose, H. J. *A Handbook of Greek Mythology.* New York: Dutton, 1959.

Ross, Michael L. "Henry James's 'Half-Man': The Legacy of Browning in 'The Madonna of the Future.'" *Browning Institute Studies* 2 (1974): 25–42.

Roth, Phyllis A. *Bram Stoker*. New York: Twayne, 1982.
———. "Suddenly Sexual Women in Bram Stoker's *Dracula*." *Literature and Psychology* 27 (1977): 113–21.
Rudwin, Maximilian. *The Devil in Legend and Literature*. 1931. Rpt. New York: AMS Press, 1970.
Rupprecht, Carol Schreier. "Enlightening Shadows: Between Feminism and Archetypalism, Literature and Analysis." *C. G. Jung and the Humanities*, ed. Karin Barnaby and Pellegrino D'Acierno, 279–91. Princeton: Princeton University Press, 1990.
Saliba, David. *A Psychology of Fear: The Nightmare Formula of Edgar Allan Poe*. Lanham, Md.: University Press of America. 1980.
Samuels, Andrew. "Beyond the Feminine Principle." *C. G. Jung and the Humanities*, ed. Karin Barnaby and Pellegrino D'Acierno, 294–306. Princeton: Princeton University Press, 1990.
———. *Jung and the Post-Jungians*. London: Routledge & Kegan Paul, 1985.
Schapiro, Barbara A. *The Romantic Mother: Narcissistic Patterns in Romantic Poetry*. Baltimore: Johns Hopkins University Press, 1983.
Schneidermann, Leo. "E.T.A. Hoffmann's Tales: Ego Ideal and Parental Loss." *American Imago* 40.3 (Fall 1983): 285–310.
Schroeter, James. "A Misreading of Poe's 'Ligeia.' " *PMLA* 76 (1961): 397–406.
Schwartz, Jerome. "Aspects of Androgyny in the Renaissance." *Human Sexuality in the Middle Ages and the Renaissance*, ed. Douglas Radcliffe-Umstead, 122–31. Pittsburgh, Pa.: University of Pittsburgh Press, 1978.
Scott, Sir Walter. "On the Supernatural in Fictitious Compositions." *Essays on Chivalry, Romance and the Drama*, 455–72. London: Chandos Classics, n.d.
Shaw, Edward Pease. *Jacques Cazotte*. Cambridge, Mass.: Harvard University Press, 1942.
Shulman, Robert. "Poe and the Powers of the Mind." *ELH* 37 (1970): 245–62.
Sicker, Philip. *Love and the Quest for Identity in the Fiction of Henry James*. Princeton: Princeton University Press, 1980.
Siebers, Tobin. *The Romantic Fantastic*. Ithaca: Cornell University Press, 1984.
Smith, Albert B. *Théophile Gautier and the Fantastic*. University, Miss.: Romance Monographs, 1977.
Smith, Allan Lloyd. "On the Other Side: The Uncanny." *ESQ* 30 (1984): 260–72.
Snyder, Robert Lance. "*Klosterheim*: De Quincey's Gothic Masque." *Research Studies* 49 (September 1981): 129–42.
Stevens, Anthony. *Archetypes: A Natural History of the Self*. New York: Morrow, 1982.
Stoker, Bram. *Dracula*. New York: Bantam, 1981.
Stovall, Floyd. "The Conscious Art of Edgar Allan Poe." *College English* 24 (1963): 417–21.
Straub, Peter. *Ghost Story*. New York: Pocket Books, 1979.
Sullivan, Jack. *Elegant Nightmares: The English Ghost Story from Le Fanu to Blackwood*. Athens: Ohio University Press, 1978.
———. "Psychological, Antiquarian, and Cosmic Horror, 1872–1919." *Horror Literature*, ed. Marshall Tymn, 221–80. New York: Bowker, 1981.
Summers, Montague. *The Gothic Quest*. London: Fortune Press, 1938.
Tatar, Maria M. "E.T.A. Hoffmann's 'Der Sandmann': Reflection and Romantic Irony." *Modern Language Notes* 95 (1980): 585–608.

Taylor, Ronald. *Hoffmann*. London: Bowes & Bowes, 1963.

Tennant, P. E. *Théophile Gautier*. London: Athlone Press, 1975.

Thompson, G. Richard. "The Apparition of This World." *Bridges to Fantasy*, ed. George Slusser, Eric Rabkin, and Robert Scholes, 90–107. Carbondale: Southern Illinois University Press, 1982.

———. *Poe's Fiction: Romantic Irony in the Gothic Tales*. Madison: University of Wisconsin Press, 1973.

———. "Washington Irving and the American Ghost Story." *The Haunted Dusk: American Supernatural Fiction, 1820–1920*, ed. Howard Kerr, John W. Crowley, and Charles L. Crow, 13–36., Athens, Ga.: University of Georgia Press, 1983

———. ed. *Romantic Gothic Tales, 1790–1840*. New York: Harper & Row, 1979.

Thompson, Stith. *Motif Index of Folk Literature*. 6 vols. Bloomington: Indiana University Press, 1955–58.

Todorov, Tzvetan. *The Fantastic*. Trans. Richard Howard. Ithaca: Cornell University Press, 1975.

Twitchell, James B. *Dreadful Pleasures: An Anatomy of Modern Horror*. New York: Oxford University Press, 1985.

———. *The Living Dead: A Study of the Vampire in Romantic Literature*. Durham, N.C.: Duke University Press, 1981.

Tymms, Ralph. *Doubles in Literary Psychology*. Cambridge: Bowes & Bowes, 1949.

Tymn, Marshall B., ed. *Horror Literature: A Core Collection and Reference Guide*. New York: Bowker, 1981.

Ulanov, Ann Belford. *The Feminine in Jungian Psychology and Christian Theology*. Evanston, Ill.: Northwestern University Press, 1971.

Vaid, Krishna Baldev. *Technique in the Tales of Henry James*. Cambridge, Mass.: Harvard University Press, 1964.

Van Meurs, Joseph. "Jungian Literary Criticism." *C. G. Jung and the Humanities*, Karin Barnaby and Pellegrino D'Acierno, 238–50. Princeton: Princeton University Press, 1990.

Varma, Devendra. *The Gothic Flame*. New York: Russell & Russell, 1966.

Varnado, S. L. *Haunted Presence. The Numinous in Gothic Fiction*. Tuscaloosa: University of Alabama Press, 1987.

Veeder, William. "Carmilla: The Arts of Repression." *Texas Studies in Literature and Language* 22 (1980): 197–223.

Vetterling-Braggen, Mary, ed. *"Femininity," "Masculinity," "Androgyny": A Modern Philosophical Discussion*. Totowa, N.J.: Rowman Littlefield, 1982.

Walker, Barbara G. *The Woman's Encyclopedia of Myths and Secrets*. New York: Harper & Row, 1983.

Warren, Barbara. *The Feminine Image in Literature*. Rochelle Park, N.J.: Hayden Humanities Series, 1973.

Weissman, Judith. "Women and Vampires: Dracula as a Victorian Novel." *Midwest Quarterly* 18 (1977): 392–405.

Whitmont, Edward. "Reassessing Femininity and Masculinity: A Critique of Some Traditional Assumptions." *Quadrant* 13.2 (Fall 1980): 121–35.

Williams, Michael J. *A World of Words: Language and Displacement in the Fiction of Edgar Allan Poe*. Durham, N.C.: Duke University Press, 1988.

Winkler, Marcus. "Cazotte lu par E.T.A. Hoffmann: Du *Diable amoureux* à 'Der Elementargeist.'" *Arcadia* 23.2 (1988): 113–32.

Zabriskie, Beverley D. "The Feminine: Pre- and Post-Jungian." *C. G. Jung and the Humanities*, ed. Karin Barnaby and Pellegrino D'Acierno, 267–78. Princeton: Princeton University Press, 1990.

Ziolkowski, Theodore. *Disenchanted Images: A Literary Iconology*. Princeton: Princeton University Press, 1977.

Index